Praxis II
Geography (5921) Exam

SECRETS

Study Guide
Your Key to Exam Success

Praxis II Test Review for the
Praxis II: Subject Assessments

Dear Future Exam Success Story:

Congratulations on your purchase of our study guide. Our goal in writing our study guide was to cover the content on the test, as well as provide insight into typical test taking mistakes and how to overcome them.

Standardized tests are a key component of being successful, which only increases the importance of doing well in the high-pressure high-stakes environment of test day. How well you do on this test will have a significant impact on your future, and we have the research and practical advice to help you execute on test day.

The product you're reading now is designed to exploit weaknesses in the test itself, and help you avoid the most common errors test takers frequently make.

How to use this study guide

We don't want to waste your time. Our study guide is fast-paced and fluff-free. We suggest going through it a number of times, as repetition is an important part of learning new information and concepts.

First, read through the study guide completely to get a feel for the content and organization. Read the general success strategies first, and then proceed to the content sections. Each tip has been carefully selected for its effectiveness.

Second, read through the study guide again, and take notes in the margins and highlight those sections where you may have a particular weakness.

Finally, bring the manual with you on test day and study it before the exam begins.

Your success is our success

We would be delighted to hear about your success. Send us an email and tell us your story. Thanks for your business and we wish you continued success.

Sincerely,

Mometrix Test Preparation Team

Need more help? Check out our flashcards at: http://MometrixFlashcards.com/PraxisII

TABLE OF CONTENTS

Top 20 Test Taking Tips.. 1
Introduction to the Praxis Series.. 2
    Why am I required to take this Praxis Assessment? 2
    Two Kinds of Praxis Assessments 2
    ETS.. 2
Map and Globe Skills.. 3
Physical Geography.. 16
Human Geography.. 43
Political Geography.. 69
Regional Geography... 83
Practice Test... 107
    Practice Questions.. 107
    Answers and Explanations 120
Secret Key #1 - Time is Your Greatest Enemy 138
    Pace Yourself 138
Secret Key #2 - Guessing is not Guesswork 138
    Monkeys Take the Test.. 138
    $5 Challenge.. 139
Secret Key #3 - Practice Smarter, Not Harder 140
    Success Strategy 140
Secret Key #4 - Prepare, Don't Procrastinate 140
Secret Key #5 - Test Yourself 141
General Strategies.. 141
Special Report: How to Overcome Test Anxiety 147
    Lack of Preparation.. 147
    Physical Signals 148
    Nervousness 148
    Study Steps.. 150
    Helpful Techniques.. 151
Additional Bonus Material 156

Top 20 Test Taking Tips

1. Carefully follow all the test registration procedures
2. Know the test directions, duration, topics, question types, how many questions
3. Setup a flexible study schedule at least 3-4 weeks before test day
4. Study during the time of day you are most alert, relaxed, and stress free
5. Maximize your learning style; visual learner use visual study aids, auditory learner use auditory study aids
6. Focus on your weakest knowledge base
7. Find a study partner to review with and help clarify questions
8. Practice, practice, practice
9. Get a good night's sleep; don't try to cram the night before the test
10. Eat a well balanced meal
11. Know the exact physical location of the testing site; drive the route to the site prior to test day
12. Bring a set of ear plugs; the testing center could be noisy
13. Wear comfortable, loose fitting, layered clothing to the testing center; prepare for it to be either cold or hot during the test
14. Bring at least 2 current forms of ID to the testing center
15. Arrive to the test early; be prepared to wait and be patient
16. Eliminate the obviously wrong answer choices, then guess the first remaining choice
17. Pace yourself; don't rush, but keep working and move on if you get stuck
18. Maintain a positive attitude even if the test is going poorly
19. Keep your first answer unless you are positive it is wrong
20. Check your work, don't make a careless mistake

Introduction to the Praxis Series

Praxis exams are used to assess your knowledge of the subject matter that you are intending on teaching. Many states in the United States use this as part of the teachers licensing procedure. The Praxis series is a national exam meaning that the subject matter covered in this study guide is applicable to all states using the Praxis series. The advantage to this national exam is that once you take the exam your score is transferable to other states however scores considered as passing vary from state to state. If you would like to find out what the passing score is for your state please consult your schools College of Education. States decided passing scores based on recommendations of panels of teachers and teacher educators in each subject matter in each specific state.

Why am I required to take this Praxis Assessment?

Your state requires you to take this Praxis Assessment in order to test the breadth and depth of your knowledge in a specified subject matter. These states adopt the Praxis series in order to ensure that you have mastered the subject matter you are planning to teach before they issue your teaching license.

Because the issuance of your license ensures competence in the subject area it is important that you take studying seriously and make sure you study thoroughly and completely.

Two Kinds of Praxis Assessments

The Praxis Series consist of two different kinds of assessments multiple choice questions and constructed response test.

The multiple choice test consists of questions followed by several answer choices. From these answer choices you select the answer that you think best corresponds with the given question. These questions can survey a wider range because they can ask more questions in a limited time period.

Constructed response questions consist of a given question for which you write an original response. These tests have fewer questions, but the questions require you to demonstrate the depth of you own personal knowledge in the subject area.

ETS

ETS stands for Educational Testing Services. ETS is the company that develops the Praxis Assessments. They began the development of these exams by surveying teachers in each specified subject area to judge which skills and knowledge beginning teachers need to possess. These answers were then ranked in terms of importance and then each specific test was designed for each particular subject matter. Teachers and educators in each state evaluate the test and examine for relevance.

Map and Globe Skills

Maps and globes

A map is a diagrammatic representation all or part of the three-dimensional world on a two-dimensional (flat) surface. A given map conveys data about certain characteristics of a region, such as human settlement patterns, climate variations, or geologic quality, which is difficult to observe otherwise. Maps can also display spatial relationships between locations and natural or human-made formations.

The science of mapmaking is called cartography. General cartography entails the creation of maps for a general audience; thematic cartography involves the creation of maps with specific geographic themes.

Because Earth is a spherical object, flat maps cannot accurately convey all shapes, distances, and directions. A globe is a representation of Earth drawn to scale, which means that shapes, distances, and directions are accurately denoted. Globes are round objects mounted upon rotational axes. They are most often used to display topographical (surface) features of the planet; however, they have also been employed as representations of the ocean floor or celestial objects other than the Earth.

Latitude and longitude

Parallels and meridians constitute a coordinate system used to identify specific locations on the planet's surface. This spherical grid is referred to as a graticule.

Parallels are circles around the globe running east to west. The equator is the longest parallel, and is drawn around the planet halfway between the North and South Poles. Latitude is an angular measurement expressing the angle (in degrees, minutes, and seconds) between any point and the equator (where latitude equals zero); parallels are lines of constant latitude. The maximum latitudinal measurement (90 degrees North or South) occurs at the poles.

Meridians are semicircular arcs which run from the North Pole to the South Pole, intersecting all parallels at 90 degree angles. The Prime Meridian is the meridian which passes through Greenwich, England and is used as a reference in the same way as the equator. Longitude is an angular measurement expressing the angle between any point and the Prime Meridian (where longitude equals zero). The maximum longitudinal measurement is 180 degrees east or west.

Five main circles of latitude
Circle of latitude is simply another term for any of the parallels in the graticule. Certain of these parallels are distinguished due to their relationships with the sun.

The equator (0 degrees latitude) is one of these special circles of latitude; it is characterized by the fact that the sun passes directly over this parallel twice each year, during the respective Vernal and Autumnal Equinoxes.

T. of cancer (mexico, N.Africa

Equ.

T. of Capricorn, S.America, S.Africa, Australia

The Tropic of Cancer (23 degrees, 26 minutes, and 22 seconds North latitude) and the Tropic of Capricorn (23 degrees, 26 minutes, and 22 seconds South latitude) represent the northernmost and southernmost points areas of the globe at which the sun may be seen directly overhead (during midsummer and midwinter, respectively).

The Arctic Circle (66 degrees, 33 minutes, and 38 seconds North latitude) and the Antarctic Circle (66 degrees, 33 minutes, and 38 seconds South latitude) represent the northernmost and southernmost locations which may experience days without sunrises.

Scale as it is used in map interpretation

In order to provide relatively accurate representations of Earth's surface, cartographers utilize specific scales in map creation. The term map scale refers to the size of the representation of an element on a map as compared to its actual size on Earth's surface. The smaller the area represented on a map, the larger the scale; a larger scale provides more detail about a region.

Map scale is usually expressed proportionally, as a ratio of the distance on a map to that actual distance on Earth's surface. This ratio is often expressed as inches to miles. For example, 1:63,360—one inch on the map equals one mile on the surface.

Knowledge of a map's scale can provide information about the intended use of that map. For instance, large scale maps typically convey information about small, specific areas, such as planned housing developments. Smaller scale maps (such as world land use maps) represent larger areas of the surface in less detail.

Nominal and ordinal scales of measurement

The types and qualities of the maps drawn by geographers are dependent on the "levels" of the measurements they collect. There are four scales of measurement.

1. At the nominal level, also referred to as the classificatory level, variable attributes are identified through the use of *numbers* or symbols. For example, a land use map may use green shading to identify woodland areas. Different symbols are seen as equivalent; they involve no hierarchical ordering of attributes.
2. At the ordinal level, numbers and symbols serve both to identify objects and to express their relations to other objects. In this type of measurement, therefore, attributes may be rank-ordered. For instance, a cartographer might use dots of different sizes to convey the relative sizes of individual human settlements.
3. In interval measurement, the distance between objects is relevant. Variable categories are actual numbers (rather than convenient labels); the intervals between adjacent categories anywhere on the scale are equal. The ratio between any two points depends upon the unit of measurement. Temperature in degrees provides an example of an interval scale: the difference between 7 degrees and 8 degrees equals that between 78 degrees and 79 degrees. Interval scales are rarely utilized in cartography.

classifactory Level → shading

Ordinal level → relative size of settlements

Interval Variable Categories are actual #s

-4-

4. Ratio scales represent the highest level of measurement. Variables measured at this level possess all the properties of the lower measurement levels, and also include absolute zeros. This means that the ratio of any two points is independent of the unit of measurement. For instance, "income in dollars" is a ratio-level variable. Categories are represented by symbols (one dollar, two dollars, etc.), ranked (two dollars is more than one dollar), and display equal intervals, and it is possible to have zero dollars. The ratio scale is used in cartography to represent, for example, population density.

Ratio scale = pop. Density

Symbols and legends

Symbols are a vital part of any graphic representation of Earth's surface. Symbols may be utilized in cartography to signify features existing at certain points, such as buildings or dams. Generally, dots of different sizes are used to convey the relative sizes of cities and towns (larger dots for larger, more populous settlements).

Linear symbols identify features like roadways and rivers on maps. For instance, major highways are typically represented by double lines. Area symbols, created through the use of patterns, color, or shading, represent land conditions, land use, or land cover.

Many symbols used in cartography are universally recognized. However, thematic maps may contain symbols which are unfamiliar to the general user. All maps include legends, or keys, which identify the scale of a map, as well as information about the symbols used and what they represent.

Compass rose, hemisphere, and International Dateline
A compass rose is a symbol on a map or navigational chart which conveys the orientation of the four cardinal directions (north, south, east, and west) and often the intermediate directions (northeast, northwest, southeast, and southwest) as well. Modern compass roses are comprised of a large circle displaying the true (geographic) cardinal directions and a smaller inner circle displaying the magnetic (geomagnetic) cardinal directions.

The graticule divides Earth's surface into four hemispheres, or half spheres. The equator separates the Northern Hemisphere from the Southern Hemisphere. The Prime Meridian is most widely (though not universally) accepted as the dividing line between the Eastern and Western Hemispheres.

The International Dateline is the meridian opposite the Prime Meridian; it follows the line at 180 degrees longitude. This imaginary line serves as a time zone boundary—the date to the east of the international dateline is one day earlier than the date to the west.

The process of map creation

A cartographer must determine a map's target audience and make attendant decisions about style, content, and scale before her or she can begin to create a useful map.

The foundation of mapmaking is observation. Cartographers make use of several different observation techniques.

Aerial survey, the practice of collecting information about Earth from an aircraft, supplies valuable information to mapmakers. This information is conveyed through detailed photos developed from large-format film; aerial survey is a form of remote sensing (the collection of information about an object or region from a distance).

Cartographers also make use of conventional land surveys, which describe the locations and measurements of boundaries and land forms (artificial or natural).

Satellite photos may also be useful in cartography. Once a mapmaker has collected all relevant data, he or she then plots the location of many points on a grid which corresponds to that which will be used in the final product. Color-coded versions of the map are printed on plastic and layered to create a complete representation.

GIS

The GIS, or Geographic Information System, is basically a system of computers and software which collects, records, analyzes, and displays (potentially) limitless amounts of geographic information about the Earth. This data is usually based on aerial surveys, existing maps and surveys, and remote sensing. Once the information is entered into the GIS, users request specific information about certain regions, and then the system analyzes the relevant data and responds. The GIS is thus an interactive mapping system, rather than a static representation of certain aspects of the world. This technology has recently become available in certain automobiles.

Processing information from a spatial perspective

Maps are useful as abstract representations of physical and human aspects of Earth's surface which cannot be observed from any single point on that surface. Each human observes the world from one location at a time. Graphic depictions of large portions of the surface enable the identification of the patterns and spatial organizations of physical and human surface features and may be used to report information about a region's subsurface characteristics (natural or artificial). Maps illustrate how natural landmarks such as rivers and mountains are oriented in relation to one another; they show how oil resources are distributed across the surface; they convey the arrangement of human settlements. The information provided by maps facilitates the formation of mental maps and an understanding of the layout of the world in many different respects. Depending on the intended use of a particular map, different physical and cultural characteristics of Earth's surface are reported and emphasized.

Components of patterns of spatial organization

A key aspect of geographic study is the identification and analysis of patterns of spatial organization. These patterns are made up of four main components.

Points are specific sites on Earth's surface. For instance, a city courthouse may be considered a point. These points are connected by lines, usually roadways or other transportation routes. For example, the roads around which a courthouse is situated serve to connect it to other points and areas (such as neighborhoods or parks).

The fourth component of geographic patterns is volume; lakes, for example, have volume.

[Handwritten left margin: Spatial pattern = a perceptual structure, placement, or arrangement of objects on earth.]

[Handwritten next to heading: Points, lines, areas + volume]

[Handwritten bottom: → Spatial pattern of organization = how things fit together in physical space → where 1 thing exists in relation to another.]

- 6 -

diffusion — spread and/transfer of ideas, people from place to place —main mechanism in cultural change.
linkage — shared trait
accessibility
movement.

After identification of the components of a pattern, one may examine concepts such as location, density, direction, and arrangement to discover the relationship between elements of the pattern.

Finally, the geographer must analyze the revealed pattern, using concepts such as diffusion, linkage, accessibility, and movement. This analysis provides reasons for the patterns and functions of phenomena on Earth's surface.

Quantitative and qualitative methods of geographic analysis

Quantitative analysis involves the use of mathematics and statistics to explain and make predictions about geographic data. This method of study entails the synthesis of factual geographic information, such as population data. Maps, charts, and graphs are helpful in this type of analysis. The use of quantitative techniques allows geographers to objectively process large quantities of data and many variables. Often, geographers use quantitative inquiry to formulate hypotheses about spatial trends and patterns; they then test these theories through qualitative methods.

Qualitative analysis involves the first-hand examination of geographic phenomena in situ. In human geography, for example, one conducting qualitative research might interview inhabitants of an area for their perspective on a certain trend or issue. In the social sciences, qualitative analysis generally involves extensive fieldwork.

Mental maps

A mental map is a person's internalized representation of all or part of Earth's surface in a spatial context. Mental maps exist on a variety of scales. They may depict regions as small as a person's kitchen or as large as the entire surface of our planet. Because they are formed through the fusion of objective knowledge (such as facts about mountain elevation, the locations of cities, and the areas of countries) and subjective knowledge (such as priorities placed on knowledge of certain areas and impressions of places), each person's mental map is unique. Mental maps are vital in understanding the world. People use their internal maps during travel or when selecting a new place to live. These individual representations of the world are constantly growing and changing with the acquisition of new information, which may be gained through personal experience or secondhand from any source. As details are added to a person's mental map, he or she becomes more knowledgeable about and comfortable in the surrounding world.

Accuracy of a mental map

Just as some people possess "natural" aptitudes for algebra or drawing, some people are more able than others to envision human activity spatially. Geographic scholars refer to this capacity as spatial cognition.

The quality of a person's mental map is also affected by the geographic education he or she has received. For example, when asked to sketch a map of the world, many people across the globe would orient their maps with the North Pole at the top, the South Pole at the bottom, and Europe in the center. This is so because of educational conventions held over from the colonial period in America.

One's exposure to and study of certain areas may also affect his or her mental map. Naturally, the more one knows about, for example, a state, the larger that state will seem on one's mental map. Logically, the quality and accuracy of one's mental map may be improved through geographic study.

Location versus place

The location of a point is its precise spatial situation on Earth's surface. Locations are often identified through the use of maps and globe. The absolute location of a point is its definitive location on Earth's surface in a specific coordinate system. At the global level, it is usually expressed using the graticule. For example, Baltimore, Maryland, is at 39.3 degrees N, 76.6 degrees W. Locally, absolute location may be expressed as a specific street address. For example, the Texas State Capitol Building is located at 1100 Congress Avenue. The relative location of a point is its location in relation to something else, such as a well-known landmark. For example, in giving a friend directions, you might say that your house is "two blocks north of the market." On a global scale, one might say that Chile is west of Argentina.

The term place refers to the human and physical qualities of a location. A place's combined array of natural and manmade characteristics distinguishes it from any other place.

Site versus situation

A location's site is defined as the physical characteristics of the place it occupies. These qualities include topography, elevation, climate, soil, resources, as well as spatial organization. In other words, site refers to a location's internal locational attributes.

A place's situation is its relative location or regional position with regard to surrounding places; it refers to the location's external locational attributes. These include its location relative to outside areas of productive capacity, other political entities or settlements, transportation routes, and barriers to access and movement.

Site and situation are especially important to geographers studying the evolution of urban areas. For example, the original site of the city of Paris was an island in a highly-trafficked area of the Seine River; eventually, the island became too densely populated, and the city grew along the river's banks. Paris's situation was conducive to growth, for the city was surrounded by fertile areas of agricultural production and many land and water routes for transportation and trade.

Map projections

Any representation of the spherical globe on a flat map entails a degree of distortion. However, maps are more practically useful than globes—maps are smaller and easier to transport. A given map can only accurately represent selected globular features at the expense of others. The practice of mathematically transferring information about the Earth to a flat surface is called projection. This is generally accomplished through the creation of a projection surface, which is then flattened. To create such a surface, cartographers conceptually "touch" one or more areas of the surface to the globe; the regions touched by the projection surface exhibit the least distortion in map form.

- 8 -

Map projection classification

The surfaces of map projections may be oriented at different global coordinates:

- A polar map is aligned with Earth's rotational axis
- An equatorial map is centered on the equator, and
- An oblique map is not aligned with the equator or Earth's axis, and is used to display a specific region.

As globes are spherical objects, any attempt to transfer information found on a globe to a flat map involves distortion of one or more aspects of the original representation.

A projection may be described as conformal if it preserves the angles between points.

Equidistant maps hold true to the distances of the original map.

Equal-area projections are those which accurately portray areas.

A gnomonic projection displays great circles as straight lines; this type of projection is the oldest. Retroazimuthal maps preserve direction in the transfer from a spherical to a flat surface.

Cartographic manipulation

Cartographic manipulation is the process by which the actual sizes and shapes of areas or countries are distorted on maps. This manipulation may be accidental or intended. A certain degree of manipulation is inherent to the creation of map projections—the Earth's surface cannot be accurately represented on a flat piece of paper. Also, unintended distortion may occur due to a lack of cartographic knowledge or poor map design; maps used by media often suffer from this type of distortion.

Intentional cartographic manipulation may be employed to convey a certain side of an issue. For example, if a community group wishes to protest the erection of a nuclear power plant near their neighborhood, they may create a map which shortens the distance between the potential plant and surrounding homes.

Cartographic aggression is the use of map distortion by a nation to lay claim to territory over which they have no legal authority. For instance, prior to Operation Desert Storm, Iraq's officially sanctioned maps portrayed Kuwait as a province of Iraq.

Standard line, bearing, and loxodrome, geodesics

Due to discrepancies between the spherical globe and a flat map, scale is almost never constant on a map. A standard line is a line on a map which corresponds in scale and distance to a line on Earth; such lines are rarely straight. A map which displays a well-defined set of standard lines may be referred to as equidistant.

A bearing or course is a standard direction. A loxodrome or rhumb line is a line of constant bearing which represents the easiest route between two points. Loxodomes are often distorted in map projections.

The shortest route between two points on a spherical surface such as a globe is part of a geodesic line (also called a great circle path, orthodrome, or geodetic). These lines run through the two given points and are centered on the sphere. The equator is an example of a great circle.

Cylindrical map projections

There are several different methods of projection; each creates a different type of map for a different purpose. On a cylindrical map projection, lines of latitude are parallel to one another, equally spaced, and perpendicular to lines of longitude. Lines of travel are consistent on such a projection, while size and shape distortion increase with distance from the equator (the coordinate origin of cylindrical projections). Therefore, cylindrical map projections are rectangular; if such a map was rolled up, it would form a cylinder without end caps. The most famous cylindrical projection is the Mercator projection.

Some notable variations of the cylindrical map projection:
- A pseudocylindrical map projection illustrates parallels and the Prime Meridian (though not the other meridians) as straight lines. Scale remains constant along any single parallel, but varies among multiple parallels (meaning that they are unevenly spaced).
- Pseudocylindrical projections tend to be equal-area. The Robinson projection is a widely-used pseudocylindrical map. It is neither completely conformal nor completely equal-area; instead, it occupies a space between the two extremes. In this type of map projection, distortion is severe near the poles but decreases quickly moving away from them.
- Another notable pseudocylindrical projection is the Winkel Tripel projection. This kind of map is actually a hybrid of several equidistant cylindrical projections, namely those devised by Aitoff.

Conic map projections

A conic projection is created as though the surface of a globe was wrapped around a cone with the point oriented at the North Pole (the coordinate origin of this type of map). On conic map projections, longitudinal lines (meridians) are straight and equidistant; they may or may not converge at a pole. Latitudinal lines (parallels) distorted into concentric circles. Conic projections may be equal-area (areal relationships are maintained) or conformal (local angles and scale are preserved). The Lambert conformal projection is a type of conic projection which is often used in the creation of aeronautical charts.

Pseudoconic projections

Normally, pseudoconic projections display parallels as circular arcs with common central points. Unlike "true" conic projections, pseudoconic projections do not represent meridians as straight lines. This type of projection produces different kinds of maps. Codiform (heart-shaped) maps in the normal aspect exhibit similarities. First, the Prime Meridian is a straight standard line, second, all other meridians are curved lines, and third, parallels are drawn in equal liner scale as circular arcs centered at a pole (usually the North Pole). Variations among codiform projections (also called Stabius-Werner projections for their creators) occur due to differences in the scale used for the parallels. All codiform maps are equal-area and convey Earth's spherical quality.

The Bonne projection is another type of pseudoconic projection. Bonne maps include parallels which are equally-spaced concentric circular arcs and are all standard lines. Each Bonne map has one parallel as its center, making all such maps different. This type of map has virtually no areal distortion and slight shape distortion (except far from the center).

Azimuthal map projections

The azimuth of a surface is the angle a person at a reference point a. and looking at one point b. must turn to face another point c.. On a sphere, lines AB and AC are geodesic lines. Azimuthal (or planar) map projections use the azimuth as a reference point and often have polar orientations. Such projections accurately represent direction (but not necessarily distance) from the azimuth to any other point.

On any azimuthal projection (regardless of its orientation), all straight lines touching the central point are geodesics; distortion varies with distance from the center.

- Azimuthal orthographic projections portray the Earth as viewed from space (at any distance)
- Orthographic projections exhibit severe distortion around their edges.
- Azimuthal stereographic projections are conformal and preserve circles. They are most useful in the examination of one hemisphere.
- Azimuthal gnomic projections are similar to stereographic maps; however, every geodesic is mapped as a straight line, resulting in pronounced distance distortion and some direction distortion.

Tissot's Indicatrix

Tissot's Indicatrix is a tool used in cartography to assess the distortion inherent in all flat maps. First, many small circles are drawn onto the original sphere. Then, the same circles are mapped onto the flat projection. After undergoing this process, a given circle may change in size or shape. A comparison of the circles on each surface thus reveals the distortion patterns of shape, size, and angle on the projected map. For example, examination of indicatrices on the Mercator projection, in which the Tissot circles retain their shapes and parallels remain parallel to one another and perpendicular to the straight meridians, proves that this type of projection is conformal, preserving shape, angle, and scale. The sizes of the circles changes when they are mapped from the sphere to the Mercator projection (on the Mercator map, the circles increase in size with distance from the equator), indicating that areas are distorted.

Counteracting distortion

An oblique map is one in which neither the equator nor the Prime Meridian is centered on or aligned with the map axes. Oblique maps generally preserve area and shape but distort properties relating to the graticule orientation of the original sphere. They are usually created to move a large area of interest from an area of high distortion to a region of lower distortion.

Interrupted maps are those which are "cut" at certain (arbitrary) lines. The resultant sections (called lobes or gores) then project separately from the map. Interrupted maps are used in attempts to overcome shape, area, or distance distortion on "normal" projections. Goode's interrupted projection is a notable equal area map: it accurately portrays size and shape but distorts distance.

A polyhedral map is created by projecting separate regions of the globe onto different faces of a polyhedron. The polyhedron may then be cut and disassembled into a flat map (a net or fold out).

Map classifications

A map is classified primarily by its purpose and content (i.e. topographic map, weather map, road map). Maps may also be classified by scale or derivation (the source of the data represented).

- A topographic or reference map conveys general information about a geographic area, including ground elevation, natural formations (such as lakes and mountains), and structures erected by men (such as roadways and dams).
- Thematic or illustrative maps are those which represent a specific geographic theme, such as demography, geology, or land use. Such maps are created for a specific purpose. For example, land condition maps delineate surface areas which are especially susceptible to flooding, mass movements, or earthquakes; these maps are used by engineers for city planning or related activities. Land use maps, tourist maps, road maps, and mineral maps are other kinds of thematic maps.
- An analytical map is one which represents a geographer's hypothesis about the relationship between two or more elements of Earth's surface; the ideas suggested in analytical maps are tested using mathematics.

Proportional symbol maps

In creation of a proportional symbol map, a cartographer selects a particular symbol form to represent a particular variable. Proportionally-sized symbols are oriented in specific areas to convey the relative quantity of the variable in those areas. This method of mapping may be utilized when data occur at points (or can be aggregated at points) and when data can be measured as absolute values.

The symbol most commonly used in the creation of proportional symbol maps is the circle, for circles are easy to construct to scale. Circles are also visually stable, aiding map readers in their interpretations. Variables such as population density are often represented on this type of map. A map reader forms an image of the spatial distribution of, for example, population density through observation of the pattern created by the differently-sized symbols.

Choropleth maps

In creation of a choropleth map, a cartographer selects a unique color, shading technique, or pattern to identify a certain variable characteristic. This symbol is then applied to the appropriate chorogram. A chorogram is a discrete statistical area, such as a voting district, or administrative district, such as a state or township. This method of mapping may be utilized when data occur in or may be attributed to a distinct spatial unit. Also, the data to be conveyed should be derived rather than "raw." For instance, a choropleth map may display population density but not population distribution. In other words, ratio-level data should be used. Cartographers typically utilize idiographic data classification, which involves the delimitation of intervals between variable classes based on the array of data (i.e. natural breaks, equal intervals, etc.). A map reader analyzes the use of color or shading to determine to which symbol class a particular chorogram belongs.

Cartograms

Cartograms, which are also referred to as value-by-area maps, are similar to proportional symbol maps, in that the cartographer adjusts the sizes of artificial collection units (chorograms) to convey the relative data value for each; chorograms are thus proportionally sized. This type of map is useful when there is no data generalization (as occurs in choropleth maps). Also, the data (which may be absolute or derived, and of the interval or ratio measurement level) must be aggregated in chorograms. Cartograms are most effective when data values correlate negatively with the areas or sizes of the chorograms (when large chorograms have small values and small chorograms have large values). This method of visual representation aids in the display of spatial idiosyncrasies which could be obscured in conventional maps (due to wide variations in the sizes of the collection units).

Geologic map

Unlike a topography map, which represents landforms on the Earth's surface, a thematic geologic map represents rock or mineral ore formations which exist underneath the surface. An outcrop is a portion of a formation which is exposed at the surface, usually due to weathering and erosion. Often, outcrops are blanketed by sediment, soil, and/or vegetation. A contact is a plane which separates two rock formations. On a geologic map, common rock types (such as limestone, shale, and granite) are represented by graphic patterns or colors. Lines are used to delineate contact planes. Cartographers use certain symbols to indicate the presence of horizontal beds, vertical beds, axes in folded rocks, etc. These maps are extremely useful in the location and recovery of mineral resources and fossil fuels. These formations are identified through analysis of field research data and aerial photography.

Relief representation

The term relief refers to the variations in elevation across a portion of Earth's surface. This includes the heights of landforms such as mountains as well as the depths of erosion landforms such as valleys. Inclusion of this dimension in a map enhances its accuracy as a representation of a region. In the past, cartographers used specific symbols to indicate the presence of different landforms; however, due to its attendant inaccuracies, this mode of conveying disparities in elevation has been foregone in favor of the use of contour lines. Contour lines on a map connect points of equal elevations and show the shapes of landforms. Typically, cartographers select a contour interval (for example, 50) and then draw contour lines for a series of elevations (such as 50 miles, 100 miles, 150 miles, and so on). The contour interval is contingent upon the scale of the map and the amount of relief in the area being represented. The distance between subsequent contour lines indicates the steepness of slopes between contour intervals.

Geographic instability

The term geographic instability refers to the transitory nature of boundaries and place names in certain areas of the globe. Periods of geographic change often follow events such as the colonization of a new area or the fall of an empire. For example, upon the disintegration of the former Soviet Union, cartographers faced a deluge of changes. New boundaries were created, forming new countries and provinces, and certain cities were renamed. Similarly, when China switched from its old spelling system to the new Pinyin system, all maps displaying the former spellings of place names became obsolete. Because we do not live on a static Earth, boundaries and place names will continue to change. This simply means that cartographers must continue to update existing maps to keep pace with geographic instability.

Graphs and charts

A graph is a visual representation of the relationship between sets of data. The term chart may be used as a synonym, or it may refer to a specialized kind of map, such as a nautical chart. There are many different methods of displaying data in graphs and charts; most include the plotting of data in two dimensions. Many of these diagrams include several basic features. First of all, a title indicates the purpose and content of a graph or chart. Most diagrams have a horizontal axis (the x axis) and a vertical axis (the y axis); the intersection of these axes, where the value of each variable equals zero, is referred to as the origin. These axes are labeled to identify the variable being plotted and/or the range of values of that variable. Generally, independent variables (such as time) are represented on the x axis and dependent variables (such as temperature) are represented on the y axis.

Nautical charts and aviation charts

A nautical chart, which may also be called a hydrographic chart, is a thematic map intended for use by sea-faring sailors in navigation. This type of map includes a latitude-longitude grid which aids marine navigators in the identification of potential hazards to a ship, such as massive coral reefs. In addition, a nautical chart conveys the locations of lighthouses and other artificial landforms, the relief and constituent materials of the sea floor, and the shapes of topographic features like shorelines or islets.

An aviation chart (also called an aeronautical chart) is another kind of thematic map. It resembles a nautical chart but for its emphasis on airways, land topography, the heights of potential obstructions in an aircraft's path, and radio beacons.

Pie charts and 100 percent bar charts

A pie chart, also referred to as a circle graph, is a method of data representation which does not utilize the axes common in other kinds of graphs, and which therefore does not involve the plotting of data in two dimensions. Circle graphs are based on percentages of a total quantity; a full circle represents one hundred percent. This type of chart is useful when this quantity is known and the chart's creator wishes to convey the relative sizes of the "pieces" which add up to that total. For example, if a geographer knows the total number of people worldwide who identify themselves as having religious beliefs, he or she might create a pie chart to show what percentage of that total describe themselves as Muslims, Christians, Jews, etc. Percentages are converted to numbers of degrees and represented as sections of the circle. A 100 degree bar chart utilizes the same principles as a circle graph; in this type of chart, percentages are represented as proportional sections of a bar.

Line graphs

A line graph is a type of chart which is useful in representing relationships between sets of data. Line graphs are often used to show changes in a variable over time. For instance, in a graph of sale trends for a major company, a time scale (such as years or months) is laid out along the x axis and an amount scale is oriented along the y axis. Then, the respective sales figures corresponding to each time unit are plotted on the graph; these data points are connected with a line whose curvature conveys general tendencies about changes in sales over time. This feature of line graphs enables viewers to make educated predictions about future trends as well. In economics, a line graph may be used to show the relationship between quantity (on the x axis) and price (on the y axis). By connecting plotted points with lines, economists can identify changes in price as they relate to changes in the available quantities of goods.

Bar graphs

Bar graphs are useful in comparing quantities. This type of chart is similar to a line graph in that each involves the placement of variables along two axes. Instead of displaying values as points on the grid, however, a bar chart uses rectangular bars extending from an axis and leveling off at the appropriate points. In other words, the length of a bar representing a particular variable conveys the value of that variable. Bar graphs may be vertical (in which independent variables are oriented along the x axis and the rectangles extend vertically) or horizontal (in which independent variables are laid out along the y axis and the rectangles extend horizontally). This type of graph aids in the observation of differences among similar things. For example, a bar chart may display the variations in population among several major cities. In a pictograph, small icons or figures relating are used in lieu of rectangles to represent values. This type of graph is eye-catching and instantly conveys the purpose of the graph.

Scatter plots

Like bar and line graphs, scatter plots use x and y axes to plot data points. However, their specific purpose is to display how one variable affects another. This relationship is referred to as correlation. Correlation between variables is identified through the examination of a large quantity of data, represented on the graph as points. The closer the points come to forming a straight line, the stronger the relationship (and the higher the correlation) between the variables. If the line formed by the points extends from a high point on the y axis to a high value on the x axis, the correlation is negative. Conversely, if the line extends from the origin to high x and y values, the correlation between the two variables is positive. One might use a scatter plot to examine the relationship between education and income by aligning education level along the x axis of a graph and yearly income along the y axis, and then plotting data points for a group of individuals.

Physical Geography

Physical geography is the scientific study of life environments. These environments exist in the life layer, the space where the four realms (the atmosphere (the layer of gases which surrounds Earth), the hydrosphere (the water on Earth), the lithosphere (the solid Earth), and the biosphere (life on Earth)) interact. The life layer encompasses the lower atmosphere and the upper lithosphere, where land and water bodies meet. The science of physical geography examines systems and cycles within the life layer; these continuous processes cause modifications in the life layer (in different areas and on different time scales), creating Earth's diverse physical environments.

Concept of systems

In physical geography, the term system is used to refer to the processes (often cyclical) which operate to modify and diversify various physical environments. Physical systems are usually natural flow systems, in which something (such as energy, water, or a chemical element) moves along one or more pathways from one place to another due to a natural power source. A system may be open, in which case matter enters and exits the system. All energy systems are open. A system may also be closed. Closed systems are referred to as cycles; in these systems, no matter is inputted or outputted from the system. The hydrologic (water) cycle is an example of a closed system. Feedback is the mechanism by which the flow in one pathway influences the flow in another pathway. Positive feedback speeds up a process, while negative feedback retards a process. Equilibrium is the state of a system in which the flow rates on all the system's pathways are constant and nearly the same.

Earth's layers

The crust is the outermost layer of the planet Earth. It is located 0-35 kilometers below the surface. Earth's crust is composed mainly of basalt and granite. The crust is less dense, cooler, and more rigid than the planet's internal layers. This layer floats on top of the mantle. Located 35-2890 kilometers below the Earth's surface, the mantle is separated from the crust by the Mohorovicic discontinuity, or Moho (which occurs at 30-70 kilometers below the continental crust and at 6-8 kilometers beneath the oceanic crust). The mantle is made up of rocks such as peridotite and eclogite; its temperature varies from 100 to 3500 degrees Celsius. Material in the mantle cycles due to convection. The innermost layer of the Earth is the core, which consists of two layers (a liquid outer layer and a solid inner layer). It is located 2890-6378 kilometers below the surface. The core is thought to be composed of iron and nickel, and is the densest layer of the Earth.

Earth's sub-layers
The lithosphere consists of the crust and the uppermost portion of the mantle of the Earth. It is located 0-60 kilometers below the surface. The lithosphere is the cooling layer of the planet's convection cycle, and thickens over time. This solid shell is fragmented into pieces called tectonic plates. The oceanic lithosphere is made up of mafic basaltic rocks and is thinner and generally denser than the continental lithosphere (composed of granite and sedimentary rock); the lithosphere floats atop Earth's mantle.

The asthenosphere is the "soft," topmost layer of the mantle. It is located 100-700 kilometers below the surface. A combination of heat and pressure keep the asthenosphere's composite material "plastic."

The mesosphere is located 900-2800 kilometers below the surface, and therefore spans from the lower part of the mantle to the mantle-core boundary. The liquid outer core exists at 2890-5100 kilometers below surface level, and the solid inner core exists at depths of 5100-6378 kilometers.

Plate tectonics

Plate tectonics is a geological theory which was developed to explain the process of continental drift (the separation and movement of the continents based on shifts in a "plastic" layer of the Earth's interior, caused by the planet's rotation). The theoretical separation of the Earth's lithosphere and asthenosphere is based upon the mechanical properties of the materials in the two respective layers, and is distinct from the chemical separation of Earth's crust, mantle, and core. According to the theory of plate tectonics, the Earth's lithosphere is divided into ten major plates: African, Antarctic, Australian, Eurasian, North American, South American, Pacific, Cocos, Nazca, and Indian; it floats atop the asthenosphere. The plates of the lithosphere abut one another at plate boundaries (divergent, convergent, or transform fault), where the formation of topological features of Earth's surface begins.

Sources of tectonic plate motion

The energy driving plate motion comes from the dissipation of heat from the mantle in the relatively weak asthenosphere. This energy is converted into one of two forces to incite the motion of plates. Gravity is one such force; geologists subdivide this category into ridge-push and slab-pull:

- In the phenomenon of ridge-push, the motion of plates is instigated by the energy which causes low-density material from the mantle to rise at an oceanic ridge. This leads to the situation of certain plates at higher elevations; gravity causes material to slide downhill.
- In slab-pull, plate motion is thought to be caused by cold, heavy plates at oceanic trenches sinking back into the mantle, providing fuel for future convection.

The other main source of plate motion is friction. Friction is subdivided into mantle drag and trench suction:

- Mantle drag suggests that plates move due to the friction between the lithosphere and the asthenosphere.
- Trench suction involves a downward frictional pull on oceanic plates in subduction zones due to convection currents.

Divergent plate boundaries

A divergent, or constructive, boundary exists when two adjacent plates move away from one another. Observation of activity at diverging boundaries provided unquestionable proof of the seafloor spreading hypothesis. At this type of plate boundary, kinetic energy generated by asthenospheric convection cells cracks the lithosphere and pushes molten magma through the space left by separating tectonic plates. This magma cools and hardens, creating a new piece of the Earth's crust:

- In the oceanic lithosphere, diverging plate boundaries form a series of rifts known as the oceanic ridge system. The Mid-Atlantic Ridge is a consequence of undersea diverging boundaries.
- At divergent boundaries on the continental lithosphere, plate movement results in rift valleys, typified by the East African Rift Valley.

Convergent plate boundaries

The Earth's diameter remains constant over time. Therefore, the formation of new plate material at diverging plate boundaries necessitates the destruction of plate material elsewhere. This process occurs at convergent (destructive) plate boundaries. At this type of boundary, adjacent plates move towards one another. One plate slips underneath the other at a subduction zone. The results of converging plates vary, depending on the nature of the lithosphere in said plates. When two oceanic plates converge, they form a deep underwater trench. If each of the converging plates at a destructive boundary carries a continent, the light materials of the continental lithosphere enables both plates to float above the subduction area. They crumple and compress, creating a mid-continent mountain range. When a continental plate converges with an oceanic plate, the denser oceanic lithosphere slides beneath the continental lithosphere. The result of such convergence is an oceanic trench on one side and a mountain range on the other.

Transform fault plate boundaries

A transform (conservative) plate boundary exists when two tectonic plates slide past each other laterally and in opposite directions. Due to the rocky composition of lithosphereic plates, this motion causes the plates to grind against each other. Friction causes stress to build when the plates "stick;" this potential energy is finally released when the built-up pressure exceeds the "slipping point" of the rocks on the two plates. This sudden release of energy causes earthquakes. This type of plate boundary is also referred to as a "strike slip" fault. The San Andreas Fault in California is the most famous example of such a boundary.

Fault mechanics terms

Slip is a measurement of the net relative displacement of structural surfaces along a fault.

Dip, in fault mechanics, is the angle that a rock body or structural rock surface makes with the horizontal surface plane. True dip is quantified through downward measurement of the angle in the direction of greatest inclination; apparent dip is the measurement of dip in any direction. Dip is equal to zero in the direction of strike and has its maximum measurement in the direction of true dip.

Strike is the direction of a line of intersection drawn between the horizontal surface plane and the surface of an uptilted rock structure.

Three types of geologic fault

A geologic fault is a fracture in the Earth's surface, created by movement of the crust. The majority of faults are found along tectonic plate boundaries; however, smaller faults have been identified at locations far from these boundaries. There are three types of geologic faults, which are named for the original direction of movement along the active faultline. The landforms on either side of a fault are called the footwall and the hanging wall, respectively:

1. In a normal fault, the hanging wall moves downward relative to the footwall.
2. A reverse fault is the opposite of a normal fault: the hanging wall moves upward relative to the footwall. The dip of a reverse fault is usually quite steep; when the dip is less than 45 degrees, the fault is called a thrust fault.
3. In the third type of geologic fault, the strike-slip fault, the dip is virtually nonexistent, and the footwall moves vertically left (sinstral) or right (dextral). A transform plate boundary is a specific instance of a strike-slip fault.

Geologic folding

A geologic fold is a region of curved or deformed stratified rocks. Folding is one process by which Earth's crust is deformed. Rock strata are normally formed horizontally; however, geologists have identified areas where these strata arc upwards or downwards. Anticlines are upfolded areas of rock; downfolds are called synclines. In anticlines, the rocks are oldest along the axis (a horizontal line drawn through the point of the fold's maximum curvature), and in synclines, the youngest rocks are at the axis. Monoclines, or flextures, are rock structures which slope in one direction only, and often pass into geologic faultlines. The process of folding usually occurs underneath the Earth's surface, but surface erosion eventually exposes these formations. Folding is generally thought to be caused by the horizontal compression of the Earth's surface, which is related to the movement of tectonic plates and fault activity.

Orogenesis

Orogenesis refers to mountain-building processes, specifically as they relate to the movement of tectonic plates. An individual orogeny can take millions of years. Generally, mountains are created when compressional forces push surface rock upward, resulting in a landform which is higher than the land around it.

There are four broad categories of mountains (which are not mutually exclusive); these categories are based on the mountain's formative origin:

1. Folded mountains, formed from the long-term deformation and metamorphosis of sedimentary and igneous rocks, usually occur in chains. This type of mountain often forms at convergent plate boundaries.
2. Fault-block mountains occur at normal or reverse faults with high dips. Portions of Earth's crust are vertically displaced along the faults.
3. Oceanic ridges are formed at divergent boundaries beneath the ocean. When plates move apart, material from the mantle rises up and creates long mountain chains.
4. Volcanic mountains form from the accumulation of products of volcanic eruptions, such as ash and lava. They often occur singularly, unlike other mountain types which usually exist in chains.

Volcanic eruption process

Generally, a volcanic eruption entails a build-up of magma (a silicate solution formed of melted rocks) in a magma chamber. Gases present in the magma, such as water vapor, carbon dioxide, and sulfur dioxide, cause increasing pressure in the material. Often, the vent which would enable release of the built-up pressure is blocked by solidified magma. The viscosity of the magma also affect the release of gas pressure—the more viscous the magma, the more pressure will build up. A volcano erupts when the pressure becomes too great to be contained and the gases are suddenly and violently released. The freed gases expand, forcing magma and solid materials upward. The products of a volcanic eruption include ash, lava, and solid igneous rocks.

Volcanic activity at different types of plate boundaries
Divergent plate boundaries are also known as constructive plate boundaries because new crustal material must be formed to fill the void created by the separation of tectonic plates. This process occurs most often under the ocean. As oceanic lithospheric plates pull apart, magma rises from beneath to fill the gap; the increased temperature and magma concentration breeds volcanic activity. At convergent, or destructive, plate margins, friction creates the heat energy necessary to melt crustal rocks into magma. Also, the subduction of one plate under another pushes crustal material into the mantle, where temperatures are higher. The presence of volatiles (such as water and carbon dioxide) at subduction zones can force magma out through vents in the Earth's surface. Occasionally, volcanic activity occurs at locations far from any plate boundary. These locations, called hotspots, are thought to exist over particularly active mantle zones which shoot "plumes" of molten material up toward the crust.

Earthquakes
An earthquake is a sudden movement of a portion of the Earth's crust. Strain energy, built up in the lithosphere, is swiftly released in the form of seismic waves which, among other things, cause vibratory ground motion. The majority of these events occur at high-stress tectonic plate boundaries.

The rupture zone is the total size of the fault that slips; the larger the rupture zone, the greater the effects of the earthquake.

The focus or hypocenter of an earthquake is the location from which the seismic waves seem to emanate.

The epicenter is the location on the Earth's crust above an earthquake's hypocenter.

Earthquakes are classified according to their focus depths: shallow (0-70 kilometer below the surface), intermediate (70-300 kilometer below the surface), or deep (below 300 kilometer deep).

The rock cycle
The rock cycle is the process whereby the materials which make up the Earth transition through the three types of rock: igneous, sedimentary, and metamorphic.

Rocks, like all matter, cannot be created or destroyed; rather, they undergo a series of changes and adopt different forms through the functions of the rock cycle. Plate tectonics and the water cycle are the driving forces behind the rock cycle; they force rocks and minerals out of equilibrium and force them to adjust to different external conditions. Viewed in a generalized, cyclical fashion, the rock cycle operates thusly: rocks beneath Earth's surface melt into magma. This magma either erupts through volcanoes or remains inside the Earth. Regardless, the magma cools, forming igneous rocks. On the surface, these rocks experience weathering and erosion, which break them down and distribute the fragments across the surface. These fragments form layers and eventually become sedimentary rocks.

Sedimentary rocks are then either transformed to metamorphic rocks (which will become magma inside the Earth) or melted down into magma.

The formation of igneous rocks:
Igneous rocks can be formed from sedimentary rocks, metamorphic rocks, or other igneous rocks. Rocks which are pushed under the Earth's surface (usually due to plate subduction) are exposed to high mantle temperatures, which cause them to melt into magma. The magma then rises to the surface through volcanic processes. The lower atmospheric temperature causes the magma to cool, forming grainy, extrusive igneous rocks. The creation of extrusive, or volcanic, rocks is quite rapid. The cooling process can occur so rapidly that crystals do not form; in this case, the result is a glass, such as obsidian. It is also possible for magma to cool down inside the Earth's interior; this type of igneous rock is called intrusive. Intrusive, or plutonic, rocks cool more slowly, resulting in a coarse-grained texture.

The formation of sedimentary rocks:
Rocks of any type (igneous, metamorphic, or sedimentary) which are exposed to the atmosphere on the surface of the Earth experience weathering and erosion due to elements such as wind and water. These processes break down exposed rocks and transport the resultant fragments. Fragmented material (small pieces of rock, organic debris, and the chemical products of mineral sublimation) is deposited and accumulates in layers, with top layers burying the materials beneath. The pressure exerted by the topmost layers causes the lower layers to compact, creating solid sedimentary rock in a process called lithification.

The formation of metamorphic rocks:
Igneous, sedimentary, and metamorphic rocks are all subject to metamorphic processes (those which result in the creation of metamorphic rocks). In metamorphism, high temperatures and levels of pressure change preexisting rocks physically and/or chemically, which produces different species of rocks. In the rock cycle, this process generally occurs in materials which have been thrust back into the Earth's mantle by plate subduction. Regional metamorphism refers to a large band of metamorphic activity; this often occurs near areas of high orogenic (mountain-building) activity. Contact metamorphism refers to metamorphism which occurs when "country rock" comes into contact with high-heat igneous intrusions (magma).

The plate tectonics rock cycle as it relates to the traditional rock cycle
The plate tectonics rock cycle expands the concept of the traditional rock cycle to include more specific information about the tectonic processes which propel the rock cycle, as well as an evolutionary component. Earth's materials do not cycle endlessly through the different rock forms; rather, these transitive processes cause, for example, increasing diversification of the rock types found in the crust. Also, the cycling of rock increases the masses of continents by increasing the volume of granite. Thus the tectonic rock cycle is a model of an evolutionary rock cycle. In this model, we begin with the creation of new oceanic lithosphere at divergent plate boundaries. This new crust spreads outward until it reaches a subduction zone, where it is pushed back into the mantle, becomes magma, and is

- 21 -

thrust out into the atmosphere. It experiences erosion and becomes sedimentary rock. At convergent continental plate boundaries, this crust is involved in mountain building and the associated metamorphic pressures. It is eroded again, and returns to the lithosphere.

The role of water in the cycling of Earth materials

Water obviously plays an important role in the rock cycle through its roles in erosion and weathering: it wears down rocks, it contributes to the dissolution of rocks and minerals as acidic soil water, it carries ions and rock fragments (sediments) to basins where they will be compressed into sedimentary rock. Water also plays a role in the metamorphic processes which occur underwater in newly-formed igneous rock at mid-ocean ridges. The presence of water (and other volatiles) is a vital component in the melting of rocky crust into magma above subduction zones.

Rock cycle terms

The rocks at Earth's surface experience physical, biological, and chemical processes which are much different from the processes ambient during their formations. The operation of these processes on Earth materials is called weathering.

Mechanical weathering causes disintegration of rocks and minerals. In this process, the affected rocks break apart into small fragments but retain their chemical compositions. This type of weathering occurs due to the presence of joints, or cracks, in rocks which allow the penetration of water and vegetative roots. Mechanical weathering occurs most often in cooler climates.

Chemical weathering refers to the processes by which rocks experience chemical changes (such as decomposition and decay) due to the influence of organic acids. Chemical weathering occurs most often in high temperature, high humidity climates. The two types of weathering are not mutually exclusive; they often occur side by side.

Erosion also occurs simultaneously with weathering. This term refers to the transportation of Earth materials by wind, water, gravity, and sometimes living organisms.

The subtypes of mechanical weathering

Pressure release, or surface unloading, occurs when erosion removes materials overlying rock. Decreased pressure causes the underlying rocks to expand and fracture. Exfoliation often occurs in regions with some moisture which experience substantial diurnal temperature changes. Rocks are subjected to heat during the day, which causes them to expand. At night, the much cooler temperatures cause the rocks to compact. The repeated expansion and contraction creates stress in the outer layers of the rocks, which eventually begin to "peel" off in thin layers. Exfoliation can also be caused by pressure release. Freeze-thaw operates when water which has penetrated the joints of a rock freezes and expands. The resultant pressure widens the joints and can even shatter the rock. If the rock does not fracture, the thawing of ice in the joints admits water further into the rock. Continuous, long-term freeze-thaw activity weakens rocks. In salt-crystal growth, the evaporation of saline solutions within rocks leaves salt crystals behind. Pressures accompanying this crystallization can be very high.

The subtypes of chemical weathering

Hydration occurs when salt minerals which are part of a rock expand and change due to the absorption of water. For example, anhydrite changes to gypsum with the addition of water.

- 22 -

Hydration can cause rocks to fragment mechanically. The process of hydrolysis involves a chemical reaction between acidic water and a rock-forming mineral. The interaction breaks the rock down into new materials. For instance, the chemical reaction between feldspar and acidic water produces quartz and clay. Most rocks contain iron-bearing minerals in some measure. Oxidation, or rusting, which results in yellow, brown, or red discoloration, occurs in these minerals when they are exposed to the atmosphere. Solution is the weathering process whereby an organic acid interacts with certain minerals in a rock, producing ions which are then washed away by erosion. Solution, therefore, is a gradual dissolving process. It produces underground channels and caverns.

Mass movement

A mass movement (also called mass wasting) is the downward movement of large amounts of rock and debris due to gravitational forces. The speed at which the material will move and the amount of dislodged material are affected by several factors: the amount of water in the affected material, the climate, the type and extent of weathering, the steepness of the incline, the presence or absence of rooted vegetation, the type of bedrock present and its condition, and the presence or absence of seismic activity. Mass movements cause changes in the landscape of an area. They can also place humans and animals in the affected area in danger.

Rockfall

A rockfall is a mass movement wherein various amounts of rock material fall very rapidly (at speeds of 99 miles per hour or more) from a cliff face. This movement may involve a single rock or boulder or may spur an avalanche of tons of rock. The pile of rocks which results from a rockfall is termed a talus. When it occurs at a mountain base, a talus may prevent weathering of the mountain. A rockfall may be triggered by an earthquake, excessive rain, ice wedging (common on mountains), or human activity. Such a mass movement may, in turn, spawn an avalanche, a rockfall which contributes to a debris flow. The materials in motion in a rockfall often leave "scars" on the slope from which they fall.

Landslide

The term landslide may be used to designate several different downslope movements. Normally, a landslide involves the movement of soil and rock as a more or less coherent mass down a slope, although either the bedrock itself or the soil which overlays it may move independently. There are two main categories of landslides. Glides, or translational slides, which entails a large portion of rock detached from its bedrock which "glides" outward and downward along a slope. A slump (or rotational slide) involves the motion of a relatively cohesive mass along a concave plane—the upper part of the sliding mass ends up below ground level, and the bottom part of the mass ends up above it.

Flow

Flow is a type of mass movement which entails "viscous" motion of surface materials. Flows are characterized by motion of the internal grains of the moving mass (unlike slides). Also, they do not include a clear barrier between the flow material and a stable surface underneath. The velocity of a flow is widely various, dependent on the slope upon which it travels and the presence or absence of water. Flows generally involve one of three types of material: earth, mud, or debris. An earth flow is often initiated at the end of a slump slide, when the block of sliding material breaks apart. A mud flow involves the motions of soil and relatively high proportions of water. Increased water content increases the velocity of the moving mass from that of an earth flow. Mud flows are common in deserts. A debris flow is

- 23 -

similar to a mud flow; often, the only distinction between the two is the size of the particles in motion. The motions of both debris flows and mud flows tend to follow pre-existing channels.

Creep

Creep is a landscape-altering mass movement. It involves a shallow mass of soil material moving slowly downward. This type of movement usually occurs so slowly that no one notices it. Creep can be caused by freeze-thaw or wet-dry cycles, depending on the characteristics of the bedrock materials. As with other types of mass movements, the introduction of high amounts of water into creep material will cause it to move more quickly. Though creep does not pose an immediate threat to human or animal life, it can be dangerous through long-term effects on the foundations of buildings, trees, or other structures.

Solifluction is an intensified form of creep. The existence of permafrost (a layer of earth that remains in a long term state of freeze, which occurs in very cold climates) prevents absorption of surface water. The excess water then enters the topmost "active" layer of soil. That layer is thus more vulnerable to the process of creep than a comparable layer of soil in a warmer climate because of its increased fluidity and the frozen surface over which it slides. Solifluction tends to result in a "wrinkled" landscape with smooth terrain.

An erosion landform

An erosion landform is a landform created by the processes of weathering and erosion. For example, a cliff is an erosion landform. Cliffs are formed when relatively strong rocks are exposed to centuries of wind and water weathering and erosion. Sandstone, limestone, and basalt are examples of rocks which commonly become cliffs. The canyon provides the classic instance of an erosion landform. Canyons are formed from many years of weathering and erosion processes (often water based), usually operating on a plateau (a mountain which has been eroded down to a flat but elevated surface). Strata of rocks which resisted the destructive processes remain visible in the canyon walls.

Stream deposition

Stream deposition is the last phase in the weathering and erosion process performed by water, specifically streams. Stream erosion occurs when the movement of water in a stream detaches material from the sides and bottom of the channel through which it flows. This can carve out valleys and wide, meandering streams. Streams then carry the weathered material, as well as material deposited in the stream by other erosive processes, out to sea. Streams transport sediment in three ways.
1. The solid load consists of the suspended load (sediment grains of various sizes floating in the water) and the bed load (the materials dragged along the bed of a channel by the moving water).
2. The bed load performs much of the erosion of the sides and bottoms of the channel.
3. A stream's dissolved load is composed of ions produced in the chemical weathering process. Stream deposition occurs when the stream drops its load of sediment. This can occur due to flooding or intersection of the stream with a larger body of water.

River and Stream erosion terms

The movement of water in streams and rivers plays a key role in landscape evolution. The long-term effect of rivers and streams is to erode the land around them down to sea level, the base level of erosion.

One theory of the way this occurs is backwasting. **Backwasting** entails the wearing down of river valley slopes parallel to themselves. When the surface between valley slopes is worn down to the base level of erosion, the slopes retreat in parallel layers until all of the land above the widening platform is eroded to the same level.

Downwasting is another theoretical process which explains landscape evolution. This process involves the diminishing of valley slopes through mass movements of soil and rock decomposition.

A **peneplain** is the result of the erosive process of the land around streams. It is a wide, nearly flat plain of bedrock which exists just above the base level of erosion.

A **monadnock** is an anomalous portion of especially tenacious rock which rises above a peneplain.

Ecosystems and common characteristics

An ecosystem (an abbreviated term for ecological system) is a system in the biosphere which consists of a biotic community (a regional group of living organisms) and the surrounding environment, called a biotope. Ecosystems may be studied at different scales. For example, an ecosystem may be as small as an area within a pond or as large as the entire planet.
- Ecosystems exist in dynamic equilibrium, a relatively steady state maintained by various symbiotic (interactive) processes such as predation (wherein one organism, a predator, overwhelms and consumes another, the prey) and mutualism (interspecies relationships which benefit both parties).
- Ecosystems receive energy inputs (mainly from the sun); this energy is transformed through the process of photosynthesis and transferred among constituents via the food web.
- Ecosystems also produce natural resources utilized by human beings, including structural materials, food, and fuel.
- Ecosystems are broadly described as terrestrial (those which include land animals and exist atop continents) or aquatic (those dominated by water and marine or freshwater life).

Ecological succession
Ecological succession is the process which occurs after a significant disturbance or disaster has simplified an ecosystem.
- Primary succession follows a disaster which eliminates all living organisms in a region (such as a volcanic eruption).
- Secondary succession refers to the process which succeeds a disturbance in which some life survives (such as deforestation).

Ecological succession is the change of a biotic community from a simpler state to one which is more diverse and complex. Through this process, members of an ecosystem mature and develop more intricate relationships. Though ecologists in earlier times envisioned a climax stage which represented the end-point of ecosystem development, this idea is largely absent in current ecological discourse. Rather, modern ecologists believe that ecosystems are always changing and reacting to various degrees and frequencies of disturbances, making a climax community unreachable.

Photosynthesis

Photosynthesis is a chemical process, fueled by energy received through direct sunlight in the form of photons, by which plants containing chlorophyll convert carbon dioxide and water into glucose and oxygen. The light energy is converted to chemical energy and stored in the bonds of glucose. During the light dependent process, the interaction of photons with chlorophyll serves to decompose water into oxygen, which is released into the atmosphere, and hydrogen. This reaction converts light energy to chemical energy, which acts on the hydrogen and carbon dioxide to produce glucose in the light independent process. Photosynthesis is vital to life on Earth because it releases a vast amount of oxygen (necessary for respiration) into the atmosphere. Also, glucose is the basic building block of carbohydrates, and is thus a main energy source for living organisms.

The food web

The food web or food network is a model used to describe the transfer of energy (in the form of sustenance) between organisms in an ecosystem. Organisms feed on one another to stay alive; this process also helps to regulate the populations of species within an ecosystem. Organisms in a food web are generally organized into trophic levels which reflect their relative positions in this system. Primary producers, usually photosynthetic plants and algae, exist at the base of a food web. These organisms produce vital biochemical molecules (including carbohydrates) from light energy derived from the sun's energy. The primary producers are consumed by small primary consumers, such as insects and fish. These organisms are in turn eaten and digested by secondary consumers, which are later preyed upon by larger organisms, and so on. Decomposers are soil-dwelling microorganisms which rely on detritus (decaying organic materials) for sustenance. Because energy is lost in transfer throughout the food web (due to respiration), the number of organisms and their sizes decline up the chain.

Respiration

Respiration is the process whereby energy is burned by an organism to keep it alive. It is basically the opposite of photosynthesis. This chemical process involves the decomposition of carbohydrates, which then combine with oxygen, releasing water, carbon dioxide, and heat energy into the atmosphere. Organisms' cells store the chemical energy produced through respiration; this energy is later used to create vital biochemical molecules. Respiration is thus a counterpart of photosynthesis in the cycling of elements through an ecosystem. Due to the energy loss inherent to the process of respiration, only 10-50% of the energy stored in organic matter at one level of the food web moves up to the next level.

The process of transpiration

Transpiration is the mechanism by which water evaporates into the atmosphere from the leaves or stems of plants. Plants absorb water into their roots through osmosis. Then, as explicated by cohesion-tension theory, water moves upward from the roots of a plant to its leaves. Some transpiration occurs directly through surface cells on the stem of a plant. More often, however, water escapes through pores in its leaves called stomates. Water droplets on the exterior surface of the leaves (usually on the bottom of the leaves) are consequently subjected to the process of evaporation. The process of transpiration enables photosynthesis, which in turn releases vital oxygen into Earth's atmosphere. Transpiration also has a cooling affect on the surface and air around the plant.

Biogeochemical cycle

The term biogeochemical cycle refers to one of several chemical processes in which chemical elements are (re)cycled among biotic (living) and abiotic (nonliving) constituents of an ecosystem. The theory of relativity necessitates the presence of such cycles in nature by virtue of its supposition that energy and matter are not created or destroyed in a closed system such as Earth's ecosystem. Generally, a biogeochemical cycle operates as follows:

1. Inorganic compounds, such as carbon, are converted from water, air, and soil to organic molecules by organisms called autotrophs.
2. Heterotrophs consume the autotrophs; some of the newly formed organic molecules are transferred.
3. Finally, the organic molecules are broken down and processed once again into inorganic compounds by secondary and tertiary consumers and replaced within water, air, and soil. Carbon, nitrogen, and phosphorus provide examples of nutrients which are recycled in the Earth's ecosystem.

Biome

A biome is the broadest general subdivision of terrestrial ecosystems. This term is used to describe a region which exhibits the distinctive plant and animal life best adapted to an area's particular soil type and climate. This concept is associated with the interrelationships between organisms and their environment. Since vegetation is more abundant than any other species in the biosphere, biomes are often classified according to climax vegetation type (the type of vegetation which exists in mature or old-growth ecosystems). The global distribution of biomes is closely related to climate and soil variations at different latitudes. The subdivision of biome may be further differentiated into formation classes, based upon the structural and dimensional characteristics of regional vegetation.

The forest biome and outline some characteristics of the low-latitude rainforest, monsoon forest, and subtropical evergreen forest formation classes:

- The forest biome is typified by an abundance of soil and moisture, as well as warm temperatures for at least a portion of the year. Trees are the dominant vegetation type in this biome.
- The low-latitude rainforest formation class exists in equatorial and tropical climate zones. This class is characterized by many different species of tall, densely spaced trees, normally with broad leaves. The canopy created by this vegetation casts shade on the ground below, inhibiting the growth of flora on the bottom layer.
- Monsoon forests may also be found in tropical latitude zones; however, this formation class exists in regions which experience a wet season and a dry season, during which the many tree species lose their leaves. This enables the growth of vegetation on the lower layer of the forest.
- The subtropical evergreen forest may be broadleaf or needleleaf (found only in the southeastern United States). This formation class consists of fewer, shorter tree species than the low-latitude rainforest. It also includes a lush lower layer of vegetation.

The forest biome classes characteristics

The *midlatitude deciduous forest formation class* is common in regions of the northern hemisphere with distinct seasons. During the warm summer season, the tall broadleaf trees in this type of forest form a nearly closed canopy. In the winter season, these trees lose their leaves. The lower level vegetation also varies with the season, growing in the spring and dying out with the summertime formation of a dense upper canopy.

A *needleleaf forest* is made up largely of conifers (cone-shaped trees with short branches, straight trunks, and small, thin leaves reminiscent of needles). Many trees in this type of forest (usually found at higher latitudes or regions where orogenies and/or plateaus are found) are evergreen, meaning that they shed their leaves once every several years. The spacing of the trees in this formation class may be dense, preventing the growth of vegetation on the ground.

The *sclerophyll forest* contains widely-spaced trees with are able to survive dry, hot seasons (short, with low branches, tough, thick bark, and short, thick leaves).

The savanna biome

The savanna biome exists between forest and grassland on the spectrum of biomes. It is often situated near the boundary of an equatorial rainforest. This type of biome is commonly found in regions which experience a wet-dry tropical climate. The lack of moisture in the soil during the dry season causes trees in the savanna biome to grow in spacious patterns. This enables the growth of a dense lower layer of grasses and other plants. The trees of the savanna biome are similar in height and shape to those found in the monsoon forest. Though fire is a fairly common occurrence in savannas during the dry season, the vegetation in these regions tends to be quite fire resistant. In fact, many geographers believe that such fires prevent rainforest vegetation from overrunning the savanna biome.

The grassland biome

The grassland biome is commonly subdivided into two types. The tall-grass prairie subdivision is characterized by an absence of trees and a high occurrence of tall grasses and broad-leaved herbs called forbs. This kind of biome usually forms in regions with distinct summer and winter seasons, in subtropical or midlatitude climates.

The other subdivision of the grassland biome is the steppe, or short-grass prairie. The steppe is typified by sparse clumps of short grasses, existing alongside the occasional shrub or small tree. Many grass species and forbs populate this kind of region. Steppes are usually found in midlatitude areas with dry continental climates; vegetation grows in wet spring months and becomes dormant during dry summer months.

The desert biome

The desert biome may be subdivided into two types. The semidesert type is found at a wide range of latitudes. It is characterized by thinly spaced xerophytic shrubs (those adapted to survival in arid climates). Steppe regions may be converted to semidesert through, for example, high levels of cattle moving through the area, treading upon and consuming regional vegetation. The thorntree semidesert is found in the tropical zone, which experiences a long, dry hot season and a short, severe rainy season. Thorny vegetation (such as cacti), called thornbush or thornwoods, populate the thorntree semidesert.

The other subdivision of the desert biome is the dry desert. The dry desert is even barer than the semidesert. Only tough xerophytes, such as cacti and hard grasses, can survive under desert conditions. Many dry desert areas display no plant life at all, due to the unfertile sand which covers the ground.

The tundra biome

The tundra biome may be arctic or alpine. The arctic tundra exists at very high latitudes near the poles. During the brief summer season in these areas, low vegetation such as herbs, mosses, and grasses are able to grow because above-freezing air temperatures enable melting of the surface layer. The type and occurrence of plant species depends upon the moisture levels in the (usually frozen) ground during the warm season. In the cold season, frost action snaps roots in the ground. Freezing wind and snow kill plants above the ground. Alpine tundra is located at high elevations, above the tree line and below bare mountain tops. Physically, the alpine tundra is quite similar to the arctic tundra.

Earth's rotation and its effects

The Earth rotates eastward (from the equator) about its rotational axis (an imaginary line running north to south through the center of the planet). This motion exposes each section of the Earth to direct sunlight for a limited period of time, thus creating the sensations of day and night. Due to minute variations in the sidereal day, which is defined as the exact amount of time it takes for reference star to cross an imaginary north-south line above an observer (a meridian), we use the mean sidereal day (a period of exactly 24 hours) in timekeeping. Earth's rotation creates diurnal (daily) variations in air humidity, air temperature, and air motion. These patterns affect plant and animal life on the planet, and also influence the hydrosphere, causing tidal movement and the Coriolis effect.

Earth's revolution and its effects

Earth revolves around the sun in an orbit. This process takes just over 365 days (our calendar year). The consequence of the elliptical shape of Earth's orbit is that the distance between the planet and the star varies over time. At perihelion, the minimum heliocentric distance, Earth is 147 million kilometers from the sun. At aphelion, the maximum heliocentric distance, Earth is 152 million kilometers from the sun. Earth's revolution about the sun and the tilt of the planet's rotational axis (approximately 23.5 degrees from its orbital plane) produce the seasons we experience on Earth—certain areas of the surface receive different amounts of sunlight throughout the year. For example, during the portion of Earth's orbit when the Northern Hemisphere tilts toward the sun, it is exposed to higher amounts of nearly-direct sunlight than any other time of year (for days are longer and the direction of sun's rays striking the surface is nearly perpendicular). This time period is summer in the Northern Hemisphere and winter in the Southern Hemisphere.

Global energy flow system

A main tenet of physics is that energy, like matter, cannot be created or destroyed in a closed system such as the Earth. This fact necessitates the recycling of energy from the sun to the Earth and back again. The Earth receives energy from the sun in the form of light and heat. It moves through the atmosphere as short-wave radiation and is converted to different forms, fueling nearly all of the natural physical phenomena which occur on the planet in one way or another (either directly or indirectly). Solar energy is also "lost" due to scattering and absorption in the atmosphere. The rate of this incoming energy, which is nearly constant, is referred to as the solar constant. Long-wave radiation is emitted from the Earth into space, often through the release of gases like carbon dioxide and water vapor. The pathways through which energy travels between the sun and the Earth, including its storage as well as its losses in the atmosphere, make up the global energy flow system.

Weather

Weather is the result of transfers of kinetic (heat) energy due to differences in temperature between objects as well as transfers of moisture in Earth's atmosphere. Meteorology, the study of weather, entails the observation of natural phenomena such as rain, fog, snow, and wind. The processes which occur at different stages in the hydrologic cycle form the basis of meteorological events. Most of the activity which produces the weather we experience on Earth takes place in the troposphere, the lowest level of the atmosphere (0-15 kilometers above Earth's surface). Atmospheric pressure, temperature, humidity, elevation, wind speed, and cloud cover are all factors in the formation of weather. A weather system is an organized atmospheric state, associated with a particular weather pattern such as cyclones or tornadoes.

Cycles of air temperature
Due to Earth's rotation, insolation (interception of solar energy by an exposed surface) varies from location to location with the angle at which solar rays hit the Earth and the length of time a particular location is exposed to direct sunlight. Net radiation is the difference between incoming and outgoing radiation. This quality is positive when more energy is flowing in than out, and vice-versa. During daylight hours, a surface location experiences positive net radiation, causing it to gain heat; at night, the location loses heat. This pattern is the daily air temperature cycle. The annual air temperature cycle results from Earth's revolution. When a region of the Earth experiences summer, the region's net radiation is positive. In wintertime, net radiation is low. Air temperature is also affected by altitude (temperature generally decreases as altitude increases), location (continental or oceanic—air temperature in maritime areas is less variable), and surface features (which may absorb or reflect heat waves). Isotherms are lines on a map connecting points with equivalent air temperatures.

The hydrologic cycle
The hydrologic, or water, cycle is the circulation of water in the Earth's hydrosphere (below the surface, on the surface, and above the surface of the Earth). This continuous process involves five physical actions. The first, evaporation, entails the change of water molecules from a liquid to gaseous state. Liquid water on the Earth's surface (often contained in a large body of water) becomes water vapor and enters the atmosphere when its component molecules gain enough kinetic (heat) energy to escape the liquid form. As the vapor rises, it cools and therefore loses its ability to maintain the gaseous form. It begins to condense (return to a liquid or solid state) and forms clouds. When the clouds become sufficiently dense, the water falls back to the Earth as precipitation. Water is then either trapped in vegetation (interception) or infiltration (absorption of water into the surface). Runoff, caused by gravity, physically moves water downward into oceans or other water bodies.

Precipitation
Precipitation is water which falls back to Earth's surface from the atmosphere. This water may be in the form of rain, which is water in the liquid form. Raindrops are formed in clouds due to the process of condensation. When the drops become too heavy to remain in the cloud (due to a decrease in their kinetic energy), gravity causes them to fall down toward Earth's surface. Extremely small raindrops are called drizzle. If the temperature of a layer of

air through which rain passes on its way down is below the freezing point, the rain may take the form of sleet (partially frozen water). Precipitation may also fall in the form of snow, or water molecules sublimated into ice crystals. When clumps of snowflakes melt and refreeze, hail is formed. Hail may also be formed when liquid water accumulates on the surface of a snowflake and subsequently freezes.

Four main types of clouds

A cirrus cloud forms high in a stable atmosphere, generally at altitudes of 6,000 meters or higher. Temperatures at these altitudes (in the troposphere) decrease with increased altitude; therefore, the precipitation in a cirrus cloud adopts the form of ice crystals. These usually thin traces of clouds may indicate an approaching depression.

A cumulous cloud is a stereotypical white, fluffy ball. They are indicators of a stable atmosphere, and also of the vertical extent of convection in the atmosphere—condensation and cloud formation begin at the flat base of a cumulous cloud. The more humid the air, the lower a cumulous cloud will form.

A nimbus cloud is, generally speaking, a rain cloud. Nimbus clouds are usually low, dark, and formless, sometimes spanning the entire visible sky.

A stratus cloud is basically a cloud of fog which forms at a distance above the Earth's surface. This type of cloud forms when weak convective currents bring moisture just high enough to initiate condensation (if the temperature is below the dew point).

Four cloud subtypes
A cumulonimbus cloud is produced by rapid convection in unstable air. This type of cloud (which is often dark) is formed as a large, tall "tower." Collections of these towers (squall lines) often signal a coming cold front. Thunderstorms often involve cumulonimbus clouds.

A cirrostratus cloud is an ultra thin formation with a white tint and a transparent quality.

An altocumulus cloud forms at an altitude from 1,980 to 6,100 meters. Clouds of this type, which appear to be flattened spheres, often form in clumps, waves, or lines.

A stratocumulus cloud forms as a globular mass or flake. Stratocumulus clouds usually come together in layers or clumps.

Humidity
Humidity is a measure of the amount of water vapor in the air:
- Specific humidity is the expression of humidity as a ratio of aqueous vapor to dry air; it is expressed as a ratio of mass of water vapor per unit mass of natural (dry) air.
- Absolute humidity measures the mass of water vapor in a given volume of moist air or gas; it is expressed in grams per cubic foot or per cubic meter. The equilibrium (or saturated) vapor pressure of a gas is the vapor pressure (created by the movement of molecules) of water vapor when air is saturated with water vapor.

- Relative humidity, usually expressed as a percentage, is the ratio of the vapor pressure of water in air (or another gas) to the equilibrium vapor pressure. In other words, it is a ratio of the mass of water per volume of gas and the mass per volume of a saturated gas.

Atmospheric pressure

Atmospheric pressure is the pressure exerted by air in the atmosphere on the surface beneath it. This pressure subsists because the air's mass is continuously being drawn toward the Earth's surface by the force of gravity. The amount of atmospheric pressure increases with proximity to the surface due to the fact that there is more mass above the lower layers. Pressure causes air mass to compress; therefore, the layer of air nearest Earth's exterior is denser than air at higher altitudes. Atmospheric pressure is measured as force per unit area. This may be the pascal (Pa), which is one newton per square meter, or the milibar (mb); one milibar equals 100 Pa. These measurements are taken with a barometer. An isobar is a line on a map which connects all points with equal levels of atmospheric pressure.

Prevailing winds and wind belts phenomena
Wind (the horizontal movement of air with respect to Earth's surface) forms due to pressure gradients (differences) in the atmosphere. Air tends to move from areas of high pressure (such as the poles) to areas of low pressure (such as the tropics).
- Prevailing winds, or trade winds, are the winds (named in meteorology for the direction they come from) which blow most frequently in a particular region. For instance, the prevailing winds most common in the region from 90 to 60 degrees north latitude blow from the northeast, and are generally called the Polar Easterlies.
- Wind belts are created in areas where prevailing winds converge with other prevailing winds or air masses. The Inter-Tropical Convergence Zone (ITCZ), where air coming from tropical areas north and south of the equator come together, is an example of a wind belt.

Air mass

An air mass is a sizeable region of air which displays consistent levels of moisture and uniform temperature throughout. The characteristics of a particular air mass develop in a source region, where air remains stable for a period of time long enough for said air to adopt the moisture and temperature qualities of the surface below. Air masses move due to atmospheric pressure gradients or the influence of winds. Corresponding changes in the surface environment may cause an air mass to take on new properties. These pockets of air are named for the qualities of the surface environment (maritime or continental), which determine the humidity of the mass, as well as the latitudinal position at which they form, which determines the temperature of the mass. For example, an air mass which forms over a continent at a high latitudinal location is called a continental polar air mass (denoted as cP).

Air stability in the atmosphere
Heated air rises because it is less dense than the surrounding air. As a pocket of air rises, however, it will expand and become cooler with changes in atmospheric pressure. If the ambient air into which rising air ascends does not cool as quickly with altitude as the rising air does, that air will rapidly become cooler (and heavier) than the surrounding air and

descend back to its original position. The air in this situation is said to be stable. However, if the air into which the warm pocket rises becomes colder with increased altitude, the warm air will continue its ascent. In this case, the air is unstable. Unstable air conditions (such as those which exist in depressions) lead to the formation of large clouds of precipitation.

Cyclones and anticyclones

Both cyclones and anticyclones are weather systems in which air masses move in spirals. Most such systems move across Earth's surface, affecting weather as they travel. A cyclone occurs when low pressure in the interior of an air mass draws air inward and upward. The risen air often forms clouds which in turn produce cyclonic precipitation. A cyclone which involves large pressure disparities produces intense weather referred to as a cyclonic storm.

In anticyclones, the movement of air is opposite to that in cyclones—air pressure in the center of an air mass is higher than the surrounding air, forcing air outward and downward. Because descending warm air does not produce precipitous clouds, anticyclones are often referred to as fair weather systems.

Weather front

A front is the distinct boundary which usually forms between an air mass and the surrounding air. This boundary may be sloped or nearly vertical in orientation, depending on the relative movement of abutting air masses. When a cold air mass moves into an area inhabited by a mass of warm air, the attendant front is referred to as a cold front. In this situation, the colder, denser air mass remains near the surface, pushing the warmer mass upward. When the ascending air is unstable, this movement may create severe weather, such as thunderstorms. A warm front is formed when a warm air mass enters an area of colder air. Again, the warmer air ascends, creating precipitation. An occluded front occurs when a cold air mass (which generally moves more quickly than a warmer mass of air due to its higher density) overtakes a moving mass of warm air near Earth's surface. As in other front systems, the coldest air remains near the ground, forcing the warmer air to rise.

Wave cyclones

A wave cyclone is a type of cyclone which forms at mid- to high latitudinal regions. This kind of weather system forms at the boundary between dry polar air masses and humid tropical air masses, called a polar front. The cyclone forms, intensifies, and ebbs repeatedly in a low-pressure trough between the converging masses. Cyclonic motion begins with the initial contact between the two air masses; the motion of both air bodies intensifies. Then, when the colder mass overtakes and elevates the warmer one, an occluded front forms in the middle of the weather system. The polar front is then reestablished, and the process begins anew. Wave cyclones affect wind, temperature, cloud formation, and precipitation in the surface regions over which they occur.

Tornado

A tornado is a particularly intense cyclone, which may exhibit wind speeds of up to 400 miles per hour. Tornadoes often form alongside mid-latitude thunderstorms over continental North America; they are also commonly observed inside of tropical hurricanes. In fact, tornadoes are most often formed at a cold front where maritime polar air forces warm, moist tropical air upward. This type of cyclone is bred from cumulonimbus clouds moving ahead of a cold front. A dark funnel-shaped cloud extends downward from a dense cumulonimbus cloud. The funnel's base appears especially dense, due to the accumulating moisture, dust, and debris being swept up by the formation. When the base of a tornado makes landfall, it can be completely devastating.

Tropical cyclone

Tropical cyclones are potentially the most destructive and dangerous type of cyclone. Such a formation is referred to as a hurricane when it occurs over the Atlantic Ocean or as a typhoon when it occurs over the Pacific or Indian Oceans. Tropical cyclones develop at low latitudes (specifically, between 8 and 15 degrees North or South latitude) when the surface waters below reach temperatures of 81 degrees Fahrenheit or above. From their zone of origination, tropical cyclones often travel westward through the trade-wind belt; westerly winds may push the storm northward as well. This type of cyclone is associated with high wind speeds and high levels of rainfall. A tropical cyclone also displays extremely low pressure in its center, or eye, where weather conditions are fair (in contrast to the rest of the storm). These weather systems occur seasonally: in the Northern Hemisphere, cyclonic activity is highest from May to November; in the Southern Hemisphere, the cyclone season is roughly opposite.

Tropical and equatorial weather system terms

An *easterly wave* is formed in the belt of tropical trades. This formation is a trough of low pressure, which travels slowly through the belt. Easterly waves occur above oceans at latitudes of 5 to 30 degrees North or South. The influence of surface winds forces the air in an easterly wave upward, causing light rainfall and occasional thunderstorms.

A *weak equatorial low* is a disturbance which occurs near the center of an equatorial trough (area of low pressure). Moist air masses meet at this point, creating precipitation.

When a small region of frigid polar air reaches low latitudes near the equator, this air is referred to as a *polar outbreak*. This type of air mass enters a low-latitude region as a cold front, which is followed by clear but cold weather and strong winds. While polar outbreaks are not inherently dangerous, the low temperatures involved can damage crops in low-latitude regions.

Lightning

Lightning is a natural electrostatic discharge which produces light and releases electromagnetic radiation. It is believed that the separation of positive and negative charge carriers within a cloud is achieved by the polarization mechanism. The first step of this mechanism occurs when falling precipitation particles become electrically polarized after they move through the Earth's magnetic field. The second step of the polarization mechanism involves electrostatic induction, the process whereby electrically charged particles create charges in other particles without direct contact. Ice particles are charged though this method, and then energy-storing electric fields are formed between the charged particles. The positively charged ice crystals tend to rise to the top of the cloud, effectively polarizing the cloud with positive charges on top and negative charges at the middle and bottom. When charged clouds conglomerate, an electric discharge (a lightning bolt) is produced, either between clouds or between a cloud and the Earth's surface.

Thunderstorm

A thunderstorm is a weather phenomenon which includes lightning, thunder, and usually large amounts of precipitation and strong winds. Thunder is the noise made by the rapid expansion and contraction of air due to the heat energy produced by lightning bolts. A thunderstorm develops when heating on the Earth's surface causes large amounts of air to rise into an unstable atmosphere. This results in large clouds of rain and ice crystals. The associated condensation releases high levels of heat, which in turn power the growth cycle of the cloud. The clouds created during thunderstorms are immense, sometimes reaching widths of several miles and extending to heights of 10,000 meters or more. The precipitation in such clouds eventually becomes heavy enough to fall against the updraft of unstable air; the consequent downpour is often short but intense. The differential speeds at which light and sound travel through the atmosphere enable one to estimate the distance between oneself and the storm by observing the interval between a lightning bolt and a thunderclap.

Climate

Climate is usually defined as the "average weather" in a particular area on Earth. The time span over which climate is measured is variable, but it is generally accepted that the climate of an area does not vary during a human life span (though climate is extremely various in geologic time). This may change, however, due to the increasing greenhouse effect.

Meteorologists measure climate by averaging certain quantifiable elements such as rainfall or temperature. Climate may be studied on several different scales:
- Local climate refers to the climate of small geographic areas (generally up to tens of miles wide). The local climate of an area is affected by things like its location relative to an ocean and the presence of mountains near the location.
- A regional climate is the climate of a larger geographic area, such as a country; a regional climate may also be delineated due to climate features that are distinctive from the surrounding climate.
- Global climate refers to the average weather experienced across the Earth.

Climate zones
Climate zones are areas of regional climate. These zones are created by the general circulation of the air in Earth's atmosphere. Generally, the warmest air moves from the equator (where the greatest amount of solar energy is received) toward the higher latitudes at the poles. The latitudinal temperature gradient produces atmospheric pressure. At the equator, solar energy heats air near the surface, causing it to rise and decreasing air pressure. The risen air is transported by winds to cooler areas at higher latitudes, where the air then descends (because cool air is heavier than warmer air), creating an area of high pressure. The descended air is then moved by surface winds, either back to the equator or up to higher latitudes, where it encounters colder air. The air then rises again in an area of low pressure. The air in polar regions is very cold, which causes it to sink, creating high pressure. Winds are thus generated to move air from warmer regions to colder ones.

Tropical, subtropical, and polar climate zones
The tropical (low-latitude) climate zone covers the area around the equator. This area receives a large portion of the sun's solar energy, making average temperatures in this zone fairly high. The consistent levels of hot air in the region indicate that air is often moving

upward. This convective process, in turn, produces large levels of precipitation in the area, resulting in a humid climate. Seasons in the tropical zone are delineated by the amount of rainfall, instead of by changes in temperatures.

Subtropical (mid-latitude) climate zones are found about thirty degrees north and south of the equator. These zones generally consist of dry descending air, clear skies, and high atmospheric pressure. Desert climates (extreme heat during the day, cold temperatures at night, and lack of precipitation) are common in these zones.

Polar (high-latitude) climate zones are found at the north and south poles. They are characterized by high air pressure (due to descending air), low temperatures (rarely above freezing), and lack of precipitation (because air cannot evaporate from frozen water).

Maritime, continental, and temperate climates
Maritime climates are greatly affected by airflow from nearby oceans. This influence prevents extreme temperatures in such regions, which normally experience cool summers and mild winters. Also, maritime climates are usually quite humid, with large amounts of precipitation.

Continental climates, unlike maritime climates, experience variations in temperature with changes in seasons, i.e. cold winters and hot summers. This is so because rock and soil have lower heat capacities than water, which serves to moderate ambient temperatures. Continental climates are usually relatively dry.

A temperate climate is one with low variation in average temperature. Temperate climates may be maritime or continental.

Mountain influences on climate
At the level of local climate, the presence of mountains forces air to rise to travel above them; this contributes to increased formation of clouds and consequently, increases in levels of precipitation. Mountain chains can affect regional and even global climates by deflecting air flow. The Coriolis force causes most of Earth's atmospheric air flow to move east and west. Therefore, the presences of north-south oriented mountain chains can force alter general circulation patterns. For example, the Rocky Mountains in western North America force air to move northward; it cools near the North Pole before blowing back down. This causes winter temperatures in Canada and parts of the United States to be very cold.

Interactions between the atmosphere and the hydrosphere
Oceans store much higher quantities of heat energy than the atmosphere is able to hold. Energy in the oceans, like energy in the atmosphere, is transferred around the globe, redistributing heat from areas of low latitudes to areas of high latitudes.

Water on the surface of the ocean is driven by atmospheric wind patterns. Energy transfers between the oceans and the atmosphere affect temperatures and precipitation in regions across the globe. For example, the Gulf Stream is an ocean current which exerts an important influence on the climates of the United Kingdom and northwest Europe. This surface current originates in the Gulf of Mexico and carries warm water (about 25 degrees Celsius) northeast across the Atlantic at speeds of three miles per hour.

When the ocean cools down at night, it releases warm air, regulating the temperatures of the regions mentioned above. Without the activity of the Gulf Stream, those regions would be as cold as Canada (which is at roughly the same latitude).

The Coriolis force
The Coriolis force, which gives rise to the Coriolis effect, is not really a force at all. Rather, it appears to be there to us because the Earth is a rotating frame of reference and we are inside it. In the atmosphere, air tends to move from areas of high pressure to areas of lower pressure. This air would move in a straight line but for the Coriolis force, which appears to deflect the air and cause it to swirl. Really, however, the Earth moves underneath the wind, which creates the impression of swirling air to someone standing on the Earth's surface. The Coriolis force causes winds to swing to the right as they approach the Northern Hemisphere and to the left as they approach the Southern Hemisphere.

El Nino
El Niño refers to the unusual warming of surface waters near the equatorial coast of South America. This phenomenon occurs during the winter approximately every two to seven years, lasting from a few weeks to a few months. El Nino can cause torrential rains, violent winds, drought, and dangerously high temperatures in surrounding areas.

El Nino is caused by a reversal of the atmospheric pressures on the eastern and western sides of the Pacific (normally, pressure is high on the eastern side near South America and lower on the western side near the Indonesian coast). This reversal causes a wave of warm water to flow eastward and sea levels to fall on the western side. The changes in air pressure and ocean temperature cause moisture levels in the western Pacific to rise drastically while the region east of the Pacific experiences drought. The air pressure changes also weaken the region's trade winds, which normally serve to distribute heat and moisture.

The relationship between Earth's physical systems and human systems

Each of the people who live on Earth has several basic needs, including food, water, and shelter. The planet's physical systems provide many natural resources (those which may be used by humans to meet a need), such as timber for building shelter, rainwater to drink, and plants and animals which may be consumed by humans. However, human involvement in these systems may be detrimental to their function. For example, high levels of human activity (including logging and the clearing of land for agricultural purposes like crop cultivation and animal grazing) are threatening rainforest ecosystems in low-latitude areas. When humans eliminate portions of a rainforest for their own purposes, the delicate balance among native plants and animals is damaged, sometimes irreparably. With increasing awareness of the threat to Earth's natural resources, some nations have created restrictions on their acceptable use. If the harvesting of natural resources for human use is practiced in small amounts with minimal use of dangerous chemicals, a balance may be achieved between Earth's physical and human systems.

Environmental Transformation
The Environmental Transformation, one of two eras of change which altered human life and its relationship with the environment, began approximately 10,000 years ago. Prior to this time, humans subsisted by hunting animals and gathering native plants for food. With the onset of the Environmental

Transformation (which probably began in the Middle East), people began to domesticate plants and animals—they started practicing agriculture (cultivating and storing certain plants for food) and herding (taming and raising animals specifically for human use). These developments allowed groups of people to settle in one area, rather than roaming the land in search of their basic needs. They irrigated lands and built stable, permanent shelters of wood collected from trees. With stable sources of food, shelter, and clothing, populations began to expand. People had more time to practice other activities, which often bred technological advancements. Individual members of societies began to specialize in, for example, pottery creation or leatherwork. Increasing specialization eventually produced vast civilizations, which influenced the world as humans know it today.

Scientific Transformation
The Scientific Transformation was the second period of major change in human history. This period (approximately 1500-1750 AD) involved intellectual and geographic explorations which produced many scientific and industrial advances in human civilization. Geographic expeditions, such as the ones undertaken by the (in)famous Christopher Columbus, were enabled by technological developments in the fields of cartography, ship building, and navigation. Such explorations taught Europeans about the physical and human geography of different regions and about the layout of land on Earth's surface.

Scientific exploration, practiced by noted thinkers such as Isaac Newton and Galileo Galilei, was enabled by inventions such as the microscope and the telescope. With these and other new tools, people made discoveries about our world and its function which are considered fundamental today. The Scientific Transformation eventually gave rise to the Industrial Revolution, which produced a plethora of new inventions, factories, and opportunities for the attainment of wealth. It also produced inequalities (still observable today) between societies with these technological capabilities and those without.

Environmental effects of burning fossil fuels
Burning fossil fuels (naturally-occurring hydrocarbon compounds which may be used by humans for fuel), especially coal, releases harmful elements into the atmosphere. The chemical reaction of coal combustion produces, for example, large amounts of carbon dioxide. When these gases reach the atmosphere, they inhibit the release of infrared photons into space—carbon dioxide molecules absorb the photons and may reflect them inward, back toward the Earth. This phenomenon is called the greenhouse effect. While the greenhouse effect is desirable, to a certain degree, to maintain a comfortable climate on the planet, increased levels of carbon dioxide can change the balance of energy in the atmosphere. This is termed global warming. Coal burning can also cause acid rain. Sulfur dioxide, a byproduct of burning coal, rises to the atmosphere and combines with water molecules to form sulfuric acid. This acid rain falls back to Earth, where it can cause harm to plants, animals, water bodies, and exposed structures. Burning gasoline can also contribute to the formation of acid rain.

Earth's ozone layer
The ozone layer is the region of the stratosphere with a high concentration of ozone (a form of oxygen) particles. These molecules are formed through the process of photolysis, which occurs when ultraviolet light from the sun collides with oxygen molecules (O_2) in the atmosphere. The ultraviolet radiation splits the oxygen atoms apart; when a free oxygen atom strikes an oxygen molecule, it combines with the molecule to create an ozone particle

(03). Ozone molecules may be broken down by interaction with nitrogen-, chlorine-, and hydrogen-containing compounds, or by thermal energy from the sun. Under normal conditions, these creative and destructive processes balance the levels of ozone in the stratosphere. The concentration of ozone molecules in the atmosphere absorbs ultraviolet radiation, thus preventing this harmful energy from reaching the Earth's surface. Ozone particles form in the region of the atmosphere over the equator, which receives the most direct sunlight. Atmospheric winds then disperse the particles throughout the rest of the stratosphere.

Ozone depletion
Prolonged exposure to ultraviolet radiation can damage the eyes or immune systems of humans and animals, and can lead to the development of skin cancer. Such radiation also inhibits plant growth, thereby limiting the processes of photosynthesis which provide vital oxygen. The ozone layer protects the Earth from the ultraviolet radiation emitted by the sun. Ozone particles absorb the electromagnetic energy before it reaches the surface. The release of certain chemicals into the atmosphere contributes to the destruction of atmospheric ozone particles. Ozone depletion occurs when the balance between creation and destruction of ozone particles in the stratosphere is tipped toward destruction.

Chlorofluorocarbons (or CFCs) are chemicals created by humans for use in, for example, refrigeration, aerosol cans, and cleaners. When these chemicals interact with sunlight in the atmosphere, chlorine atoms are released; these free atoms participate in processes which destroy ozone particles. An ozone hole (an area of severe ozone depletion) has been identified over Antarctica, where spring sunlight contributes to the chlorine-ozone reactions which destroy the latter molecule.

Human activity affects average surface temperatures
Humans change the Earth's surface for reasons other than those which are agriculturally motivated. For example, the building of cities involves the elimination of native vegetation as well as the pavement of large sections of land (which effectively covers natural, usually moist soils). This, in turn, prevents naturally-occurring plants from practicing transpiration. It also concentrates solar heat at the surface, for there are no leafy trees to intercept and diffuse the energy. Materials such as concrete and stone repel rainwater and absorb and trap heat. Thus, the net effect of city building is the production of an urban heat island. Air temperatures in a city are often several degrees higher than the temperatures of surrounding suburban or rural areas. The absence of heat-mediating plants and soils, taken with the high instance of heat-absorbing materials, creates an area in which air temperatures do not drop immediately with the sunset—heat collected during the day remains in the region after nightfall.

United States climate groups

The United States is an extremely large nation with a varied topography, so a number of climate groups are represented. In the continental United States, there are humid oceanic, humid subtropical, humid continental, desert, semiarid, highland, and subtropical dry summer regions. Climate is significantly impacted by major topographical features, like the Pacific Ocean, Rocky Mountains, and Great Lakes. The highest average temperature is 78.2 degrees Fahrenheit, in Death Valley, California, while the lowest average temperature is 9 degrees Fahrenheit, in Barrow, Alaska. It was near Barrow that the lowest temperature ever was recorded: -80 degrees Fahrenheit on January 23, 1971. The highest recorded temperature is 134 degrees Fahrenheit in Death Valley on July 10, 1913.

Humid oceanic

A humid oceanic climate region exists in a narrow band that runs down the northern Pacific Coast of the United States, from Washington State almost to San Francisco. The eastern boundary of this climate region is the Cascade/Sierra Nevada mountain group. A humid oceanic climate region is characterized by a moderately warm summer and a moderately cold winter. In other words, temperature variations are slighter in this region than in others. Humid oceanic climates are typical of the western side of continents, where the prevailing winds blow east from the sea onto the land. These regions have a moderate to high level of precipitation throughout the year, mostly in the form of rain. There are very few droughts, heat waves, or thunderstorms. In general, the relative stability of the ocean's water temperature translates into stable temperatures just inland.

Humid subtropical

A humid subtropical climate region covers much of the Southeastern United States, and extends up the Atlantic coast as far as New York City. This climate region exists even over the higher elevations of the southern Appalachian range. It extends into western Texas and Oklahoma. In this climate region, there are very hot summers and relatively mild winters. There is a medium amount of precipitation in all seasons. No season gets significantly more precipitation than the rest. In the winter, there are often large snowstorms related to the rapid passage of westward winds over the open spaces. There are frequent summer thunderstorms, and the southeast coast occasionally encounters tropical storms and hurricanes as well.

Humid continental

A humid continental climate region covers the Northeast and much of the upper Midwest. It encompasses New England and broadens as it extends west, taking in Missouri and eastern Colorado as well as Minnesota. Humid continental regions are characterized by mild summers and extremely cold winters. These regions experience an average amount of precipitation in all seasons. Farther inland, the variation between winter cold and summer heat is likely to be greater. Indeed, in places like northern Minnesota the difference between summer and winter average temperatures can be as much as 65 degrees Fahrenheit. These inland locations also tend to have a bit more precipitation during the summer. The humid continental climate region in the United States is often covered by snow for most of the winter. This snow perpetuates the cold temperatures by reflecting heat back into the atmosphere.

Desert and semiarid

There are desert and semiarid climate regions in the western United States, particularly in the southwest and in the northern regions on either side of the Rocky Mountains. The deserts are concentrated in southern New Mexico, Arizona, and California. In both semiarid and desert regions, there is very little precipitation. The variation between day and night temperatures in these regions is often severe, in part because the air is typically very clear and dry. Moisture in the air would tend to mitigate wild swings in temperature, and clouds would retain some of the heat from the day. Deserts receive less precipitation than semiarid climates, though not by much. The semiarid regions are generally at a slightly higher elevation.

Highland

Some isolated highland climate regions exist in the United States along the higher points of the Rocky Mountain and Cascade ranges. To some extent, this climate region even extends south along the Sierra Nevada range. The highland designation actually encompasses a number of distinct climate types that are present at different elevations. The progression of climates along the ascending edge of a mountain is not unlike that encountered during travel away from the Equator: as one gains elevation, the climate becomes closer to tundra or even an icecap. Air becomes thinner, vegetation becomes more sparse and low-lying, and precipitation is more likely to be snow or ice. At the highest points of the highland region, the temperature may never rise above freezing.

Subtropical dry summer

A subtropical dry summer climate region exists in the United States in southern California, from the Pacific Ocean west to the Sierra Nevada Mountains. The subtropical dry summer zone extends up the coast to San Francisco, and slightly farther north just inland. Los Angeles is around the southern tip of this climate zone. A subtropical dry summer climate region is characterized by hot, dry summers and mild winters. There is a moderate amount of precipitation in the winter, and very little in the summer. This is the climate typical of the Mediterranean countries in southern Europe. The subtropical dry summer climate is generally found on the western edge of a continent. In the section of the region closest to the water, the temperatures are more moderate and there is less variation between summer and winter weather.

Subarctic and tundra

Subarctic and tundra climate regions only exist in the United States in Alaska. The lower two-thirds, approximately, of the state is considered subarctic, while the top third is tundra. In a subarctic climate region, summers are cool and brief, while winters are long and extremely cold. There is considerably more precipitation during the summer, but any during the winter is likely to be snow and to remain on the ground until spring. Indeed, subarctic regions are typically covered for most of the year. Tundra is drier and colder. The tundra is too cold to support trees, so the only vegetation there is low grasses. A common feature of tundra is permafrost, or permanently frozen ground just under the surface. It is virtually impossible to farm in tundra.

Topography

The physical features of a landmass have a significant influence on the climate. For instance, there are distinct climate patterns on the alternate sides of a mountain range. The windward side of a mountain, which in the United States is typically the western side, will have more precipitation. The leeward side, on the other hand, is arid and less cloudy. The dry valleys that extend out from the eastern side of mountain ranges in the United States are often said to have a rain shadow. The formation of clouds is affected by mountains as well. As air is forced up by mountains, it cools and forms clouds. This is why the tops of mountain ranges are frequently misty or cloudy. Bodies of water also affect climate. Water heats and cools more slowly than land, so places where air arrives from over a body of water will also have less extreme variations in temperature.

- 41 -

Characteristics of the United States

Mineral resources and soil of the United States
The rise of the United States to global prominence was due in large part to the abundance of natural resources. With regard to minerals, the United States has significant deposits of coal, iron ore, natural gas, and petroleum. However, the enormous energy needs of the nation require it to import still more petroleum and iron. There are also large mining operations based on the extraction of gold, lead, sulfur, zinc, and silver. The soil of the United States is for the most part exceptionally fertile, particularly in the Midwest and South. There is a nutrient-rich, thin soil called loess that makes farming possible in Washington State. The Mississippi River brings a rich soil known as alluvium to the region around the Gulf of Mexico.

Water, fisheries, and forests
The United States contains abundant water resources. There are massive freshwater lakes, rivers and streams, and underground water tables to supply all the water needed for industry, agriculture, and consumption. Americans use about 450 billion gallons of water every day. The majority of this water is used for irrigation or steam power plants. There are also plentiful supplies of fish in the nation's waterways, though these supplies are being threatened by overfishing. The species most commonly drawn from the Pacific are cod, halibut, tuna, and salmon. The Atlantic Ocean supplies abundant cod, flounder, herring, lobsters, and other shellfish. The Gulf of Mexico is known for its abundant supplies of oysters and shrimp.

Agriculture
Massive improvements in agricultural technology have reduced the energy and manpower required for American agriculture, even while increasing the overall yields. American farms grow enough to feed every American with some left over for the rest of the world. Indeed, about a quarter of American farm income comes from exports. The most lucrative product of American farms is beef cattle. These profitable animals are primarily raised on massive ranches in the West. Dairy cattle operations are more likely to be found in the northern states, primarily in a strip extending from New York to Minnesota. The other major crops and livestock in the United States are milk, chickens, eggs, corn, soybeans, wheat, hogs, and cotton.

Mining
Many of those who bemoan the United States' dependence on foreign energy sources would be surprised to know that the nation ranks only behind Saudi Arabia and Russia in the production of petroleum, and only behind China in the extraction of coal. The largest deposits of petroleum are in Alaska, California, Louisiana, New Mexico, Oklahoma, and Texas. The most productive coal mines are in the Appalachian Mountains, particularly in Pennsylvania, Kentucky, and West Virginia. Some of the other products that are lucratively mined in the United States are copper, gold, cement, clay, granite, iron ore, zinc, salt, and sand. There are mining operations in virtually every state, though mountainous regions remain the most heavily mined.

Human Geography

Human geography is the subdiscipline of geography which involves identification and analysis of the ways humans interact with the physical Earth. It focuses particularly on the causes and effects of the spatial distributions of humans and human activity on the planet's surface. Human geography draws upon cultural, economic, political, and social data about particular regions to reveal patterns about the ways human beings interact with their environments. This field of study includes several of its own subdisciplines which focus on certain aspects of human life, such as medical geography, feminist geography, military geography, and religion geography. While the focal point of human geography is human activity, it is impossible to discuss such activity without knowledge of the physical landscape upon which it occurs.

Terminology

A **country** is a geographical territory. Many countries are independent entities, with their own governments, constitutions, militaries, and tax regulations; however, some are non-sovereign (which means they are governed by a separate government) and some have an overseas dependency (which means that they control the government of a separate country).

The term **state** is conventionally defined as a political entity which inhabits a specific territory. States have independent governments, through which they exercise internal and external sovereignty. Some social thinkers have offered alternate conceptualizations of a state. For example, Max Weber defined state as "a state is a human community that (successfully) claims the monopoly of the legitimate use of physical force within a given territory."

A **nation** is a cultural entity. Historically, the term has been used to refer to a group of people who share a commonality in ethnic ancestry, descent, or parentage. The criteria used to identify members of a nation are widely variable. A state which is recognized as a nation's "homeland" is called a nation-state.

Population refers to the conglomeration of people or organisms of a certain species in a particular area. This variable is especially important in the study of human geography, which deals with (among other things) changes in the population of a region and why those changes occur.

Demography is the study of human populations. This field examines the characteristics of a population such as its size and distribution, the way it changes over time, and the religions, ethnicities, and languages of members of the population. The term demographic refers to specific population attributes, especially as used in marketing or opinion research.

A society's **standard of living** is a quantitative and qualitative assessment of the material goods and services available to members of that society. It is often measured through observation of the average yearly income per person (adjusted for inflation); however, variables such as the literacy rate and cultural resources of a society may also be taken into account in estimation of that society's standard of living.

The **gross national product (GNP)** of a country is defined as the aggregate value of all goods and services generated by a society in a particular year. When the GNP is divided by the population of the country, the per-capita GNP is revealed.

Literacy is the ability to read and write; the **literacy rate** of a society is the percentage of people in that society who are literate.

Population density is defined as the number of people per specified unit of area.

The **life expectancy** of a society is the average lifespan of people living in that society.

The **birth rate** of a society refers to the number of births per 1,000 people in a society. This figure, usually expressed as the crude birth rate (CBR), is calculated without consideration of the sex or age of the population.

The **death rate** of a society is figured in the same manner but with regard to deaths rather than births and is expressed as the crude death rate (CDR).

The fertility rate of a society is the average number of children which would be borne by a woman during her "childbearing" years. **Replacement fertility** is the fertility level at which women on the average are birthing just enough children to "replace" themselves and their partners in the population.

Population momentum is the phenomenon whereby a society's population persists after the attainment of replacement fertility. This occurs at the end of Stage Three in the demographic transition model, due to the relatively high concentration of people of the same age in their "childbearing" years.

The delineation of the developed world
When used in human geography and related fields, the terms developed world and technological world refer to those regions of the planet where people were able to cultivate natural and human resources using technology made available by the Scientific Transformation. Developed countries had direct access to the tools and information discovered in this era. Today, the "developed world" encompasses most of Western Europe, some of Eastern Europe, including the former U.S.S.R., North America, Japan, and Australia and New Zealand. These regions share several characteristics. For one, people living in developed countries are generally well-educated and highly literate. Public education systems are relatively sophisticated, and young people spend many years in a structured school environment. Education of a developed society's youth is often seen as a precious human resource. Countries of the developed world also display low rates of population growth; some are experiencing negative growth. Another characteristic of the developed world is that most people work in the service or manufacturing industries (as opposed to the agricultural industry).

The delineation of the developing world
In fields which study humans and their behaviors, the term developing world refers to regions in which the advancements offered by the Scientific Transformation were either slow to arrive or ignored by inhabitants of these regions. Today, Latin America, Africa, The Middle East, South Asia, China, and Southeast Asia are considered members of the developing world. Many of these countries are attempting to modernize; however, the

process is very expensive and people in developing regions have relatively little money. Several characteristics distinguish this part of the world from the developed countries. For example, many people in developing societies have not had time to receive thorough educations because they must work to provide sustenance for themselves and their families from a very young age (most people work in agriculture, rather than in the manufacturing or service industries). This means that most people cannot read and write in their own language, much less in a European language in which scientific or technological literature is written.

The Malthusian Catastrophe

Thomas Malthus (1766-1834) was an English political scientist and demographer. His relatively pessimistic views were developed as a rebuttal to the hopeful theorizing of his peers. For one, Malthus believed that the global population would increase exponentially unless methods to check such growth were implemented. The Malthusian Catastrophe (also referred to as the Malthusian Disaster, Dilemma, or Crisis) is Malthus's prediction that the world population would eventually surpass the global food supply. He felt that after a certain point, society would return to subsistence-level food production (the level at which people consume only enough food to survive), due to a decrease in the amount of available nourishment per person. Obviously, this catastrophe has not yet come to pass. Malthus underestimated the rate at which agricultural and economic production would increase with technological, scientific, and industrial advancements in those fields. Also, the rate of global population expansion has not undergone continuous growth, as evidenced by the demographic transition model.

Phases of the demographic transition model

The demographic transition model is a representation of changes in population in industrial societies, created by demographer Warren Thompson. This model describes variations (transitions) in birth and death rates in developed nations over the past 200 years. The demographic transition model encompasses four transitional phases.

Stage One is associated with pre-modern (that is, pre-industrialized) society; it characterizes most regions of the world through the 17th century. In this stage (the high stationary stage), birth and death rates are high and nearly equivalent, indicating that population growth is slow.

The second stage in the demographic transition model is differentiated by a sharp increase in a society's population due to a dramatic decrease in the death rate. This transition occurred in the late 18th century in Western Europe and spread outward. The onset of Stage Two is associated with advances in public health such as the creation of food handling regulations and sewage disposal, as well as advances in agricultural practices (including crop rotation) which helped to create a stable food source.

Stage Three of the demographic transition model involves a decrease in a society's birth rate (following the rapid population growth in Stage Two). Most developed nations entered this phase late in the 19th century. Many hypotheses have been advanced to explain this phenomenon. For example, some have suggested that the decline in birth rates observed in developed societies is related to urbanization, which dilutes the high value traditionally placed on fertility; also, the costs attendant to urbanization make it less financially desirable for a family to have many children. The decline in birth rates has also been said to relate to medical advancements which decreased the rate of childhood mortality, or to improvements in contraceptive technology (though this occurred later, in the second half of the 20th century).

The populations of societies in Stage Four of the demographic transition model are either stable or declining. After the decline in birth rates, the general population grows older. If the fertility rate dips below replacement, the population experiences a rapid decline.

Demographic transition models for more-developed and less-developed societies

An alternate demographic transition model exists which applies demographic analysis to less-developed nations. There are several differences between the transitions observed in more-developed countries and those observed in less-developed countries. For instance, less-developed societies experienced a more pronounced decrease in death rates (about 50 years, as compared to 150 years in more-developed societies) in Stage Two of the transition model. This is so because of medical advancements as well as increases in the female literacy rate (behavioral changes) due to exposure to more-developed countries. Rather than being "(re)discovered," this type of information was imported by less-developed countries and quickly applied.

Another difference in the demographic transition models for more- and less-developed societies is that less-developed societies experienced a later (20th century) Stage Three transition (decline in birth rates). This difference stems from the fact that the technological advancements which accompanied the decline of birth rates in more-developed societies were unavailable in less-developed societies at the time.

Human settlements
A human settlement is defined as any area inhabited by humans. The term may refer to a newly established region of residency for a group of people, or it may refer to a single home. Settlements are described as nucleated if residents live very closely together; settlements are dispersed when people live separately. A village is an example of an agglomerated rural settlement, in which people reside together in small groups. There are several different general types of settlements. The temporary residences set up by nomadic peoples (those constantly traveling due to their pastoral responsibilities, or in search of employment or food) constitute a type of settlement. There are also several types of permanent settlements.

Rural, urban, and suburban communities
Permanent human settlements are classified by their economic activities and layouts. Rural settlements are those in which a majority of land is used for agricultural purposes. Inhabitants of rural areas often work in the agricultural industry, serving their own community.

An urban settlement is typified by many nucleated buildings. Most residents of urban areas work outside of the agricultural industry, serving outside communities. Cities and larger towns are examples of urban areas.

A suburban community is one which exists just outside a large urban area; it is generally smaller and less nucleated than the major urban community it abuts. Often, city workers reside in a suburban area and commute to work, aiming to avoid unsavory elements of urban life, such as crowding and pollution.

How environmental factors affect patterns of human settlement

Site factors are those taken into considerations by humans in the selection of an ideal location to create a settlement. There are several environmental characteristics weighed by settlers deciding where to place their communities. While many of these factors were more important in the pre-modern past, many of them are still relevant today. Water supply is an important site factor. Used for drinking, washing, cooking, and agriculture, settlements cannot thrive without a consistent, adequate supply of water. Settling in an area prone to flooding or on marshy land can also be dangerous for budding towns. Though modern settlements do not rely singularly on natural sources for water supplies, it is still important for communities to be within piping distance of a central water source. A related factor is the proximity of rivers to an area. In addition to drinking water, rivers provide transportation or act as natural boundaries. Aspect is the direction a site faces; this affects the amount of direct sunlight in an area, which affects temperature and agriculture.

Central Place theory

Central Place Theory is also referred to as Christaller's Theory for its formulator, Walter Christaller. This theory describes typical size and spacing of human settlements. It rests on the idea that centralization is a natural principle of order which manifests itself in human settlement patterns. Christaller's Theory predicts that a large central market will have several smaller towns around it at equal distances; the smaller towns purchase goods and services from the central hub. From several assumptions, Christaller derived laws for the determination of the size, number, and distribution of towns. These assumptions include the even distribution of population and resources, similar purchasing power among all consumers, a flat, expansive surface, and providers of goods and services who cannot earn excess profits.

The principle laws of Central Place Theory are:
- That the number of settlements is inversely proportional to the size of the settlements
- That the larger the settlements, the greater the distances between them will be
- Three, that as settlements increase in size, services become increasingly specialized.

How settlements are ordered

Following Central Place Theory, the goods and services available for purchase in settlements varies with its size. Settlements may thus be classified by these factors. For example:
1. In a high-order settlement, such as a conurbation (a large urban city or capital), one might expect to find the following services: government buildings, museums and theaters, churches of various religions, multiple medical centers, transportation terminals, and large shopping complexes.
2. A middle-order settlement (a city or town) might house a hospital, multiple retail stores, a few specialized medical practices, a high school football team, and a cathedral.
3. In low-order settlements, such as hamlets and villages, one may find a single church, a main store, a tavern, and a small junior high school; the lowest-order settlements offer no services whatsoever.

Settlement order may be displayed in a hierarchical pyramid, in which lowest-order settlements make up the bottom level (they are most plentiful) and highest-order settlements are at the top of the pyramid (they are fewest).

Common settlement forms
Study of the shape (form) of a settlement can reveal information about their origins and development.

An *isolated settlement* is a single structure, such as a farmhouse. This settlement form is often found in areas where physical conditions make survival difficult or uncomfortable. Historically, isolated settlements were common in the early stages of pioneer settlement.

A *dispersed settlement* consists of 2 to 3 buildings which are 2 kilometers or farther from the next dispersed settlement, possibly forming a hamlet.

A settlement typifying the *nucleated form* includes many buildings grouped together for a social, economic, and/or defensive purpose; they often form around crossroads.

A community of the *loose-knit form* is similar to a nucleated settlement, but the buildings are spaced farther apart.

Lineated settlements consist of buildings spread out in lines along a river, canal, or dike, allowing all residents access to the waterway.

Finally, *planned settlements*, usually made up of crescent-shaped estates housing several small buildings, are typically constructed near one or more major cities which support the workforce.

Concentric Zone Model
Burgess's Concentric Zone Model was developed in 1925 by Ernest Burgess, based on his observations of Chicago and other American cities. This model of land use and urban development suggested that towns grow outward from a central "downtown" area, creating concentric circles (zones) of building and activity; this indicates that the ages of structures decreases with distance from the central hub. Burgess's model also implies that inner zones have tendencies to expand into the outer regions. This characterizes urban growth as a process of expansion and reconversion of land uses. While this model is less complex than actual cities existing in the twenty-first century, it is still useful as a theoretical approximation of urban growth patterns. The descriptions given of the zones in Burgess's model are based upon observation and analysis of modern city growth.

Inner Zones :
1. The central zone in the Burgess Concentric Zone Model (Zone A) is the central business district (CBD). Land in the CBD is more expensive than in any other zone. As the area accessible to the largest number of people, the CBD houses retail shops, banks, health care facilities, and office buildings. This zone tends to be densely developed, with high levels of traffic and a lack of vegetation.
2. Zone B is referred to as the Transition Zone or the Twilight Zone. This area may be subdivided into a (declining) industrial sector and a section of low-class residential housing (older buildings arranged in tight grids with no yard space). In a continually

- 48 -

developing city, Zone A's growth, coupled with attempts to renovate older areas of the region, create constant activity in Zone B, characterizing it as a transition zone.
3. Zone C, called the Council Estates, houses middle-class residencies; there are fewer apartment buildings with more yard space than in Zone B.

Outer zones:
4. Zone D of Burgess's model is the region often referred to as the suburbs or the commuter zone. The suburbs are typified by high-class (expensive) residential buildings. Houses abut garages and other outbuildings; nearly every residency has a yard. Theoretically, the most affluent members of a community are able to reside at a distance from the CBD because they have the means to procure transportation into the downtown area to work and purchase goods and services.
5. The countryside zone (Zone E) was not present in Burgess's original formulation of his model. Rather, it has been added to represent the residents of an area who wish to live as far as possible from the busy CBD while retaining the ability to utilize the employment opportunities and services available in the innermost zone of the city. The countryside zone is a rural area with large areas of natural vegetation and a less nucleated form than that of zones closer to the CBD.

Hoyt's Sector Model
The Sector Model, formulated by Homer Hoyt in 1939, is essentially a modification of Burgess's Concentric Zone Model. Based on observations of the development patterns of many American cities, Hoyt deduced that most large urban areas centered around major transportation routes, such as railways and sea ports. Commercial entities and industrial facilities were often erected around high-access thoroughfares, and low-income housing was often found near railroad lines. Hoyt updated Burgess's model to account for these patterns. He suggested that cities grow outward from the Central Business District in wedged sectors along major transportation routes. In the Sector Model, commercial businesses remain in the CBD while manufacturing and warehousing interests (a portion of Burgess's Zone B) forms in a wedge around major paths of transportation. The low-income housing in Burgess's Zone B abuts the wedge of industrial activity (for pollution and noise affect the quality of life in this region, decreasing the land value). As in Burgess's model, middle- and high-income housing in Hoyt's model are situated away from the CBD.

The Multiple Nuclei Model
Edward Ullman and Chauncy Harris developed the Multiple Nuclei Model in 1945 to explain urban growth patterns which did not fit the somewhat outdated Concentric and Sector Models. By this point in the development of American cities, many suburbs were growing rapidly and operating as small business districts. Ullman and Harris found that land use patterns formed around these nuclei or nodes of economic activity, which were specialized to the needs of residents with certain levels of incomes and certain leisure patterns. The Multiple Nuclei Model retains the Central Business District as the main commercial region, from which retail and manufacturing companies spanned outward along transportation routes. In this model, heavy industry is located near the outskirts of a city, possible near areas of low-income housing. The small communities surrounding suburban nuclei filled the urban periphery.

<u>Population density</u>
Population density is a measurement of the population per unit (usually miles or kilometers squared). Population density may be an indicator of economic development; however, this is not so for many less economically developed countries.

There are several factors which commonly influence population density:
1. The level of industrial activity in an area the area's population—major industrial areas provide many job opportunities, which draw people into the region, increasing population density.
2. The climate of a region also affects its population density, for people generally gravitate toward temperate climates rather than extremely cold or hot areas.
3. Urbanization affects population density in that people often move into cities where resources, services, and employment are readily available because they no longer have to work in agriculture.
4. Natural disaster areas influence population density as well. Although potential danger exists for residents of these regions, many large population centers are located in or near them; often, this occurs for historical or agricultural reasons. For example, the byproducts of volcanic eruptions can create extremely fertile soil.

Human migration

Human migration is simply the movement of people from one location to another. Human migration may be international or internal. International migration is movement from one country of residence to another. This kind of migration generally covers permanent movements, thus excluding such transitory activities as migrant labor, nomadism, tourism, and commuting. When leaving a country, migrating peoples are referred to as emigrants; when they arrive in a new country, they are called immigrants.

Migration may be voluntary or forced:
1. Voluntary migration (movement based on uncoerced personal decisions) occurs for many reasons: proximity to family and friends, expansion of territory, a search for employment and economic opportunity, an attempt to improve one's quality of life, and the settlement of undeveloped territory.
2. Forced migration occurs when a person or group of people is compelled to move regardless of their individual preferences. This type of migration has many possible causes: slavery, overcrowding, racial, religious, or political persecution and/or discrimination, natural disaster (such as hurricanes or flooding), and war.

<u>Population transfer</u>
The term population transfer refers to actions taken by a political authority in a state or country to drive large groups of people out of a particular region (forced migration). Historically, population transfer has been used to force groups of people with ethnicities and/or religious beliefs different from the dominant norm into isolated regions. This forced migration is often detrimental to the well-being of the ousted people, for no consideration is made for the suitability of the new region to the group's way of life. The "Indian Removal" which occurred in the United States in the 1830's is a classic example of population transfer. Native Americans were forced off of their homelands onto isolated, federally-owned reservations. The mass expulsions of Jews, Muslims, and Gypsies which took place in various European countries numerous times throughout history are also instances of population transfer. Though these discriminatory practices were considered "humane"

resolutions to religious, ethical, and cultural conflicts for centuries, they are considered violations of international law in modern times.

Internal migration
Internal human migration is the movement of people within a country; this type of migration may be permanent or temporary.

Permanent internal migrations include urbanization (the migration of people from less developed rural areas to more developed urban areas, which often occurs when people seek access to the wide variety of services usually available in urban areas), urban depopulation (the opposite of urbanization, which occurs when people seek residencies in quieter, less polluted, less crowded areas), and regional migration (a general trend of movement within a country, such as from northern areas to southern areas).

Temporary internal movements such as commuting to work or school are referred to as daily migrations. Seasonal migration is that practiced by transhumant nomads and farm workers. The movement of people from one region to another for a significant period of time (but with the intent of returning to the original region) is referred to as semi-permanent migration. Workers on ships and oil rigs engage in this type of movement.

Push/pull factors
Push and pull factors are features of regions which cause people to want to leave or move to a particular region. Push factors are those which encourage residents to depart an area; they are viewed as negative aspects of a region. There are several common factors which "push" people from, for example, rural to urban areas: overpopulation and overgrazing result in scarce resources, which decreases income levels; agricultural endeavors are subject to unpredictable and sometimes harsh physical forces (such as drought or flooding); the possible lack of health and educational services so far from a downtown district; mechanization of agricultural labor may decrease the number of available jobs.

The perceived pull factors of urban areas also contribute to urbanization: utilities such as water and electricity may make housing more comfortable, theoretically increasing a migrant's quality of life; food sources are ostensibly more reliable in urban areas than in agricultural rural areas; there are more job opportunities in larger urban regions; more goods and services are available for purchase in cities.

Early human migrations
The migrations of early human beings helped to shape the path of human development throughout history. The first anatomically modern Homo sapiens evolved in Africa between 100,000 and 150,000 years ago. These prehistoric beings probably practiced hunting and gathering, meaning that they moved constantly in search of food. These communities became more organized, developing more sophisticated tools and cooperative predation tactics. The population grew as they quickly migrated to other regions, inhabiting each of the continents but Antarctica within 50,000 years. Hunting alone could not sustain the increasing population, spurring the transition from hunting and gathering to migratory slash-and-burn agriculture; crops spread across the globe. People began to settle in permanent, stable agricultural communities. The innovation of sailing vessels encouraged human migration, resulting in new settlements bred from colonization and/or conquest. Seafarers and nomadic pastoralists aided in the distribution of new technologies to various regions. The sharing of increasingly specialized knowledge enabled the rise of several early

empires. New social circumstances then bred new (increasingly violent) forms of human migration.

Modern human migrations
Due to increases in the population, as well as advancements in technology, modern human migrations have surpassed earlier movements in terms of size and scope. The many technological innovations associated with the Industrial Revolution facilitated, among other things, transportation over long distances. This factor, combined with economic, cultural, environmental, and political forces, led to many massive migratory movements. The Great Atlantic Migration, which involved the relocation of many people from Europe to North America in the mid- to late-1800's, was the largest such migration. This period of mobility began with the immigration of many Irish and German people to the United States; these migrants left their countries in search of ample food after failure of the potato crop in Ireland and southern Rhineland led to famine in those areas. The mass movement of residents of developing countries to more industrialized nations is another major migration which has taken place in modern times.

Population structure
The population structure of a society is a description of that society in terms of the ages and sexes of its members. The study of demographic structure includes, by extension, analysis of crude birth and death rates and infant mortality rates (the number of infants in a society who die before they reach one year of age divided by the number of live births per year). Practitioners in this field also examine natural increase, which is the rate at which a society's population grows due to a difference between the birth rate and the death rate.

A society's population structure is usually represented by a population pyramid. This type of diagram is created through the placement of two bar graphs (one denoting females and one denoting males) side by side. The x-axis shows the percentage of people of each sex who fall into a certain age group as shown on the y-axis.

The typical population pyramid of a developing country
The population pyramids of developing countries tend to be wide at their bases and increasingly narrow toward the tops of the diagrams, indicating that a sizeable portion of developing countries' populations are made up of young people, due to high birth and death rates. Improvements in the living conditions of many developing nations may decrease the CDR, resulting in a youthful population (one in which the majority of the population is teenaged or younger) and a large gap between the CBR and CDR (a high rate of natural increase). Developing countries often exhibit high birth rates for several reasons, some of which may become less applicable as a society's standard of living improves. For instance, high infant mortality rates in some societies impel parents to bear many children in the expectation of losing some of them. In agricultural societies, members of large families can share farming and household duties. High death rates in developing nations result from insufficient access to medical services and unsanitary and/or insufficient food and water supplies.

The typical population pyramid of a developed nation
Generally, the population pyramid of a developed country is slightly narrow at the base, consistently wide through the middle, and narrower at the very top. A population pyramid of this shape indicates relatively low birth and death rates—the number of babies born is less than the number of adults, and a majority of children reach late adulthood. The small

discrepancy between the CBR and CDR implies a low rate of natural increase. Decreasing birth rates can result in an ageing population, in which a large number of people are over age 65. Developed nations often exhibit low birth rates because women are likely to have access to reproductive and family planning services, which gives them control of their own fertility. Also, it can be expensive to raise a large family in a developed country. Death rates (including infant mortality rates) in developed countries are usually lower than those observed in developing countries because of better access to medical services, clean water, food, and adequate housing in the former.

Social trends
The study of population structure supplies geographers with useful information about social trends and patterns. On a national scale, the examination of population structure provides clues as to the economic status and standard of living of a nation, as evidenced by the patterns observed in the population pyramids of developed and developing nations. On a regional scale, variations in population structure may result from migratory processes or from the presence of institutions which attract and concentrate people of a certain age in a given area. For example, the existence of a large university in an urban area will decrease the average age of the area's residents. The study of a region's population structure and changes in that structure is helpful in city planning, for different age groups have different physical and social needs and engage in different sorts of leisure activities. Also, examination of the number of males and females in each age group can aid in the prediction of future variations in population structure.

Culture
Culture is the acquired knowledge which people use to interpret the world around them and to guide them in social behavior. Therefore culture is not behavior itself; rather, it a body of shared knowledge which causes people to act and interact with others in certain ways. Also, culture is not genetic. From a young age, members of a group learn about the (arbitrary) aspects of that group's culture from observation of and participation in social activity. Culture may be tacit, meaning that its transmission occurs unconsciously (for instance, certain linguistic conventions), or explicit, meaning that its transmission is purposeful and articulated (for example, religious education). Culture is a complex system of interrelated parts. While some aspects of culture are shared by all members of a particular society, each person in that society is a member of multiple groups with their own cultural knowledge. For example, one is likely to behave differently in the presence of his or her family than in the presence of friends.

Ethnicity
The term ethnicity refers to the classification of a group by its distinctive cultural traits; these traits form a comprehensive cultural entity. Members of an ethnic group feel strong ties to the group's cultural traditions and knowledge and identify themselves as a "people" rather than simply a statistical population.

Ethnicity may be expressed through music, dance, dress, kinship patterns, moral and value systems, food, religious beliefs and activities, language, literature, etc. In an ethnic group, these cultural qualities are common throughout the society, and are seen as unique with respect to other ethnic groups. Often, an ethnic group will share a common history and territorial "homeland."

The concept of ethnicity differs from that of race, which divides people into arbitrary categories based on perceived differences in people's physical and biogenetic characteristics. The labeling of a group as either a race group versus an ethnic group is thus determined by the criteria used to define it.

Terminology

Historically, dominant groups have been wary of ethnic diversity. In less enlightened societies, people tend to believe that their own cultural norms are "natural" and therefore superior to other belief systems; this attitude is referred to as **ethnocentrism**. Ethnocentric beliefs have led to the discriminatory and hostile treatment of minority groups throughout history. The actions taken by Nazis against Jews in World War II Germany provide an extreme example of the attempted elimination of a particular ethnic group.

Pluralism, on the other hand, is a doctrine which advocates the autonomous participation of differing ethnic, racial, religious, and/or social groups in a common civilization.

Cultural relativism is a theory which suggests that it is possible to observe other cultures without making value-based judgments. This can only be achieved through complete detachment from one's own cultural beliefs. Cultural relativism proposes that each group's cultural "reality" is equally valid and worth preserving, and that aspects of a particular culture can only be fairly evaluated in terms of that culture as a whole.

Assimilation is the process whereby individuals of a minority ethnic group are absorbed into and internalize cultural characteristics of a dominant group. Assimilation may be voluntary or forced:
1. Voluntary assimilation often occurs when immigrants arrive in a new country. As they learn about the dominant culture through contact with and participation in their new societies, many immigrants gradually begin to abandon their previously-held cultural beliefs and practices in favor of those predominant in those societies; this helps them to thrive in a new culture. For example, learning the dominant language is extremely important in the creation of economic and educational opportunities.
2. Forced assimilation occurs when one group invades and conquers the territory of another group. The conquering group forcibly impels the native group to forsake their ethnic beliefs and practices in favor of those of the newly dominant group. Forced assimilation constitutes an attempt to create artificial unity, which may help them retain control of the region.

Though assimilation is common among new members of a society different from their own, it is rarely complete. More often, assimilating peoples adopt certain useful characteristics of the dominant culture while retaining certain important aspects of their culture. In cultural studies, the process whereby a society becomes ethnically mixed is termed **amalgamation** or hybridization. Examination of Mexican culture reveals that nation's amalgamated society. Throughout centuries of contact, certain aspects of Native American cultures and Spanish cultures have been extracted, modified, and synthesized to create a new society. The hybrid natural of this society may be observed in, for example, spoken dialects, religious beliefs and practices, and architectural styles.

Language

A language is a conventionalized system of sounds, gestures, and signs used for communication. It is an important and distinctive aspect of any culture. Human language relies heavily (though not exclusively) on vocalizations. The activities which produce vocal sounds are referred to as speech; speech is generated and interpreted through language. In language, words act as symbols which refer to something else. We learn to associate particular words with particular referents. For example, the symbol "wall" refers to a barrier between spaces.

Symbology in language simplifies the task of communication; it enables us to communicate about things which are not present. Symbols in language may also be nonlinguistic. Posture, eye contact, clothing, and material goods are symbols through which information may be communicated.

Sociolinguistic rules are cultural conventions which govern the ways humans communicate in different social situations. For example, a person is likely to speak differently during a job interview than he or she would among peers at a social gathering.

The subsystems of language
Phonology is the subsystem of language which deals with the formation and ordering of sounds. Sounds are classified as phonemes, the basic units used in word construction. Phonemic categories are culturally defined. For example, in English, the "t" sound is treated as a single phoneme; in Hindi, the same sound is divided into four distinct phonemes. Grammar is the subsystem of language which provides categories and rules regarding the combination of vocal symbols. Morphemes are categories of the smallest vocal units intrinsic to meaning. They may be words (categorized, for example, as nouns or verbs) or parts of words. For example, "s" is a morpheme when used to pluralize a word. Semantics is the aspect of language which deals with the categories and rules for relating vocal symbols (words) to their referents.

Semantic rules tell us how to combine words with what they stand for. For example, the semantics of the English language instruct us to associate the word "chair" with an object upon which we sit.

The Sapir-Whorf Hypothesis
Many people believe that language mirrors reality, that words are simply symbols for what already exists. This viewpoint is an example of naïve realism, the belief that everyone sees the world in the same way. The Sapir-Whorf Hypothesis, developed by the linguists Benjamin Whorf and Edward Sapir, directly contradicts this point of view. One's native language is completely imbedded in one's consciousness; we use our languages to formulate thoughts and to identify and classify things that we encounter in nature. Also, certain words and concepts cannot be directly translated from one language to another. Whorf believed that humans are only capable of conceptualizing ideas which may be articulated and expressed through language. Therefore, we cannot think about something we do not have the words or structures to express. The Sapir-Whorf hypothesis states that humans dissect and interpret the multitude of stimuli provided by the outside world using the linguistic systems in our minds. Consequently, people's native languages govern their views of reality and determine their perceptions of the world.

Modified Whorfism

The nature of language itself problematizes any attempt to prove the Sapir-Whorf Hypothesis. Since language is such an integral part of human consciousness, it is fruitless to ask a person how the language he or she speaks has affected his or her view of the world; no one could answer such a question objectively. Today, many social and linguistic thinkers accept "modified Whorfism," which suggests that language affects but does not dictate the reality experienced by humans. Euphemistic language, the use of words which are seen as less offensive in place of more unpleasant, direct, or harsh synonyms, lends credence to the idea that language has some affect on one's perceived reality. Though different languages may not create exclusive worldviews for their speakers, they do influence the thought patterns native speakers in distinctive ways.

Religion

People tend to feel most at ease when they are sure of themselves and the order of the world around them. When a particularly traumatic or incongruous event cannot be explained intellectually or experientially, people often turn to religion for answers. Religion is culturally shared knowledge and beliefs about the supernatural realm (that which exists beyond human experience) which people use to explain the relationship between human life and the universe. Religion can provide people with worldviews (sets of beliefs and assumptions about the origin of life and the way things work). An important aspect of religion is the emotional nature of the dilemmas it addresses. Consequently, religion can unify disparate peoples with similar beliefs or created unbridgeable divisions between different groups. In human geography, the term is often used to refer to organized religion (a structured organization of people supporting a particular religion) rather than an individual's belief system. Organized religion may be public (state-supported) or private (funded by donations from those who attend religions functions).

Governmental policies regarding religion

There are three general attitudes taken by governments regarding religion. A secular government is one which neither advocates nor discourages religious practices and beliefs. Theoretically, in a secular state, a legal separation exists between religious affairs and political affairs. The "separation of church and state" in the government of the United States of America exemplifies a secular standpoint. An atheistic state is one in which the government attempts to suppress or even prevent religious practices. North Korea is an example of an officially atheistic state, while China allows people to participate in religious practices under state supervision. A religious government is one with official links to a particular religion or branch of religion. For example, Sweden is considered Evangelical Lutheran and Nepal is officially Hindu.

Terminology

Monism is a philosophical position which avers that the universe is created of one single substance, energy, essence, or principle. Substantive monism is the belief in one substance; attributive monism is the belief that while there is only one kind of thing, that category is made up of many individual objects or beings; absolute monism is the belief that there is but one being created of one substance. Monism may also be broadly subdivided into idealistic monism (which holds that only the mind is real), neutral monism (which states that both mental and physical phenomena can be reduced to a third energetic substance), and materialism (which claims that physical reality is the only reality).

Dualism may refer to the belief in two opposing universal forces which are often personified as deities, to the perceived division between mind and matter, or to the belief that the entire world may be divided into two categories.

Pluralism holds that the universe is made up of many different substances.

Theism is the belief in a divine being. **Monotheism** is the belief in a single, all-powerful, universal deity. Zoroastrianism, Islam, and Judaism are examples of monotheistic religions. Deism, a subtype of monotheism, is the belief that although there is one God, this deity does not intervene in human affairs and may be understood only through observation of nature. Monistic theism is a type of monotheism which includes monistic and pantheistic elements as well as the belief in a universal divine being. Substance monotheism, an aspect of some indigenous African religions, claims that the many gods are manifestations of a single God.

Polytheism, on the other hand, holds that there are many deities; these gods are believed to exist in a pantheon (a set of divine beings with complex, human-like personalities and varying degrees of power in different realms). Inclusive monotheism holds that all polytheistic deities are simply alternate names for the one Supreme Being, while exclusive monotheism asserts that there is one true God and that all others are false.

Pantheism, in its original Greek translation, literally means "all is God and God is all." It is thus a type of monotheism which holds that the single divine being and the universe are one. In classical pantheism, God personifies natural order and natural law. Natural pantheism, on the other hand, equates nature with a non-sentient divinity.
Panentheism is the belief that the universe was created by a single immanent God; unlike pantheism, panentheism does not view God and the universe as one. Rather, God is seen as more powerful than and outside of the universe. Generally, faiths which are considered classically pantheistic may also be described as panentheistic. However, natural pantheism and panentheism are not equivalent concepts—natural pantheists do not believe in the existence of a conscious being that is more powerful than nature.

The largest religious bodies which originated in India
Hinduism is the oldest religion practiced in modern times, dating to approximately 4,000 years ago. Those who adhere to the principles of Hinduism are referred to as Hindus. Today, each of the several sects of Hinduism relies on the Vedas (sacred hymns and verses) as an absolute authority on fundamental truths about the universe. Also, the majority of Hindus believe in Brahman, the ultimate universal power. Reincarnation, karma, and the caste system are ideas prevalent in Hinduism. Different branches of Hinduism espouse belief systems which may be described as monistic, dualistic, or pantheistic. In principle, Hindus support religious tolerance and consider different doctrines inadequate rather than wrong.

Buddhism, which grew out of Hinduism during a period of social change in India, was founded by Siddhartha Gautama (Gautama Buddha). The goal of Buddhists is to attain the blissful state of nirvana. This can be accomplished through the purification of one's thoughts via strictly-defined behavior. Buddhism may be described as a polytheistic faith, though any otherworldly powers of Buddhist deities are deemphasized.

The largest religious bodies that originated in Eastern Asia

Both Confucianism and Taoism are considered traditional Chinese religions. In fact, most adherents to Chinese religious tradition build their faiths upon a fusion of Confucianism, Taoism, and Buddhism.

Confucianism was founded by Confucius, who lived around the same time as Buddha. This faith was designed to relieve conflict in all arenas, from that which existed among families to that between heaven and Earth. Confucius defined "appropriate" social roles for people of different ages, sexes, and social ranks; by assuming these roles, Confucians attempt to create a more peaceful world. Taoism originated in China at approximately the same time as Confucianism.

Taoism strives to create harmony between humans and the natural world. Unlike Confucianism, which has a significant political aspect and is largely monistic, Taoism values natural goodness and expressiveness over social order and is largely dualistic. Shinto is an ancient Japanese religion. A polytheistic belief system, Shinto espouses a belief in many spirits of nature called kami. Animism, the belief that all things possess consciousness, is another tenet of Shintoism.

The largest religious bodies which originated in Western Asia

Judaism, Christianity, and Islam, all of which originated in Western Asia, are the largest monotheistic religions practiced today.

Judaism is nearly as old as Hinduism. This religion centers on the belief that faithfulness to God and the Ten Commandments will ensure blessings for His followers. The Torah is the Jewish religious text, though the Talmud in practice is their main authority. Christianity has its roots in Judaism; like Judaism, Christianity claims the existence of a single, omnipresent, omniscient God. Unlike Jews, however, Christians believe that Jesus Christ was the son of God. Christian doctrine asserts that Jesus was crucified to atone for the sins of humanity and rose again three days later to ascend to Heaven. Currently, Christianity has more followers worldwide than any other religion. The Bible is the Christian religious text.

Islam, practiced by Muslims, is based upon the guidance of the Prophet Muhammad, who advocated the existence of one all-powerful god (Allah). The Koran, the Islamic religious text, calls for daily prayer, an annual month of fasting, and almsgiving. Islam, like Christianity, has roots in Judaism.

Methods of religious diffusion

As evidenced by, for example, the existence of Buddhism in the United States and the presence of Christianity in Africa, all bodies of religious thought have been diffused across the globe. As different belief systems come into contact, religious ideas are discarded, changed, and fused, branching existing religions into sects and creating new religions altogether. Historically, military campaigns have been an important vehicle in religious diffusion. The Crusades (11th to 13th centuries), a series of military forays by Catholics striving to "recapture" Jerusalem from Muslims, provide an example of religious imperialism (an approach to spreading religion to different people through the use of warfare, oppression, and persecution). Historically, colonization has often involved religious imperialism. Trade routes have played a key role in the diffusion of religions. Missionaries, those who attempt to convert others to their faith, often traveled along these routes with traders and explorers. Migration has also served to bring groups with different religious beliefs together; in fact, religious persecution has spurred many mass human migrations throughout history.

United States population and immigration trends

<u>Population</u>
In 2011, the Census Bureau estimated that the population of the United States was 311,591,917. In 2000, the Census Bureau reported the United States population as 281,421,906, while in 1990 it was 248,709,873. The population has grown almost 10 percent in the last decade. Children under the age of five years make up 6.5 percent of the population, while people under 18 make up 24 percent. Thirteen percent of the population are senior citizens, or people over 65. White people make up 72 percent of the population, and black people another 12.6 percent. Hispanics make up about 16.3 percent of the population. About 12 percent of the population was born in another country, and 20 percent speak a language other than English in the home. About 85 percent of the adult population has graduated from high school, but only 38 percent of adults have graduated from college. There are about 2.5 persons in the average American household.

<u>Original inhabitants</u>
The territory that is currently known as the United States was originally inhabited by Native Americans, Inuit, and Hawaiians. Hawaiians were descended from Polynesians who arrived on the archipelago approximately two millennia prior. Inuit and Native Americans arrived on the North American continent thousands of years ago, most likely by walking across the Bering Strait from Asia. Estimates are difficult, but many experts believe that 5 million Native Americans lived in what is now the United States before the arrival of Europeans. Native Americans were not all one people: they were divided into hundreds of tribes with vastly different lifestyles. Some of these tribes survived by farming, while others were exclusively hunter-gatherers.

<u>European immigration</u>
The first Europeans to make a large settlement in what is now the United States were the Spanish, beginning in the early sixteenth century. For a hundred years, there was very little expansion of the European population, but in the seventeenth century the race for colonial supremacy began in earnest. English colonists began sizable settlements in the Northeast. They were soon joined by immigrants from Ireland, France, Denmark, Norway, Sweden, Scotland, Holland, France, and Germany. Up until the beginning of the twentieth century, the vast majority of immigrants to the United States came from northern and western Europe. In the last hundred years, however, there has been a sharp uptick in arrivals from the Southern and Eastern Europe, most notably from Greece, Italy, Poland, Russia, and Austria-Hungary.

<u>African and Asian immigration</u>
The vast majority of African-Americans are descendants of those West Africans who were forced into slave ships and brought to American during the seventeenth, eighteenth, and nineteenth centuries. These unlucky people were primarily used as free labor in southern plantations. After slavery was eliminated, many African-Americans wanted to return to their native homeland. However, most remained in the United States and continued the struggle for civil rights. Today, there are proportionally more immigrants from East Africa than West Africa. Asian immigration to the United States did not really begin until the nineteenth century. During the early 1800s, many Chinese came to work as manual

laborers. These days, the majority of Asian immigrants come from China, Japan, India, South Korea, or the Philippines.

First wave of immigration

The first wave of immigration to the United States extended from the beginning of the colonial period to the Revolutionary War. At the beginning of this wave, the vast majority of immigrants to what is now the United States were from England. After communities were established, there was an increase in immigrants from Ireland, France, Germany, Holland, Wales, and Scotland. These immigrants had various motivations, from religious freedom to entrepreneurialism. Those who could not afford their own ticket from Europe to the colonies became indentured servants; that is, they traded a few years of labor for passage. It was also during this first wave that Africans began to be kidnapped and brought to the Americas as slaves. These unlucky souls were often the members of defeated West African tribes. The rate of immigration during the early years of colonization is difficult to estimate, but by 1700 it is estimated that there were around 250,000 people living in what would become the United States. From 1700 to the beginning of the Revolutionary War, another 450,000 people arrived.

Second wave of immigration

The years from 1820 to 1870 saw another massive influx of northern and western European immigrants to the United States. Two-thirds of these people were Irish or German. The Germans who arrived were more affluent, and therefore were able to move inland in search of land and better economic conditions. Many Germans settled in what is now the American Midwest. The Irish, on the other hand, were largely indigent and stayed close to their point of entry in major cities like New York and Boston. These Irish immigrants mainly sought refuge in the United States because of a horrible famine that beset their homeland in the 1840s. Advances in transportation made the journey across the Atlantic quicker and less expensive. There was also a rise in the number of sojourners, or immigrants who planned to repatriate after making money in the United States. In particular, there were many Chinese who came to the American West to work on railroads but intended to return home after a few years. Of course, many of these sojourners never returned to their homelands, either because they were unable to make enough money to do so or because they learned to love their new land.

The second wave of immigration created unrest and anxiety similar to that caused by immigration today. The economy of the United States was volatile during this period, and many Americans worried that new citizens would take all the jobs. Also, the rapid increase in urban dwellers created dangerous and dirty living conditions, which were decried by many social commentators. Of course, there was also a certain amount of racism in the opposition to immigration. Many of the Irish immigrants were Roman Catholic, which was anathema to the Protestant majorities in large East Coast cities. The year 1875 marked the passage of the first federal anti-immigration legislation, a law that prevented convicts and prostitutes from entering the United States. A more extreme law, the Chinese Exclusion Act of 1882, prohibited any immigration from China. This racist law followed a series of violent acts against Chinese in California. The anti-immigrant cause was taken up by the American Party, also called the Know-Nothings.

Third wave of immigration

After a brief lull, immigration to the United States again skyrocketed during the years 1881 to 1920. This third wave of immigration was characterized by a gradual shift in the immigrant's point of origin; whereas before immigrants largely came from northern and western Europe, during this period there was a sharp increase in the arrivals from Europe's south and east. In particular, there were massive numbers of Polish and Italian immigrants during the third wave. The increase in immigration was again accompanied by a nervous reaction from Americans. Congress expanded the restrictions on immigration in 1882, in legislation that forbade unaccompanied children, beggars, and the mentally disabled from entering the country. The prohibition against the Chinese was expanded in 1917 to include most Asian countries as well as Pacific Islanders. In this same law, Congress declared that men and women must be able to read and write before entering the United States.

Immigration lull

In the years between 1930 and 1945, the rate of immigration to the United States dropped precipitously. The primary reason for this is obvious: the Great Depression, which began in 1929, significantly reduced the economic prospects of aspiring immigrants. As World War II began, the U.S. government made it easier for people to immigrate, and many Europeans took advantage in the hopes of avoiding persecution and conflict. Another result of the war was an elimination of the ban on Chinese immigration. After all, China was a valuable ally of the United States in World War II. Despite these efforts, however, the fifteen-year interval beginning in 1930 marked the low point of immigration to the United States. Indeed, during several of these years more people emigrated from the United States than entered.

Fourth wave of immigration

The Immigration and Nationality Act was amended in 1965, and all quotas related to country of origin were removed. However, the amendments did place caps on the number of immigrants from the eastern and western hemispheres. The immediate result of these amendments was to increase immigration from Asia and decrease immigration from Canada and Europe. Immigration from Europe had already slowed by this time, while immigration from Central and South America rose sharply. The 1965 amendments also established a visa system, whereby preference was given to foreign citizens with special expertise or relatives already in the United States. According to these new rules, the immediate family members of United States citizens could become citizens without counting towards the overall quota for their home hemisphere. The hemisphere-based limits were removed in 1978, at which point Congress declared that 290,000 immigrants would be admitted annually.

Refugee Act of 1980 and the Immigration Reform and Control Act of 1986

The Refugee Act of 1980 expanded the number of persecuted individuals who could find sanctuary in the United States. The quotas established by the 1965 amendments to the Immigration and Nationality Act proved too small to accommodate the massive number of people displaced and driven from their homes by violence and oppressive regimes in Southeast Asia and the Caribbean. The United States has always seen itself as a source of shelter for the victims of nondemocratic governments, so Congress passed the Refugee Act in order to grant citizenship to more refugees. This law allowed 50,000 refugees to immigrate to the United States every year. The Immigration Reform and Control Act of 1986, meanwhile, granted amnesty to certain seasonal agricultural illegal immigrants and to illegal immigrants who entered the United States before January 1, 1982, and had resided there continuously.

1990 amendments to the Immigration and Nationality Act, and the current state of immigration

In 1990, the Immigration and Nationality Act was amended to allow more people to enter the United States every year. By 1995, the total number of immigrants allowed into the country was 675,000 per year. This figure does not include refugees. The amendments to the Immigration and Nationality Act also gave preference to residents of countries from which few immigrants had arrived in the past. This has led to an uptick in the number of immigrants from East Africa and the Balkan region of Europe. These days, the most common home nations of American immigrants are Mexico, the Philippines, Vietnam, the Dominican Republic, China, India, Cuba, Ukraine, Jamaica, and South Korea. Immigrant communities are largely concentrated in the East and Midwest, as well as in California and Florida. The federal government tries to settle refugees from the same country together in disparate locations around the country. This has led to some interesting enclaves, such as the huge community of Iraqis in Dearborn, Michigan.

Population shift

According to the United States Census, an area is defined as urban when it contains more than 2,500 people. Any community with fewer people is considered rural. Over the history of the United States, there has been a continuous shift of the population from rural to urban areas. The first census, taken in 1790, indicated that only 5 percent of the nation's people lived in urban areas. Now, only about 20 percent of the population lives in rural communities. There are several reasons for this shift. The industrial boom of the nineteenth century created many new jobs in city factories, and the improvement of agricultural technology reduced the need for farm laborers. Immigrants have been more likely to settle in urban areas, where they can form enclaves with people who share their heritage. The cities of the United States have increasingly become centers of culture, recreation, and education, all of which have lured young people away from their rural homes.

Urban population

Even though urban areas cover less than 3 percent of the land mass of the United States, they are host to more than 80 percent of the population. The largest city in the United States is New York. It has approximately 8 million residents, while Los Angeles, the second-largest city, has only about 4 million. The next-biggest cities in the United States are Chicago, Houston, Philadelphia, Phoenix, San Diego, and Dallas, respectively. The populations of all these cities are much larger when surrounding suburbs are included. For instance, the metropolitan area of New York, northern New Jersey, and Long Island has about 18 million people. The populations of the densest urban areas have been relatively stagnant over the past few decades, while the populations of suburbs have soared. Urban populations tend to be younger, poorer, and more ethnically diverse.

Rural population

Though farms are still the basis of the rural economy, very few Americans actually work on them. Advances in farm technology have sharply reduced the need for workers. Rural residents are much more likely to work in farm-related industries, like equipment repair or supply. The life of the rural American has become more similar to that of the urban as improvements in technology have diminished the practical distance between town and country. Rural citizens now have access to the same television and Internet services as those in big cities, and can commute into town relatively quickly. However, rural areas tend to have economies dominated by a single industry, so any unforeseen calamity can have a devastating effect on the entire community. In general, rural areas are more ethnically and culturally homogenous. Single-family homes are the most common form of housing in rural areas.

Major modes of transportation in the United States

The United States has one of the highest per-capita rates of automobile ownership in the world, as well as a vast network of roads and highways to accommodate all those drivers. For every four Americans, there are three automobiles. There are also approximately 50,000 miles of federal interstate highway, many of them built during the Eisenhower administration. A little more than a quarter of all commercial freight moves in trucks. The leading freight carrier, however, remains the rail system. Though only about 1 percent of passenger traffic takes place on the rails, close to 40 percent of commercial shipping is done on railroads. Another 15 percent of freight moves over water, whether across Great Lakes or along rivers like the Mississippi, Arkansas, and Ohio. Boats can reach the inner parts of the United States from the Atlantic Ocean by means of the Saint Lawrence Seaway. The busiest ports in the United States are New Orleans, Houston, and New York.

Major media outlets in the United States

In the United States, the media is independent from the government, though it must maintain standards of accuracy and decency. Libelous, obscene, and treasonous messages are prohibited. The United States is still served by several national newspapers, including the *Christian Science Monitor*, *Wall Street Journal*, and *USA Today*. The *New York Times* and *Washington Post* provide local coverage for residents of their respective cities, but are widely seen as national newspapers because of their excellent national and international reporting. There is an ever-increasing number of television stations. Most mid-sized cities have a local television news operation. These days, there is a television for almost every household, and many households have multiple sets. Radio is another venerable source of news and entertainment. It does not have the cultural centrality of a century ago, but it still provides relevant content.

Printing technology

Though the printing press had been around for centuries, in 1811 it became even more influential. This was the year that Friedrich Konig, a German printer, developed a system for powering the press with a steam engine. The result was a sharp increase in the speed of printing. One immediate result of this advance was an increase in daily newspapers and other periodicals. In the United States, newspapers proliferated, though the ethical standards of journalism were undeveloped. The increase in printed materials contributed to improvements in literacy. At around the same time, the U.S. Postal Service greatly improved its efficiency, which reduced the costs of mailing letters. For the next 200 years, the mail service would be a vital mode of social, commercial, and political communication.

Electric telegraph

The first viable electric telegraph was developed by the American professor Samuel B. Morse in the 1830s. Morse also created a language of dots and dashes, known as Morse code, by which extensive messages could be sent over the wires. The electric telegraph was almost immediately adopted by the burgeoning newspaper industry. Within twenty years, there were telegraph lines connecting all of the major American cities, such that information could be sent back and forth almost instantaneously. Soon after, there were telegraph lines connecting the United States to Europe. Telegraphs were quite expensive to use, so they were primarily the tool of banks, government officials, and large media outlets. Very few common people ever had occasion to send or receive a message over the telegraph. Nevertheless, this innovation revolutionized the gathering and dissemination of news, and made it possible for people in all areas of the United States to hear about important events soon after they happened.

Telephone and typewriter

The first telephone was patented by Alexander Graham Bell in 1876. Within a couple of years, there were small telephone networks in all the major American cities. This became a national telephone network in 1879. The company that spearheaded the national network was called AT&T and would dominate the industry for the next century. Telephone service was especially popular in the United States. For many years it was the exclusive province of the wealthy, but AT&T's practical monopoly allowed it to create efficiencies and reduce prices rather quickly. Another important innovation of the late nineteenth century was the typewriter. In 1868, three different American inventors patented versions of this device. The introduction of the typewriter accelerated personal communication, interaction between businesses, and the news media.

Radio

Radio was invented towards the end of the nineteenth century and quickly became an essential tool for communication. The first major job for radio was in navigation, since the early radios could only transmit in Morse code. Once it became possible to transmit speech, music, and other sound, the potential for entertainment and information expanded. One significant milestone for radio was the development of vacuum tubes that could amplify faint radio signals, thus making it possible for many people to pick up a broadcast. By 1908, there were a number of radio stations in the United States. The Radio Corporation of America (RCA), an offshoot of General Electric, set about acquiring all of the major radio equipment patents in 1919. This consolidation of technical expertise enabled RCA to quickly create a powerful network of radio stations. Commercial radio stations date back to 1920, and the first radio advertisement was broadcast in 1922. This initiated an era of sponsored and commercially driven broadcasting.

Television

Television technology evolved over a long period, but it was not until the 1930s that public broadcasts began. After World War II, the television boom began in earnest. Television brought news, sports, advertising, and entertainment into the living rooms of Americans. One result of television has been a homogenization of American culture. Since everyone watches the same television programs and absorbs the same messages, there are fewer regional differences. At the same time, the advent of nationwide news broadcasts shifted more focus onto national and international events and politics, at the expense of local and state news. The United States has always been at the forefront of television program development, and even now exports much more content than it imports. Other countries have often complained of the outsized influence of American entertainment in their culture.

Steam-powered transportation

The development of the steam-powered engine was the first major innovation in transportation in the United States, though the technology itself was developed in Britain. The United States was home to the first profitable steamboat service, and by the end of the nineteenth century steamboats had replaced sailboats as the primary shipping vessels. The steamboat increased the speed and frequency of exports and imports to and from the burgeoning American economy. At the same time, steam-powered railroads were proliferating and eliminating the need for canals. No longer was it essential for a town to be located next to a body of water. Steam-powered railroads were able to move extremely heavy loads much quicker than could canal boats. These trains were so fast that it became possible to travel from New York to San Francisco in less than a week. As these rail lines became more common, the cost was reduced and more people traveled. Also, the improved rail service bolstered the populations of cities, because people wanted to be close to the rail hub.

Automobile

The steam-powered railroad enabled millions of people to travel farther faster than they ever could have dreamed, but it was not until the early twentieth century and the development of the automobile that rapid autonomous transportation became a reality. The automobile was made possible by the invention of the gasoline engine in the 1880s. This engine led to breakthroughs in many areas of transportation: for instance, the Wright brothers used a gas engine to power their airplane. The first gas-powered cars and trucks were built in Germany in the 1890s, and by the 1920s automobiles had become the dominant form of personal transportation in western Europe and the United States. This launched a massive period of road-building in the United States, as governments struggled to improve infrastructure fast enough to keep pace with technological expansion and the increasing demands of commerce. The automobile made it possible for people to travel long distances by the fastest possible route, and to stop whenever they liked. The automobile remains a central symbol of American life, evoking freedom, independence, and personal responsibility.

Freight transportation

Freight transportation underwent exponential improvement in the twentieth century, but increases in speed and efficiency have begun to plateau. The rail system in the United States is still widely used, but many operators complain that it needs considerable maintenance. Airplanes are a growing sector in freight, though it is expensive and people who live near freight airports complain of the noise. One major advance in freight transport over the past few decades has been pipelines that move natural gas and petroleum over long distances. Interestingly, the cheapest way to ship goods is by water, hearkening back to the days when much of American shipping depended on the canal system. Most overseas shipping makes use of enormous ships loaded with standard containers, which can be stacked neatly and loaded onto rail cars. These ships can reach any destination in the world in just a few days, at a very low cost.

Public transportation

The United States at one time had the world's best public transportation: smooth multi-lane interstate highways, clean modern airports, and rapid trains connecting major cities. Now, however, cuts in infrastructure spending have allowed this transportation system to fall into disrepair. Population booms in some cities, such as Atlanta and Houston, have strained existing infrastructure. Nevertheless, the public still has a range of options with regard to transportation. Most major cities have a subway or tram system, and all have bus service. Automobiles remain relatively inexpensive in the United States, and more people than ever own one. In some cities, like Portland, Oregon, a light rail system has reduced some of the burden on traditional paths. Light rail is a railroad service designed to accommodate high-speed passenger trains. These trains are often powered by green technologies, like magnetized or electrified rails.

Zoning

Zoning is the practice of designating uses for land. For instance, in a city, land might be zoned for residences, businesses, or factories. Although the concept of zoning has existed for thousands of years, there was no municipal zoning legislation in the United States until 1912. In that year, New York City passed a major ordinance dictating where businesses and residences were permitted. Besides designating how structures in a certain area may be used, zoning ordinances also restrict their dimensions. For instance, a zoning ordinance may state that residences are not allowed to be above a certain height or within a certain distance of the street. Zoning ordinances are essential to the management of city growth. It is generally agreed that the free market will not make good development choices if left alone. This is because every developer will act in his or her own interest, without regard to the city as a whole. The result is often overpopulation, pollution, or traffic problems.

The United States was late to begin adopting zoning ordinances, in part because the enormity of the country made land use considerations less immediate. In 1916, however, New York City became the first place to pass a zoning ordinance. It was aimed at reducing the damage to property values after the construction of skyscrapers. These incredibly tall buildings blotted out the sun for most of the day, significantly reducing the value of nearby real estate. As with many issues in American history, once legislators got started with zoning they found it hard to stop. Over time, municipal zoning ordinances settled on three main categories for land use: residential, commercial, and industrial. For many years these three zones were kept apart, but in recent decades it has become popular to mix commercial and residential zones so that people can conduct most of their business on foot. This reduces traffic and pollution. As more people start to work at home, zoning ordinances will no doubt go through more change in the future.

In the United States, zoning strategies are typically Euclidean, incentive, form-based, or performance. Euclidean zoning is named not after the Greek geometrician, but after a town in Ohio. In this strategy, planners designate large areas of the city ahead of time, and force developers to abide by their rules. This model creates very clear zoning systems, but critics charge that it is inflexible. In the incentive strategy, planners establish certain baseline requirements, as well as a series of supplementary goals that developers can earn rewards by achieving. This system encourages cooperation between planners and developers. In a form-based zoning strategy, more attention is paid to the actual use of a structure than to its classification. For instance, in this system a large apartment building would be treated quite

- 66 -

differently from a single-family dwelling, even though both are residential structures. Finally, in the performance strategy, statistics about land use are analyzed to create zoning ordinances. This system is not used very often in the United States.

Major religious groups in the United States

Although more than half of Americans are affiliated with a religious group, on the whole religion plays less of a role in American life than ever before. Approximately half of all religious Americans are Protestants, while another 40 percent are Roman Catholic. The remaining 10 percent is composed primarily of Jews, Mormons, Muslims, and Eastern Orthodox Christians. Since Protestants are divided into denominations, the largest single group is the Roman Catholics, of whom there are about 70 million. Among Protestants, the most populous denominations are the Baptists, Methodists, Pentecostals, Lutherans, and Presbyterians. Throughout its history, the United States has codified religious tolerance in its law. It still is a beacon for people suffering religious persecution in other countries. Despite waning membership, religious organizations continue to provide charitable services in their communities and around the world.

Religious freedom in the United States

Religious freedom has been one of the most important factors in the development and success of the United States. Many of the original colonists left their homes in search of religious freedom. For instance, the Puritan pilgrims had been persecuted in their European homes, and sought a place where they would be free to worship. The same is true of the Quakers, who largely settled in Pennsylvania, and the Roman Catholics, who gained a foothold in what is now Maryland. Even before the drafting of the Constitution, religious freedom was a central tenet of colonial law. The Constitution establishes this freedom in the First Amendment, which states that the government may not establish any state church or give preference to any religious group. Religious persecution has been illegal for the entire history of the United States. The promise of religious freedom continues to attract immigrants from around the world.

Cultural pluralism in the United States

Cultural pluralism exists when a diverse population lives together, sharing some aspects of culture and differing in others. The United States is perhaps history's greatest example of cultural pluralism, and this quality has been responsible for much of the country's greatness. In the United States, people are proud of their religion, ethnic background, and heritage, but they also identify as Americans. The United States government has generally avoided forced assimilation, which in the long run has encouraged mutual respect and tolerance. There has assuredly been racism and cultural prejudice throughout American history, but it has gradually been removed from the law. Cultural pluralism makes the United States a vibrant society, in which people learn about each other's backgrounds and beliefs, and in which a rich conversation about and within American culture has thrived.

Human behavior

Leaving aside the debate over whether global warming is the result of fossil-fuel combustion, there are numerous other ways in which human behavior influences the climate. Urban areas are warmer and drier than nearby areas, because the asphalt absorbs heat. Also, sewer and storm water drainage systems remove standing water from the terrain, so heat that otherwise would be evaporating water instead is absorbed by the land. Industrial facilities and large numbers of automobiles also affect the climate. Smokestacks and exhaust pipes emit tiny particulates and water vapor, which encourage the development of clouds downwind. This phenomenon is assisted by the natural heat of cities. It is typical for the area immediately downwind from a large city to have more cloud cover and precipitation than would otherwise be expected.

Political Geography

Political geography (sometimes referred to as geopolitics) is the branch of geographic study which focuses on the spatial implications of power relations. In other words, political geographers investigate the relationships between political and social power, and geographic location and space. Geopolitics examines, among other things, the delineation of Earth's surface into nations, states, cities, etc, as well as regional alliances, the locations of bases of political power, and the spatial relationships of different areas to central regions. The study of political geography can be useful at international, national, and metropolitan levels.

Defining characteristics of an independent country

While countries vary greatly in size, economic strength, and military power (among many other things), each independent country shares four defining characteristics:
1. First, any independent country inhabits a specific territory (land and water) defined by boundaries. The sizes and shapes of countries differ widely.
2. Second, each country has a population which occupies its territory. The sizes and constitutions of each country are also extremely variable.
3. Third, any independent country possesses sovereignty, the freedom to control and protect its territory, population, and foreign interactions without outside influence. The geographic location and landscape of a country's territory may affect its ability to defend its sovereignty. For example, the high mountains surrounding Switzerland have served to protect the country against foreign invasion for centuries.
4. Finally, every independent country has a government, an institution which creates and enforces laws and policies and acts to further the public good (through protection, the maintenance of order, and provision of certain services). There are several types of government structures and governmental authority.

<u>Government structures</u>
Governments may be classified by the nature of the relationship between the central governing body and the smaller units (states, provinces, etc) which make up a country:
1. A <u>unitary system</u> exists when a central governmental body exerts sole control over an entire country. The principle government formulates policies applicable at all levels of government; smaller units exert power only if the central government grants it to them.
2. When certain powers are allocated to a central government and certain powers are given to regional or local governmental units, the governmental structure is referred to as <u>a federation</u>. In a federation (such as the United States), federal and local governments share political power.
3. In a governmental system of <u>confederation</u>, smaller governmental units retain their sovereignties and allow the central government only specific, limited powers (usually regarding national defense or international trade). In this type of structure, states and provinces retain a large degree of independence but still ally to address common concerns.

Governmental authority

A government may be classified by the source of its authority. Different kinds of governments are run with various degrees of public participation.

- In an anarchy, every citizen in the population is seen as a qualified participant in decision-making which will affect the country. There is no central governing body—people govern themselves.
- Democracies also involve rule by the people. However, unlike an anarchy, a democracy includes a central government which aims to serve the people. In a representative democracy, citizens exercise their political franchise or suffrage (the right to vote) in the selection of leaders, who in turn participate in governmental proceedings and make political decisions. Citizens of a democratic nation also express their opinions about certain issues by voting.
- In an oligarchy, political power is concentrated in the hands of a small group, usually made up of wealthy people with strong military influence and/or familial traditions of power. Often, the most influential participants in an oligarchic government operate outside the public eye in the economic realm.

Types of authoritarian governments

An authoritarian government is one in which the country's leaders possess all (or a majority of) political power. Until fairly recently, most countries across the world had authoritarian governments. Today, various forms of democracy are more common. There are different degrees of authoritarianism:

- A monarchy is a type of authoritarian government in which monarchs (for example, queens, shahs, and pharaohs) inherit political power simply by being born into a ruling family. Monarchs may serve as symbols of national unity, or they may rule as dictators.
- A dictatorship (the most common type of authoritarian government) is a system in which political power is held by a small group or even a unitary individual. The dictator(s) exert control through military force and intimidation; the dictator(s) attempt to control the behavior of their subordinates.
- Totalitarianism is the most extreme form of authoritarianism. In this kind of system, the ruling body tries to control every aspect of society in its territory, from economic activity to people's personal lives.

Boundaries and frontiers

A boundary is a functional through hypothetical structure which delineates territories of differing political entities or legal domains, such as countries, provinces, and states. Prior to modernized conceptions of territory, nations defined their territories as the area over which they could exert authority. Today, territories are demarcated by boundaries which are effectively material and officially designated. A map whose sole purpose is to convey the sizes and shapes of various governmental units is termed a political map. Though boundaries may run alongside physical features of Earth's surface, such as mountains, they are contrived by humans to segregate one area from another. The areas on either side of a boundary are often referred to as borders.

A frontier is an area of undeveloped land, the edge of civilization; frontiers exist outside of certain boundaries.

Throughout history, competition for the control of boundaries and frontiers has been the cause of much military and ideological conflict.

The phases of boundary formation
The processes of boundary formation and implementation occurs in four general phases:
1. During the historical precedent phase, boundaries are established and maintained based on the cultural characteristics (such as religion, language, or ethnicity) of people in an area. Different cultural groups form communities which inhabit particular areas. The recognition of boundaries in this stage may also be based on previous attempts to establish a dividing line.
2. The political definition or delimitation phase entails the official establishment of boundary lines, through the use of legal documents such as treaties. These lines are drawn on official maps. Often, the placement of a boundary is negotiated by representatives from the concerned regions.
3. During the technical demarcation phase, the boundaries agreed upon during the previous phase are practically implemented. Demarcators analyze the relevant terrain and material markers or monuments are constructed to display the location of the officially-defined boundary.
4. Finally, the characterization phase entails modification of the demarcated boundary to accommodate population growth in the border areas.

Terminology
A **natural boundary** is a boundary arbitrarily formed by landscape evolution. This type of boundary may be hydrologic, or formed by a waterway such as a river, or orthographic, or formed by a land formation such as a mountain chain.

An **artificial boundary** is an abstract line formulated by humans to aid in identifying specific locations. Geodesic lines and the lines which constitute the graticule are examples of artificial boundaries.

A **separation barrier** is a physical construction (for instance, a wall or fence) intended to separate disparate populations or to inhibit movement between two areas. The Great Wall of China, which spans nearly 4,000 miles, provides a classic example of a separation barrier. It was initially built to protect citizens against raids by conquering tribes. Another example is the border of the United States with Mexico, which was created to prevent the free entry of immigrants into the U.S.

Cultural boundaries
As displayed on maps, boundaries may appear as straight lines, as lines which follow natural landscape features, or as wiggles which seem to twist and turn for no reason. The last of these boundary types may be attributed to many (perhaps continuous) boundary disputes between cultural and/or ethnic groups on either side of the separating line. For example, the border region between Belgium and the Netherlands is sprinkled with tiny, hamlet-sized areas "belonging" to one country on the other's side of the boundary. This type of boundary is sometimes referred to as a cultural boundary. When conflict along cultural border ebbs, the formal process of boundary formation often begins, resulting in the wiggles observed along borders across the world.

Factors of production

Classical economics identifies three main factors in the production of consumable goods and services. Land is one such factor. This term refers to the physical location at which production occurs, as well as material goods (including natural fuel resources, such as coal, as well as materials like minerals and soil which are used in production). Rent is the monetary compensation paid for the use of land owned by a separate party.

Labor is the second factor of production. This term refers to the work executed by humans in the production of goods and the performance of services. The quality of labor is affected by education and training levels.

Finally, capital goods are manmade goods which are used in turn to produce other goods and services. Capital goods are also referred to as means of production. This factor includes tools, buildings, and machinery.

Natural resources

A resource is something valued by humans for its role in survival. A natural resource is a naturally-occurring material (such as water, soil, minerals, or animals) which humans use to maintain their existences. Such resources are unevenly distributed across the globe; their monetary values vary with scarcity, technology, and specific human needs. For example, petroleum became much more valuable after the invention of automobiles, which require the substance to operate.

Some natural resources are renewable, meaning that they are constantly being replenished in nature. Energy from the sun, water, and soil are all renewable resources.

Nonrenewable resources are those of which the Earth has a limited supply. Fossil fuels such as coal and oil take millions of years to form in the Earth's crust; therefore, once humans exhaust the current supply of these resources, no more will become available in our lifetimes. Most natural resources (renewable or nonrenewable) are utilized to provide energy to fuel modern industry.

Resource distribution
Resources are not evenly distributed across the globe. Fossil fuels, for example, form over millions of years (under specific natural conditions) from the remains of fossilized plants and animals. Even renewable resources such as water are not equally distributed. Certain global regions experience droughts while others withstand deluges of rain. The uneven distribution of natural resources affects the locations and sizes of human settlements, the quality of life in those settlements, and the economic activities in which certain people can participate. A lack of resources in an area may lead to mass migration to an area with a larger supply or to the formation of trade networks with countries possessing higher quantities of a particular resource.

Use of boundaries to exert control over resources
Though boundaries appear as lines along Earth's surface on two-dimensional maps and globes, they do more than separate terrestrial territories. Theoretically, boundaries exist as vertical planes, extending below the surface and into the air, effectively separating underground resources and airspace. For example, disputes about the "ownership" of an

underground oil field (inconveniently located beneath the Iraq-Kuwait border and extending into both countries) contributed to the development of a conflict which culminated in the Gulf War. Disputes over the exploitation of other underground resources, such as coal and natural gas, have been and continue to be sources of international conflict. International boundaries also extend above the surface, creating divisions of airspace (the zone above a state's territory where the rights of other states may be limited). Often, commercial aircrafts may fly through another state's airspace only with official agreement. During the communist period, for example, Soviets shot down a commercial Korean aircraft which strayed outside the narrow corridor the USSR had delimited for flights over its territory.

Maritime boundaries

The concept of territorial control of portions of the seas originated centuries ago. Seafaring peoples created maritime boundaries to claim certain fishing grounds or trading ports for themselves. The delimitations of these boundaries have become more and more specific as time passes. A critical action by President Harry Truman in 1945 hastened the rush to claim oceanic territory. Truman claimed all of the potential natural resources located on the continental shelf for the United States. After Truman's declaration, countries across the world scrambled to lay claim to their own oceanic territories.

Today, the following conventions exist regarding maritime law: states may claim up to twelve nautical miles of oceanic territory; states may claim up to 200 nautical miles as their Exclusive Economic Zones—coastal states have the sole rights to manage and exploit natural resources within these zones; coastal states possess exclusive rights over the natural resources on an beneath the continental shelf of their respective continents.

Hegemony

Hegemony is a continuous process whereby a dominant group exercises ideological control over other subordinate groups. By influencing the shared belief and value systems of others, the dominant group attempts to naturalize its own beliefs in other groups. The process of hegemonic establishment may or may not involve force or the threat of force; in fact, hegemony is more effective when it exists as a mixture of control (on the part of the dominant group) and consent (on the part of the subordinate group(s)). In practice, hegemony serves to empower certain religious beliefs, ethnic groups, political ideologies, economic systems, and cultural practices; this marginalizes alternative beliefs and practices. The creation of hegemony is both a method of attaining power and a means to maintain that power. Theories of hegemony attempt to explain the ways that dominant groups (referred to as hegemons) coerce members of non-dominant groups to accept and internalize the social, cultural, political, and economic norms of the former.

International power relations

International power refers to the ability of one state to exert control or influence over other states. Power is generally defined as the capacity of an individual or group to impose their wills on others. This may be achieved through hegemonies (soft power) or through the use of brute force (hard power). Today, states may be classified by the degree of their influences, especially in relation to the power of other states. Middle powers are those states which cannot dominate other states but still possess degrees of international influence. Such states often ally themselves with groups but do not lead them. Canada is an example of a middle power. A regional power is a state which exerts control over other states in its region but not necessarily around the globe. Great powers, global powers, and superpowers are terms for strong states which share power with a few other influential states. A hyperpower is a singular dominating state in a unipolar world. Many consider the modern United States a hyperpower.

Spheres of influence

In international politics, the term sphere of influence refers to the claim of a powerful state to exclusive or predominant control over foreign territory, often in the surrounding region; this claim may or may not be recognized as legitimate by other entities. States within a powerful state's sphere of influence often function as satellite states (states which are officially independent but influenced by the more powerful state in practice). For instance, during its prime, the Japanese Empire exerted much political power over events in the nearby states of Korea, Vietnam, and Manchuria. Historically, the term sphere of influence has been used to refer to the respective colonial territories of two or more powers in a region. For example, in the 1880's, Great Britain and Germany signed an agreement stating that neither would interfere in the other's (predefined) sphere of influence in the Gulf of Guinea. In regional geography, a major urban area may exert economic influence over the surrounding area; this is also referred to as a sphere of influence.

The Monroe Doctrine

In 1823, President James Monroe formulated a foreign policy which is known today as the Monroe Doctrine. In his annual address to Congress, Monroe indicated that the Old World (namely Europe) and the New World (namely the United States) were distinct entities with distinct systems, and should therefore exist as separate spheres. His statement included four main points: the United States would not participate in conflicts inside or between European nations; the United States officially recognized and would not interfere with existing colonies in the New World; the Western Hemisphere was off limits for future colonization; and any endeavor by a European power to influence any nation in the Western Hemisphere would be considered a hostile act against the United States. Though the Monroe Doctrine was militarily unsustainable at the time of its formulation, as the U.S. emerged as a global power in the 1870's, the Monroe Doctrine came to be viewed as a geopolitical definition of the country's sphere of influence as the entire Western Hemisphere.

Cooperation among people and nation-states

Cooperation is the practice whereby individuals and groups working together (possibly with common methods) to achieve a shared goal. Often, those working in concert accomplish more than those acting independently or in against one another (competition), though the impetus to compete against others is often a motivation for individual behavior. In fact, individuals or nation-states may cooperate with a larger group in order to be part of a larger, more competitive entity.

There are potentially infinite reasons for collaboration between people and nation-states. For instance, at the local level, a group of citizens may form a group to protest the planned construction of a large shopping center in a rural neighborhood. At the regional and national levels, organizations such as Mothers Against Drunk Driving (MADD) collaborate in attempts to change public policy and spur the passage of legislation aimed at making society safer. Internationally, the governments of nation-states and/or their citizens may join together to promote humanitarian activities; the International Federation of Red Cross and Red Crescent Societies (IFRCS).

Non-governmental organizations

A non-governmental organization (sometimes referred to as a private voluntary organization) is, as its title suggests, a cooperative group formed independently of any state government. Usually, a group of this type forms for reasons other than commercial gain, such as the advocation of social or environmental policy; non-governmental organizations are often non-profit. There are two general types of NGOs. Advocacy non-governmental organizations are formed to promote awareness of and/or support for a certain issue, which they accomplish through lobbying activities, orchestration of awareness-raising events, and press work. Operational NGOs participate in the organization and execution of relief-oriented or development-oriented projects. Most development-related groups evolve in three stages: first, the group concentrates on relief and welfare activities; next, on the development of self-reliant activity in affected areas; and lastly, on the implementation of sustainable development activities at local, state, and national levels.

The Market Effect

The Market Effect is a model which exemplifies one type of international governmental cooperation. Trade, the voluntary exchange of goods and/or services, is a vital mechanism by which nation-states who do not have and cannot feasibly produce a particular good can obtain it. In the Market Effect situation, it is assumed that it is impractical and/or impossible for a single country to produce all of the resources it needs in sufficient quantities. Therefore, it becomes desirable for each country in a system to specialize in the efficient production of one resource and trade a surplus of that resource for another material. This process requires cooperation among the participating nation-states in discussions of costs and quantities. For example, Arabic countries control a large portion of the world's oil reserves. Western countries in need of that particular resource often share technological information with Arabic countries in exchange for oil. In this manner, each country has the potential to obtain the resources it needs.

The United Nations

The United Nations (UN) is a group of nation-states (including nearly every independent country) which defines itself as a "global association of governments facilitating cooperation in international law, international security, economic development, and social equity." This organization was founded after World War II in 1945 by the victorious countries, which possessed the shared aim of preventing future conflicts and wars between nations through the establishment of a situation of collective security. This means that any aggression against any of the member states is viewed as an attack on the entire organization, which will respond as a whole. Today, the United Nations consists of several specialized agencies which deal with issues such as human rights, arms control, global health, economic development, and humanitarian assistance. As a large organization made up of nearly 200 member states, the UN does not always function perfectly. However, the group has achieved more through international cooperation than any single nation-state could accomplish alone.

Sustainable development and Agenda 21

Sustainable development is a developmental process which satisfies the needs of those living in the present without impairing the abilities of those in future generations to attain the same degree of comfort; it is development which does not exhaust the global supply of natural resources. In other words, sustainable development refers to a balance achieved between economic development, social development, and environmental protection.

Agenda 21 is a UN program which strives to reach that balance. It consists of four sections: the social and economic dimensions section, which stresses the importance of addressing global poverty in developing nations through health education, promotion of sustainable settlement patterns, and altering destructive consumption patterns; the conservation and management of resources development section, which includes information on environmental protection and the preservation of biodiversity; the section on strengthening the role of major groups, which aims to empower groups at the individual and local levels; and the means of implementation section, which describes educational, technological, financial, and international procedures for the attainment of the program's goals.

Conflict between people and nation-states

Conflict is a situation of discord and/or opposition between two or more individuals or groups. In political science, conflict is defined as a continuing state of hostility between groups of people, which often involves physical violence. Conflict must be distinguished from competition, which involves two or more groups possessing mutually exclusive goals (meaning that attempts by one party to achieve its goal compromises the ability of the other group to attain its goal). Competition (and occasionally cooperation) may lead to conflict. Individuals and nation-states may become involved in conflicts for a variety of reasons at a variety of scales. For example, two local groups may have conflicting views on a proposed tax increase. At the regional level, different religious or ethnic groups may exist in a state of conflict. Internationally, competition for scarce resources or ideological disagreements may lead to a war between countries.

Class conflict

Social classes may be defined and differentiated using various criteria. An individual's membership in a particular class may be based on his or her income, education level, possessions, reputation, manners, relationship to a means of production, or any combination of these and other factors. Regardless of how one's class status is determined, however, some measure of discord usually exists between members of different classes; this tension is referred to as class conflict. This conflict may be overtly manifest through, for instance, physical violence, worker strikes, or protests. Class conflict may also be expressed more subtly, through, for example, informal "slowdowns" in production or prejudicial treatment of members of an oppositional class. Ironically, conflict between different classes may increase the level of cooperation within a single class, as members ally to lobby public policy makers.

Terminology

The generally accepted definition of the term **indigenous peoples** is that which describes them as distinctive cultural groups whose historical associations with an area or region predate that area's colonization, annexation, or integration into a nation-state. Indigenous societies are often non-urbanized, and are frequently based on agricultural, pastoral, or hunting and gathering production methods.

Colonialism is the practice whereby a nation-state asserts sovereignty over territories outside of its boundaries, usually in order to gain control of an area's resources (natural and human) and potential markets. Colonization may occur violently, through the forcible suppression and domination of indigenous peoples, or it may occur relatively peacefully, through the hegemonic promotion of ideologies which imply that the colonizers are spreading superior (and thus beneficial) values and systems to colonized areas.

- 76 -

Imperialism is similar to colonialism in that each practice involves the extension of a nation's control over foreign territories. However, imperialism refers more specifically to the creation and/or maintenance of an empire, a set of regions officially ruled by a single emperor.

Civil war

A civil war is a conflict which occurs between antagonistic groups in the same country or empire; each faction wishes to secure control of the affairs of the state. Like any conflict, a civil war may take place due to differing political or religious views among members of the warring groups, an unequal distribution of wealth among citizens of a country, racial or ethnic prejudices, or the desires of revolutionary groups to change the social organization of a country. For example, the Nigerian Civil War (1967-1970) was bred from religious, political, and ethnic tensions between the Hausa, Yoruba, and Igbo peoples. The political boundaries of Nigeria had been created by European colonial powers with no regard for previously existent cultural boundaries, sparking conflict between the indigenous groups. The Irish Civil War (1922-1923) occurred between supporters and opponents of a treaty that created an Irish state (excluding the six countries of Northern Ireland) which was described as "free" but was actually a non-sovereign dominion of the British Empire.

Major causes of some historic international wars

An international war is a violent conflict between two or more independent states. Such conflicts frequently occur as a result of competition over land, resources, and/or sovereignty. Throughout the late 19th and early 20th centuries, many of the era's great powers competed for colonial territory and trading rights in Eastern Asia. The Russo-Japanese War (1904-1905) was fought between Russian and Japanese forces for imperial control of Manchuria and Korea (specifically, the Liaodong Peninsula). The Japanese victory in 1905 marked the first time an Asian country had defeated a European country, and firmly established Japan as a formidable global power. The Arab-Israeli conflict, an extended conflict dating back to the late 1800's, is an example of international animosity based on differences in political and religious ideologies. The spectrum of points of view among members of the concerned parties problematizes any simple definition of the cause of the conflict. However, reasons cited for the conflict tend to relate to hostilities between Muslims and Jews and the dispute over Israel's right to self-determination.

Three types of economic systems

The term economic system refers to the way in which goods and services are produced, distributed, and consumed in a society. In a traditional economy, determinations of the types and amounts of goods produced, methods of production, and distribution of goods are based on long-established customs and habits. Such economies are sometimes referred to as subsistence economies because little surplus is produced, which negates the need for markets. In a market economy, producers of goods and services are free to trade them as they see fit. The types and amounts of goods and services produced (and their prices) are determined by the laws of supply and demand, and by private individuals and organizations. Nearly every aspect of a command economy is controlled by a central government. The government often makes economic decisions based on social and political goals; for instance, a government may set the price of a gallon of milk at 25 cents even if it costs one dollar to produce so that everyone can afford to purchase it.

Economic interdependence

Resources (including natural resources such as minerals and land as well as human resources), fuel sources, and information are distributed unevenly across the globe—no single country possess all the resources it needs to subsist and thrive. Therefore, each must trade its surplus goods and services for those it lacks. Economic interdependence is a situation in which two or more countries depend on each other for any or all of the following: energy, food, manufactured goods, minerals, or labor. The North American Free Trade Agreement (NAFTA) was formed among three economically interdependent countries (Canada, the United States, and Mexico) in an attempt to ease trade restrictions on vital imports and exports in the member states.

Industry and industrial sectors

The term **industry** refers to a method of economic production, namely manufacturing, which involves the investment of large amounts of capital prior to production. An industry may also be defined as a group of businesses which produce similar products; for example, all of the businesses which participate in film production constitute the "movie industry." Industries in general may be classified into four sectors based on the resources needed for production and the type of goods produced.

The *primary sector* of industry is made up of businesses which transform natural resources into raw materials used in other industries. Agriculture, mining, and forestry are examples of activities related to the primary sector of industries.

The *secondary sector* of industry involves the manufacture of goods suitable for sale to consumers and other businesses. Businesses in this sector often make use of the materials produced in the primary sector. The clothing, tobacco, and energy industries are considered to be in the secondary sector.

The *tertiary sector* of industry is also referred to as the service industry or sector. Businesses in this industrial category provide services to consumers and other businesses. Hair salons, hospitals, and restaurants are examples of tertiary businesses which provide services directly to consumers. Members of the tertiary industry may also provide services to other businesses, such as the transportation, distribution, wholesale, or retail of goods produced by businesses in the secondary sector. While the provision of services may involve the alteration of the secondary product (like the preparation of raw foods in the restaurant industry), the focus of the tertiary sector is on interaction with consumers.

The *quaternary sector* is a relatively new categorization, having been recently distinguished from the tertiary sector. The quaternary sector involves the provision of specialized "intellectual" services, such as education, scientific research, and the distribution of information technology.

Industrial location factors

Industry owners and managers take several industrial location factors into consideration during the selection of an ideal physical location for their businesses.

Human or economic factors include the availability of a labor source (the proximity of potential workers to the location); the location of leisure facilities for workers; the market (the capital required to keep a business in operation, which depends on the wage demands of laborers in a particular area, the cost of the transportation of goods, and the size of the business's sphere of influence); the relative location of transportation routes (such as seaports, railways, and highways); the government (which may impose laws, restrictions, and/or incentives in a particular area); access to technology (such as manufacturing robots); and geographical inertia (which refers to traditions of producing particular goods in particular areas).

Physical location factors include the relative locations of natural transportation routes (such as rivers); the relative locations of raw material sources (the primary industrial location factor); and the size and relief of the prospective business site.

Labels for levels of development
Economic geographers use different terms to classify countries by their levels of economic development. Most broadly, countries may be classified as either more developed countries (MDCs) or less developed countries (LDCs). In this system of classification, distinctions are made often made based on political factors as well as economic factors.

Geographers may also categorize the level of a country's economic development as First World (capitalist), Second World (communist or socialist), Third World (underdeveloped), Fourth World (severely underdeveloped), or Fifth World (poorest). Currently, the World Bank (an international organization which monitors the economic status of countries) classifies countries as high income, upper-middle income, lower-middle income, or low income. However, any of these categorizations may be misleading when applied to an entire country. Most of the world's countries exhibit highly-developed cores as well as peripheral regions stricken by poverty. Therefore, averages of national economic statistics have lost some of their meaning. It is useful to consider the relative advantages (geographic location, resources, political stability, etc) of certain countries over others.

Measures of economic development
Gross national product, population growth, occupational structure, urbanization

Geographers examine several characteristics of a country in the determination of that country's level of economic development. A country's per capita *gross national product (GNP),* the total value of all final goods and services (those provided directly to consumers) produced per person in a year, is taken into account. The higher a nation's GNP, the more developed it is assumed to be.

Geographers also examine the annual *population growth* of a country as a measure of its economic development. Generally, poorer countries have relatively rapid rates of population growth.

The *occupational structure* of a country's labor force (the proportions of people working in the primary, secondary, and tertiary sectors of industry) is considered. In MDCs, most workers participate in tertiary activities; in LDCs, most workers participate in primary activities.

Geographers also evaluate a country's *level of urbanization* (the proportion of a country's total population living in urban areas). Urbanization is seen as progress in the process of economic development, for urban areas often provide specialized job opportunities and services.

A country's *consumption per capita* is observed as a measure of the country's level of economic development. Naturally, the higher a nation's level of economic development, the wealthier its citizens will be and, therefore, the more they can afford to consume.

Geographers also study a country's *infrastructure* in assessment of its economic status. Transportation systems, urban centers, distribution mechanisms, industrial businesses, communication systems, and service facilities such as hospitals and police stations are all considered aspects of a country's infrastructure.

A country's *social conditions* are also used as measures of economic development. These conditions include the literacy rate, the infant mortality rate, and the availability of health care. The United Nations Development Program has developed a human development index based on the national averages of three figures: life expectancy, education (assessed through examination of the adult literacy rate and the combined rates of enrollment in secondary and tertiary schools), and per capita income. A higher human development index is seen as an indicator of a higher level of economic development.

United States Government

Constitutional authority
The authority of the federal government in the United States is granted by the Constitution. The government may not overstep the boundaries established by this document. According to the Constitution, the primary mission of the federal government is to "establish justice, insure domestic tranquility, provide for the common defense, promote the general welfare, and secure the blessings of liberty." Of course, these are rather vague guidelines, so the specific duties and restrictions of the government are spelled out at greater length elsewhere in the Constitution and in the ever-increasing body of federal case law. Essentially, the federal government is allowed to establish and enforce any laws necessary for it to accomplish the above goals. However, the federal government may not violate the freedoms enumerated in the Bill of Rights. Among these are the freedoms of speech, the press, and religion.

Separation of powers
The government of the United States is divided into three branches: the executive, legislative, and judicial. The respective powers of these branches can be classified as either expressed or implied. Expressed powers are explicit in the Constitution. For instance, the Constitution declares that it is the responsibility of Congress to declare war (though this designation has been flouted routinely in recent years). Implied powers may be reasonably inferred from those expressed. The separation of powers was intended to keep too much authority from accumulating in any one branch of government. The expressed powers of each branch are designed to restrict the powers of the other. In the broadest sense, the Constitution indicates that the legislative branch will write the laws, the executive branch will enforce them, and the judicial branch will consider their constitutionality.

Federalism
Federalism is the system for dividing responsibility between the national, state, and local governments. In the United States, the Constitution establishes the respective duties of the national and state governments, while the state constitutions establish the boundaries between the state and local bodies. The federal government is restricted to those powers listed in the Constitution. The powers held by both the federal and state governments are

called concurrent powers. One of the more commonly exercised concurrent powers is taxation. The balance of power between the national and state governments has tilted over the years. In education, for instance, the state traditionally held most of the authority, though there has been more federal intervention in the last few decades. Many conservatives call for authority to be returned to the states on this and other issues.

Representative democracy

In a pure democracy, such as that of ancient Athens, every government decision would be left up to a popular vote. Of course, this system would be impossible for a nation as large and complex as the United States. The solution is representative democracy, in which the people elect officials to serve as their voice in Washington. Elections are held on a regular schedule and according to predetermined rules. In the United States, representative democracy is dominated by two political parties, the Democrats and the Republicans. To the extent that additional parties exist, it is mainly to promote particular issues or to act as a "none of the above" ballot option for disgusted voters. Third-party candidates rarely win elections.

Executive branch

The basic mission of the executive branch of the United States government is to enforce the laws passed by the legislative branch. Of course, the actual role of this branch is much more complex. The top official in the executive branch is the president. Presidents are elected every four years, and may serve no more than two terms. Presidents are not elected by a popular vote, but rather by a convoluted system known as the Electoral College. This system was developed to prevent populous states from dominating national politics. The president is considered the nation's chief executive: he or she is charged with appointing top officials, preparing the budget, and enforcing the laws of the nation. Because the president is an individual actor, he is able to respond more quickly and decisively to crises than Congress or the court system. For this reason, the president is given certain powers to be used in the case of an emergency.

Legislative branch

The legislative branch of the United States, otherwise known as Congress, is divided into two chambers: the Senate and the House of Representatives. The Senate has 100 members, two from each state. Senators serve terms of six years, and the senators from any given state do not run in the same year. The House of Representatives, on the other hand, has 435 members, who are apportioned to the states depending on population. After the conclusion of each census, the House seats are reassigned. However, each state must have at least one representative in the House. Every member of the House must run for reelection every other year. However, both senators and representatives may serve an unlimited number of terms. The founders of the United States imagined that the House would be a more volatile place, because members would be representing a smaller constituency with more extreme beliefs and more idiosyncratic needs. The Senate was designed to be a more reserved, calm body, where more secure members could consider the virtues of an issue without worrying as much about reelection.

The primary job of the legislative branch of the United States government is to make laws. The volume of legislation passed by Congress is astonishing: in each two-year session, there are likely to be about 600 bills that become law. Perhaps even more amazing is that this number represents only a small percentage of the bills that are introduced in each session. Many of these bills are on minor issues, and most are entirely uncontroversial. Congress is also responsible for investigating the executive and legislative branches (in other words, itself) when there are allegations of impropriety. The Senate is in charge of reviewing and approving the president's appointees, and the House is responsible for initiating any legislation related to taxation or spending.

Judicial branch

The federal judicial system comprises a series of courts, at the top of which is the United States Supreme Court. Cases are first heard by a trial court; if the verdict is appealed, this trial is held in an appellate court. There are a few unique lower courts that only handle certain types of cases, like the Court of Federal Claims, the Court of International Trade, the Court of Military Appeals, and the Tax Court. A district court is a trial court with federal jurisdiction; at present there are ninety-four federal district courts. A federal appellate court is known as a court of appeals. There are twelve judicial districts in the United States, each of which is served by a court of appeals. There is also a thirteenth court, known as the United States Court of Appeals for the Federal Circuit, that has national jurisdiction.

United States Supreme Court

The Supreme Court is the highest legal authority in the United States. It handles cases that are appealed from lower courts, primarily from appellate courts. Occasionally, the Supreme Court will review appeals from district courts and state supreme courts. The Supreme Court has nine members, one of whom is designated as the Chief Justice. The others are called associate justices. In order for a case to be heard by the court, at least four justices must agree to hear it. The Supreme Court prefers to hear cases that relate to a controversial, unsettled, or newly interesting aspect of federal law. A case cannot be argued before the court unless at least six justices are present. Sometimes, a justice will recuse him or herself because of a conflict of interest. Cases are decided by a majority vote. When the justices are deadlocked, the decision of the lower court is upheld. The Supreme Court hears about 100 cases in a typical year.

Regional Geography

Regional geography is the subdiscipline of geography which involves the study of the ways in which human and physical characteristics combine to form geographic regions. Geographers use a regional concept to organize Earth's surface into sections based on the presence of at least one shared characteristic. The classification of groups of places into regions enables geographers to examine the associations between historical, cultural, organizational, economic, and environmental factors within a particular region. Geographers then investigate the effects of these associations on that region's development and interrelationships with other regions. Regions may be studied at many levels, from the local to the international.

Geographic realms

A geographic realm is the largest geographical unit into which the Earth's surface can be divided. Geographic realms are sometimes referred to as "global neighborhoods." All places within a realm share at least one overarching characteristic, whether that factor is physical (such as climate type) or human (such as mode of production). Realms are also distinguished by the type of interaction which takes place between human society and the natural environment. In other words, the ways in which humans alter the land on which they live, including the features they erect upon it, affect the area's position in the global regionalization scheme. Finally, a geographic realm must encompass a "great cluster" (population concentration) of humans. China, for example, exists at the center of one such cluster. Like all regional classifications related to human activity, geographic realms change over time. Today, geographers identify twelve realms: Europe, Russia, North America, Middle America, South America, North Africa/Southwest Asia, Sub-Saharan Africa, South Asia, East Asia, Southeast Asia, Australia, and the Pacific Rim.

The Earth's three largest population clusters
East Asia, centered on China, is home to the world's largest population cluster, incorporating the eastern coastal zone from the Korean Peninsula to Vietnam. Population density is highest near the coast and ebbs as one moves inland; members of this cluster are also concentrated in the valleys of China's major rivers. The majority of people in East Asia lives in rural areas and engages in agricultural production.

India exists at the center of South Asia, the second-largest population cluster, which also includes Pakistan and Bangladesh. The highest concentration of humans in this region is located near the Ganges River. This realm is also largely agricultural. High levels of population growth in South Asia have problematized sustainable production.

The third-largest of the world's population clusters is located in Europe. In contrast to the other two largest clusters, the highest population density in this cluster runs along an east-west axis corresponding to a zone of raw industrial materials. As one of the most industrialized realms, Europe is highly dependent on these resources.

Transition zones
Like other geographic boundaries, the divisions between geographic realms are often blurred. As these boundaries are theoretical, it not surprising that they do not practically

differentiate adjacent realms. A transition zone is an area of spatial change between global neighborhoods. Such zones are characterized by gradual changes in the physical and human characteristics which differentiate one realm from another. Cultural amalgamation and international economic activities often take place in transition zones. The high degree of interaction between residents of neighboring realms which takes place in these areas often leads to regional change.

Geographic regions

The classification of areas into geographic regions is more refined than the classification of realms. In other words, a region is a smaller spatial unit than a realm; each realm is subdivided into one or more regions. There are several properties which all regions have in common.

First, all regions have area. While they are indeed theoretical constructions, regions are materially present in the real world, occupying space on the surface of the globe.

Secondly, all regions have boundaries which delineate their spatial territories. Like the boundaries of nation-states, regions' boundaries are defined by a synthesis of natural and human factors. They are occasionally rather sharp, but generally function more like transition zones.

Regional geographers may make use of political boundaries to aid in the designation of regions within realms. All regions also have location, both absolute and relative. The names of some regions (for example, Equatorial Africa) convey information about their locations.

A formal region
A formal geographic region is one which is identified based on physical and/or human characteristic(s) shared throughout the area. In other words, formal regions exhibit a high degree of homogeneity or similitude. This type of region may be political, defined by shared governmental/legal systems, as in the cases of states, countries, and cities.

Population information (including factors such as typical industrial or agricultural production techniques, ethnic heritage, per capita income, or density and distribution) may be used to designate a cultural region. For example, several large American cities include cultural regions characterized by high concentrations of people of Chinese descent practicing their cultural and social traditions, referred to as "Chinatowns."

Formal regions may also be distinguished by physical homogeneity in, for instance, the areas of climate, topology, and vegetation. For instance, the steppe region of Northern Eurasia is typified by temperate grasslands with rich soils.

A functional region
A functional geographic region consists of a central node and the surrounding areas affected by it. Often, the focal point and the proximate areas are linked by economic activities such as manufacturing, retail trading, and transportation and communication systems. However, like formal geographic regions, functional regions may be identified through the application of several different criteria. The New York metropolitan area provides an example of a functional region. This region includes parts of four states (New York, New Jersey,

Connecticut, and Pennsylvania), associated by common media distribution, commuting patterns, and trade flows.

<u>A perceptual region</u>
Perception is the process whereby individuals use their senses to collect information about their situation or environment. A person's perception is affected by his or her past experiences and cultural background. Therefore, perceptual geographic regions are those which are shaped by people's shared feelings and attitudes about an area. The delineation of these regions is thus a subjective process. Perceptual regions are often influenced by people's mental maps. The theoretical organization of parts of Earth's surface into perceptual regions may help to develop an individual's sense of the world's structure; however, since such regions are delineated based on personal viewpoints, they may reflect inappropriate (and sometimes prejudicial) stereotypes.

Cultural landscapes

People of every cultural group transform the lands upon which they live. They erect buildings, create transportation routes, till soil, and subdivide their territories into smaller parcels. The ways in which humans interact with the natural environment often differ from culture to culture. For example, industrialized societies may ignore the presence of certain vegetation or even see it as an obstacle to development, while traditional societies may view the same vegetation as an important natural resource.

Carl Sauer, a geographer who focused his cultural studies on the concept of cultural landscapes provides a straightforward definition: cultural landscapes are "the forms superimposed on the physical landscape by the activities of man." The term sequent occupance refers to the stages of evolution undergone by an area when different cultural groups successively occupy that particular landscape. The presence of a distinctive cultural landscape is a major criterion in the delineation of a cultural region.

<u>Place</u>
In geography, a place is a space on Earth's surface which has been given particular meaning by humans. A place may be as small as a room or as large as a continent. Places are differentiated by the unique combination of human and physical properties exhibited by each, and are often bounded and named. The human characteristics of a place include political systems, economic systems, languages, population statistics, and cultural norms. A place's physical characteristics include climate, vegetation types and distributions, landforms, animal life, and soils. Constant changes in these qualities affect entire places; therefore, places never stay the same for long. They may thrive or ebb, become simpler or more complex, or become altered in organization.

<u>Termininology</u>
A **culture hearth** is a principle source area and center of cultural innovation from which migrating peoples transport traditions and beliefs to their new homes. Mesoamerica, a region which spans the area between central Mexico and the northwestern boundary of Costa Rica, is an example of a culture hearth. Populations from this hearth expanded and worked for advancements in the spheres of, for instance, science, architecture, agriculture, and religion; these advancements spread to other regions and influenced further developments.

The term **cultural mosaic** is used to describe a society in which distinct ethnic, language, and culture groups exist side by side. This concept is largely synonymous with the idea of cultural pluralism, and the opposite of a culturally assimilated society.

Transculturation is the process whereby different cultures merge and converge. It refers specifically to the tendency of humans to work toward the resolution of conflicts, be they political, ethnic, or social.

Culture spheres

A culture sphere is a cultural region within a larger region. The identification of general culture spheres may be useful in the description of the cultural mosaic of a pluralist society. For instance, geographers have delineated five generalized culture spheres within the South American realm:

1. The tropical-plantation region is characterized by a dispersed settlement pattern, a high level of plantation agriculture, and a culture dominated by the descendents of African slave laborers who were brought over to work on those plantations.
2. The European-commercial region is populated largely by Europeans, specifically those with affiliations to Hispanic culture. This region is economically more developed than the rest of the realm.
3. The Amerind-subsistence region is characterized by a feudal socioeconomic structure, a holdover from former Spanish conquerors. This region contains some of the realms poorest areas.
4. Culture in the Mestizo-transitional region is a fusion of Amerind and European elements. It is also a zone of transition between the commercial and subsistence economic areas.
5. The undifferentiated region consists of regions with unclassifiable cultural characteristics.

Eastern European Terms

There are several geographic terms with roots in the region of Eastern Europe which are used to describe the collapse of established order; these terms are so designated due to the complex, transitory nature of the area.

Balkanization, named after the Balkan Peninsula, is defined as the breaking down of a society (such as a region) into smaller and more hostile units.

Eastern Europe has been depicted as a **shatter belt**, or a region located between two or more stronger, oppositional cultural-political forces. These regions are often pressured, taken over, and divvyed up by outside, rival forces.

Ethnic cleansing is another term coined from events in Eastern Europe. The phrase is a euphemism used to designate the forcible elimination of people of a certain ethnic group from their homeland by more aggressive groups in search of power. The term has been used historically by the Soviets (in reference to the "resettlement" of Poles) and by Serbs in Yugoslavia (in description of the policies of Albanians against Serbs).

Enclaves

An enclave is a piece of territory which is completely surrounded by another political territory of which the former is not a part. For example, the sovereign country of Vatican

City is enclaved within Italy. A true enclave is one which can be entered only via another country; a practical enclave is one which may be more easily accessed through another country even though it is not completely detached from the "mother" country, due to, for example, its topography or available transportation routes. A subnational enclave is a territory which belongs to one political subdivision of land, yet is attached to another. For instance, Long Island is considered part of the city of Boston, but is road-accessible only from Quincy, Massachusetts. An ethnic enclave is a community of members of a minority ethnic group which is situated in the midst of a larger ethnic group (such as a Chinatown).

Exclaves

An exclave is a territory belonging to yet detached from one political entity and surrounded by other political entities. The term is similar in meaning to enclave. However, the two are not synonymous; an exclave is not necessarily an enclave. For instance, if area C, whose motherland is country B, is located in the center of country A, area C may be referred to as B's exclave and A's enclave. If, however, area C is located along the boundary between country B and another foreign country d., it is no longer referred to as an enclave, but it is still appropriate to describe it as B's exclave. Like enclaves, exclaves may be subnational, true, or practical.

Irredentism

Originally, the term irredentism referred to the nationalist Italian movement which advocated the annexation of certain territories (which were officially held by Austria but populated by a majority of Italians) to Italy. Today, the word's meaning has been expanded to include any nationalist policy which seeks to extend cultures and possibly expand political territories through the incorporation of territories ruled by foreign entities. For instance, while the population of Hungary proper is close to 10 million, there are large concentrations of Hungarians living in Romania, Slovakia, Croatia, Serbia, and Slovenia (holdovers from a time when Hungary was more powerful and held more territory on the Balkan Peninsula). The Hungarian government appeals to these "ethnic cohorts" and seeks to protect them, if needed, from the government of the states in which they live; this behavior is referred to as irredentism.

Globalization

Globalization is the process whereby regional differences are reduced due to the increased exchange of cultural, economic, and political ideas and practices among traditionally isolate nations. Advancements in technology have bred increased interdependency among the world's countries and enabled people to interact with others on a global scale. Time-space convergence is the increasing nearness of people and places due to the technological reduction of the travel/communication times and distances between them. Social theories Arjun Appaduri has identified five categories of global connectivity:
1. Ethnoscapes are the movements of people from one region to another.
2. Financescapes are the movements of money around the world.
3. Ideoscapes are the global movements of ideas and belief systems.
4. Mediascapes are the mass distributions of images through the media.
5. Technoscapes are the movements of technologies around the globe.

Some view the changes associated with globalization as positive steps toward the development of a fully multicultural global society. Others see globalization as a synonym for imperialism.

Spatial diffusion

Spatial diffusion is the mechanism whereby ideas, practices, and innovations spread through a population over time and space. Study of the processes through which spatial diffusion takes place allows geographers to hypothesize the dispersal of cultural and economic ideas in the past and future.

Expansion diffusion is the type of diffusion in which a strong central source area emanates propagation waves in all directions. These waves affect ever-growing populations and places. Contagious diffusion is a method of expansion diffusion which relies on local proximity to spread phenomena, while hierarchical diffusion involves the diffusion of phenomena from a high leader such as a king or chief.

In contrast to expansion diffusion, relocation diffusion occurs when a phenomenon spreads after the movement and resettlement of a source population; expansion from the relocated source area typically follows.

Centripetal and centrifugal forces

In political geography, centripetal forces are forces within a state which act to unify and strengthen it. For instance, an outside threat (actual or perceived) on a state often binds that state's political system, and may consequently make it stronger. A particularly important and enduring centripetal force is the belief of the state's citizens in the state's governmental system and their committed support of that system. Historically, certain charismatic leaders, such as Charles De Gaulle in France and Mao Zedong in China, have inspired this type of loyalty.

Centrifugal forces are those which act against centripetal forces, tending to divide or degrade states. These forces are usually internal. Interracial hostilities, religious and/or ethnic conflicts, and political strife are key factors in the disunification of states. For example, clashes among ethnic groups in Yugoslavia led to much fighting and the eventual breakup of the state in 1991. The proportion of centripetal to centrifugal forces in a state affects its stability and strength.

Urban geography

Urban geography is the subfield of geography which involves the spatial analysis of city-centered settlements with high population densities. This area of study has been organized into four main sections. The historical evolution component of urban geography (also known as urban evolution) is interested in the forces behind urban development during each period of human development since the city's founding. Interurban geography is concerned with the interactions and relationships between urban systems at a national level. Areas of interest include city types, city functions, and spheres of influence. Intraurban geography deals with the internal spatial organizations of highly urbanized settlements. This includes study of the infrastructure of a city as well as observation of the distribution and activities of different population groups in that city. Urban social

- 88 -

geography is the component of urban geography which investigates the spatial arrangements of people in a metropolis, with a focus on their residences. A related field, urban economic geography, examines the distribution of commercial and recreational activities in urban areas.

Economic geography

Economic geography is the subfield of geography which investigates the ways in which people support themselves and their families, and the ways in which the goods and services they produce are spatially organized. For example, the types of goods produced in a particular geographic region may be influenced by, for example, the region's climate, political and/or social organization, infrastructure, and geology. Scholars of economic geography seek to explain how the interaction of these and other factors creates the patterns of diverse economic activity observed across the surface of the globe. Recognition of these relationships can help geographers make predictions about past and future events, and to postulate solutions to the problems of unequal economic development among the nations of the world.

Epochs of metropolitan evolution in North America

Analysis of advancements in transportation technology and industrial energy reveals five epochs of metropolitan evolution in North America.

1. The Sail-Wagon Epoch (1790-1830) was characterized by basic overland and waterway methods of transportation. North America depended on overseas trade, which was more plausible than trade with the largely inaccessible western periphery.
2. Railways dominated transportation during the Iron Horse Epoch (1830-1870); the completion of the transcontinental railroad near the close of this epoch heralded the start of the creation of national urban systems.
3. The Steel-Rail Epoch (1870-1920) was greatly affected by the U.S. Industrial Revolution, with the associated increases in production levels and railway efficiency.
4. The Auto-Air-Amenity Epoch (1920-1970) saw the invention of the gasoline-powered internal combustion engine and a consequent rise in automotive and air transportation. Much of the American workforce entered the service industry, and the national urban hierarchy matured.
5. The Satellite-Electronic-Jet Propulsion Epoch (1970-) has thus far shown increased levels of international interaction, specialization, and constraints on expensive energy sources, and the development of a global village.

The eras of intraurban structural evolution in North America

Developments in transportation technology and industrial energy affected urban areas in North America on a local scale. Intrametropolitan growth, like national urban evolution, may be organized into stages.

*   During the Walking-Horsecar Era (prior to 1888), cities had to be compact due to the time required for long travel by pedestrians.
*   The Electric Streetcar Era (1888-1920) saw the invention of a motor which could be attached to horsecars; this decreased travel time significantly and thus enabled urban expansion. This, in turn, enabled more specialized land use.

- The Recreational Automobile Era (1920-1945) was characterized by increased accessibility to the outer metropolitan ring, due to the impact of automobiles and highway expansion. The city core reached its peak during this era, which also saw an increase in suburbanization and the partitioning of residential space.
- The Freeway Era (1945-) has demonstrated the full effect of individual automobile transportation on high-speed expressways; urban sprawl has resulted in distances up to 30 miles between the city's center and outskirts.

Rostow's model

In the 1960's, economist Walt Rostow formulated a model of the process of economic development (the Rostovian take-off model). Rostow asserted that each of the world's countries follows five-stage path toward development. In the first, traditional society, people engage in agricultural production at subsistence levels. Nations in the first stage tend to adhere to a rigid social structure and resist technological change. The second stage, preconditions for take-off, involves the introduction of a progressive leader (or leaders) who steer the nation toward greater diversification and flexibility. Traditional beliefs and practices are discarded, agricultural activity and birth rates decline, and infrastructure improves. Take-off, the third stage of Rostow's model, generally involves an industrial revolution, as well as urbanization and technological advancements. The fourth stage of the model, drive to maturity, is reached when technology disperses throughout a nation, enabling industrial specialization and increased trade. A nation in the fifth stage, high mass consumption, exhibits high income levels and a majority of workers in the third and fourth sectors of industry.

Principles of spatial interaction

Human contact and interaction in the realm of economics and trade is organized around three principles.

Complementarity comes about when one area produces a surplus of a certain commodity which is needed in a second area. This principle thus occurs due to spatial variations in the supply and demand of particular resources, both natural and human.

The second interaction principle, transferability, is the ease of transportation of goods between two areas. Distance (including costs and travel time) and accessibility (including travel routes and the character of the relevant terrain) are factors in the transferability of a commodity. Therefore complementarity alone does not ensure trade between regions.

Intervening opportunity is the third component of spatial interaction. This principle states that trade between two areas, even if the conditions of complementarity and transferability are met, will occur only through the lack of a more proximate (intervening) supply source.

Areal functional specialization

Due to variations in amounts of available resources (natural and human), levels of industrialization, and amounts of available technology, certain areas and peoples specialize in the production of certain goods. This phenomenon is referred to as areal functional specialization. Europe, for example, exhibits a high degree of areal functional specialization; particular ores, minerals, manufactured goods, and agricultural products tend to be produced (in surplus) in particular areas. The needs of these specialized regions of production tend to be complementary, so each area satisfies its needs through trade with other areas. Europe, therefore, is a realm of areal (economic) interdependence.

Oil production and sale on oil-exporting countries

The production of oil and its sale have had significant effects on the countries of the North Africa/Southwest Asia realm which export it. These effects illustrate the impact of trade patterns on participating regions.

1. First of all, the high demand for oil across the globe creates higher incomes among the populations of oil-exporting countries, which tend to place these countries among those in the upper-middle income category (in contrast to those in peripheral regions of the realm).
2. Second, large oil revenues have led to increased modernization in certain countries.
3. Third, oil-exporting countries have experienced increased industrialization as an effect of oil production and sale.
4. Fourth, many workers from peripheral areas of the realm migrate to core countries; thus intra-realm migration is an effect of oil.
5. Oil-exporting countries also experience inter-realm migration.
6. Sixth, concentrated oil production in the realm has heightened regional disparities, both economic and cultural.
7. Finally, oil-exporting countries of the realm have begun to receive foreign investment, which creates further international relationships.

Core areas and peripheral areas

The core area(s) of a region or nation, which may also be referred to as heartlands, are the hubs of human and economic activity in those areas. These central regions usually exhibit at least one substantive urban area, a large population cluster, and high levels of accessibility and connectivity, which grant them influence over entire regions.

Peripheral areas (also referred to as hinterlands, a term which literally means "countries behind") are those surrounding core regions. These areas depend on goods and services produced in those core regions, which are key influences on urban development along the periphery. Heartlands and hinterlands develop due to the presence or absence of natural resources, the degree of availability of those resources, regional variations in climate, and the degree of a region's connectivity to other regions. Contrasts in development levels exist at several different scales: local, regional, national, and global.

Core-periphery relationships

Uneven development is, sadly, a fact of life on Earth. Certain countries (and regions within those nations) have advantages that other countries and regions do not have, and the gap between these haves and have-nots continues to grow. Already powerful and developed core areas continue to grow and evolve, while hinterlands remain undeveloped and often unstable. This occurs due to the structure of core-periphery relationships. These two types of regions are functionally tied together. Citizens of the periphery contribute labor and taxes to the development of the core. In other words, core regions would not be as they are without the contributions of peripheral regions. Hinterlands begin to depend on heartlands for employment (though workers from the periphery generally receive lower wages than workers in the core), specialized goods and services, and even military protection. This situation negates the possibility of economic growth in the hinterlands.

Balance of trade

The majority of the world's countries engage in trade (the exchange of goods and services) with one another. The term balance of trade refers to the relationship between the values of imported goods and services and exported goods and services. The exchange of raw materials, manufactured goods, agricultural goods, transportation, and travel are all considered in determination of a country's balance of trade. If the value of a country's imports exceeds that of its exports, the balance of trade (the trade deficit) is said to be negative. Conversely, if the value of a country's exports is higher than that of its imports, the balance of trade (the trade surplus) is considered positive. A nation's balance of trade must be distinguished from its balance of payments; this term covers any international flow of money, including investment income and transfer payments.

Trade pacts

A trade pact is a broad agreement between two or more nations which specifies which forms of production and consumption are ideal and which are undesirable. This type of agreement attempts to increase productive efficiency through the facilitation of free trade (the international exchange of goods and services without tariffs or trade barriers, such as import quotas). Trade pacts often come under political scrutiny for their roles in increasing economic interdependence between entities or altering traditional economic customs. There are several different types of trade pacts.

Four types of trade pact:
- A Trade and Investment Framework Agreement (TIFA) institutes an agenda aimed at the resolution of conflicts and expansion of trade between two or more nations.
- A Bilateral Investment Treaty (BIT) establishes the requisites for the foreign direct investment of nationals/companies of one state in another.
- A preferential trade area is a group of nations which gives preferential access to particular goods from other countries in the area. A trade pact which identifies this type of agreement usually reduces tariffs without eliminating them.
- Another type of trade pact may create a free trade area (a zone whose component states have agreed to do away with trade barriers such as quotas and preferences on most goods exchanged between them).

Trade blocs

A trade bloc is a large free trade area delimited by one or more trade pact. Trade blocs are usually regionally based. Occasionally, a state may act as a member in more than one bloc. For instance, Venezuela is a part of both the Andean Community and the Mercosur trading blocs. Generally, such pacts name formal adjudication panels, such as NAFTA's, which may allow differing degrees of member participation. The European Union, for instance, includes a democratically elected parliament, which acts as a decision-making body. A trade bloc may decide to eliminate visa requirements and (at least theoretically) borders between its member states, enabling free travel in the region. NAFTA and the EU are two of the most active trade blocs on the globe. The Caribbean Community and Common Market (CARICOM) is another active group with a state-like governing structure. There are currently 15 full members of CARICOM. The Economic Community of West African States (ECOWAS) is a regional trade bloc aimed at furthering economic integration between its member states.

Six stages of economic integration:
1. The weakest form of economic integration between economies is the existence of a preferential trading area.
2. The second stage of economic integration is a free trade area.
3. The third stage, a customs union, is a free trade area whose participating states have agreed upon a common external tariff, which involves the application of the same customs duties, quotas, and preferences on all goods entering the union.
4. The fourth stage of economic integration may be referred to as a common market or a single market. A single market exists when all states in a customs union share common policies on product regulation, and when all factors of production (goods, services, labor, and capital) move freely between them.
5. The fifth stage is the creation of an economic and monetary union, a single market with a common currency.
6. Complete economic integration (the final stage) is reached when integrated units have no individual control over economic policy. Complete economic integration is more common within countries than in supranational organizations.

The Neolithic Revolution

The Neolithic Revolution was a period of conversion from hunting and gathering methods of subsistence to agricultural methods of production; this transition began approximately 10,000 years ago. This "revolution" is so named because of the long-lasting effects of social and economic changes in human society which resulted from this conversion. The causes of these changes are climatic changes associated with the end of the last ice age (namely, warmer, drier climates), which led hunter-gatherers to settle near stable water sources, and a food crisis perpetuated by the extinction of several species of large mammals during the late Paleolithic era. The transition to agricultural production involved the development of permanent settlements (as well as a decrease in nomadic lifestyles), the domestication of plants and animals, human modification of the natural environment, the evolution of notions of land ownership, economic specialization, and the development of trading systems. Many of the characteristics of present day "civilization" (for instance, social hierarchies, advanced, specialized technologies, and cities) began with the Neolithic Revolution.

Intensive and extensive agriculture

Intensive agriculture or intensive farming is a type of agricultural production system which involves the use of high levels of chemical inputs, such as fertilizers, pesticides, and growth regulators, on relatively small plots of land to maximize the output of that land. This method of agricultural production is associated with modern farming techniques, including mechanization. While the use of intensive farming techniques can assist in the maintenance of a stable food supply, it often occurs at the expense of the environment. For example, the clearing of land eliminates local vegetation and therefore the natural habitat of the area's fauna, and can lead to soil erosion. Also, the use of chemicals creates pollution which may affect the local ecosystem and the area's water supply.

Extensive agriculture, in contrast, involves the production of crops over large areas of low-cost land without the use of pesticides and fertilizers. While this type of agricultural production is not harmful to the environment, it cannot produce crops at the same volume as intensive agriculture.

Agrarian revolution

The term agrarian revolution is used to refer to the period of transformation of agricultural production methods in Europe from the 16th to mid-19th centuries. These improvements enabled European farmers to sustain a rapidly-growing population during this time. The resultant increase in urbanization and growing markets served as impetuses for improved organization of land ownership and agrarian activities, in the forms of land enclosure and consolidated farmland; higher crop prices encouraged farmers to move from subsistence levels of agricultural production to production for a capitalist market. Other advancements included the introduction of new crops (such as potatoes from the Americas) in the realm, crop rotation (which increased the variety and amount of crops produced and also improved the quality of the soil), and the improvement of storage and distribution systems. The products of the later Industrial Revolution contributed to the ongoing process of agricultural advancement. Ultimately, the agrarian revolution marked the development of improved agricultural practices which eventually diffused throughout the realm and world.

Von Thunen's Isolated State Model

In 1826, economist Johann Heinrich von Thunen created a geographic model to explain the effects of distance and cost of transportation on the location of productive activity. Von Thunen's Isolated State model is so titled because he wanted to develop a secluded community with no outside influences on its economic activity, in order to ascertain the basic factors in the spatial organization of an agricultural region. He based his model on several assumptions: one, that soil quality and climate characteristics were homogeneous throughout the area; two, that the area was flat and contained no divisive landforms (such as river valleys or mountains); three, that the region consisted of a centrally located city surrounded by wilderness; and four, that farmers within the Isolated State would move their own products directly to the central city (meaning that transportation costs would be directly proportional to distance). Though Von Thunen's theoretical model did not represent real economic areas in Europe, the distorting factors could be applied individually to the idealized representation of agricultural economy.

The Isolated State Model

Von Thunen's Isolated State model seeks to identify the ideal spatial arrangement of agricultural activities in an isolated community. It consists of a central market city surrounded by concentric rings. The innermost ring is a zone of intensive production (including dairying); the second zone houses a forest from which firewood and timber (an important building material in Von Thunen's time) can be extracted; the third area produces extensive field crops; the fourth zone is characterized by ranching and animal husbandry. In other words, the crops which yield the highest returns and perish most easily (such as vegetables) are grown closest to the city. Extensive crops like potatoes and grains are grown further away (outside the forest zone); ranching activities take place just inside the boundary marking the distance at which transportation costs make market agricultural production uneconomical. Today, due to improvements in transportation technologies, Von Thunen's model can be expanded to a macroscale, meaning that it centers on an entire urban area rather than a single city.

The Green Revolution

The Green Revolution began in 1945 with the development of agricultural technologies which aimed to improve the agricultural output of Mexico; these techniques were eventually diffused to regions all over the globe. The technologies which spawned the Green Revolution involved the breeding of new plant varieties and the application of modern

- 94 -

farming practices, which included the heavy use of pesticides and fertilizers, irrigation methods, and machines to increase crop output. The techniques introduced during the Green Revolution did produce higher yields and decrease dependence on human labor in agriculture. However, the disadvantages of these techniques include decreased biodiversity (as fewer varieties of crop are produced), decreased crop quality (including health value), and the detrimental health effects of agricultural chemicals on plant, animal, and human life.

The Industrial Revolution

The term Industrial Revolution generally refers to the conversion from an economy based on manual labor to one supported by industry and machine manufacture, which took place in Britain during the late 18th and early 19th centuries (though other countries experienced industrial revolutions after Britain's). The numerous causes of this revolution are complex. They include the presence of a large workforce (due to improvements in disease control); the agrarian revolution (which made agriculture a less labor-intensive endeavor and forced workers into other spheres); colonial expansion (which improved Britain's international trade market and increased its available capital); the existence of a sizeable domestic market; and the availability of abundant natural resources.

Developments of the Industrial Revolution included improvements in iron smelting, based on the use of coal (converted into carbon-rich coke) as an energy source, and invention of the steam engine, adapted for use in the textile, mining, manufacturing, and transportation industries. Innovations developed during the Industrial Revolution spread through Europe and to North America, and eventually diffused across the globe.

The geographic realm of Europe

Made up of five geographic regions (Western Europe, the British Isles, Northern Europe, Southern [Mediterranean] Europe, and Eastern Europe), the geographic realm of Europe is home to one of the largest population clusters in the world. Despite the relatively small size of its territory, Europe's people and their actions have affected (and continue to affect) all the world's realms. Technological innovations, political revolutions, and vast empires have influenced the behaviors of people on each continent. European colonial endeavors have established communities and impacted the formation of ideologies the world over. Europe's natural and human resources have helped the realm to survive and grow throughout the years. For approximately the last 50 years, Europe has been engaged in a unification program known as the European Union. Currently, 25 of the realm's 48 nation-states are members of the Union.

The general economic geography of Europe

The economy of Europe is dominated by the European Union, which, if considered as a whole, has the largest economy in the world. Though the functional region of Western Europe has historically been the hub of economic activity in the realm, this situation is changing with the development of other core regions, productive complementarities, and interregional/international trade markets. Levels of economic development tend to decline as one moves from west to east across the realm; this too is changing with the growth of the economies of former member countries of the Soviet Union, and their increasing interactions with other regions and realms. Europe's agricultural and fishing sectors are highly developed, and still center on Western Europe. Europe's manufacturing sector is also quite developed. While many of the realm's industries are concentrated in Western Europe, deindustrialization in the region has resulted in the outsourcing of labor, to areas such as

Eastern Europe and China. Financial activity in the realm is concentrated in several cities, with London as the largest.

The geographic realm of Russia

Russia, the largest territorial state on Earth, is an example of a geographic realm which has undergone tremendous amounts of change throughout its existence. Tsars conquered and dominated Russian territory, which was subsequently inhabited by Soviets, who then shaped the domain and its peoples into the Soviet Union. Though World War II tested the empire, it also validated the U.S.S.R.'s status as a global superpower, which it retained until the late 1980's. Internal factors (such as mismanagement of a communist government) and external factors (including the Second World War, pressure from anti-communist leaders, and the global decline of colonialism) eventually led to the dissolution of the Soviet Union in 1991. Consequent cultural, economic, and social diversity has given rise to the establishment of four geographical regions (each of which contains subregions): the Russian Core, the Eastern Frontier, Siberia, and the Far East.

The general economic geography of Russia

The economic geography of Russia is highly varied, and characterized by discrete core and peripheral regions of economic activity. Despite the presence of substantial natural resources (such as gas and oil) and a well-educated labor force, the effects of the transition from a failed centrally-planned economy during the Soviet Era to a free market continue to hinder the development of the economies in certain regions. In the agricultural sector, production has decreased drastically with attempts at the privatization of collective farms and restructuring of the economy. Also, the harsh climate in the realm has had an effect on agricultural production. The levels of meat, milk, vegetables, and grains have decreased yearly since 1989. This has had negative ramifications in a country which is largely dependent on its own food production. The inefficiencies and inadequacies held over from the Soviet Union continue to disturb Russia's industrial sector, particularly in the extraction of raw materials and the distribution of goods. Still, Russia is the most industrialized of all the former Soviet republics.

The geographic realm of North America

The geographic realm of North America is home to two countries, Canada and the United States (which is currently considered a global superpower). This realm is characterized by pluralistic (diverse) societies which, unfortunately, are often plagued by social inequalities. It is also a postindustrial realm, which means that the economies of Canada and the United States each experienced increases in the amount of available information technology and rapid expansions of the tertiary (service) sector of industry after the industrialization processes in those countries. The eight regions of North America (many of which stretch across the U.S.-Canada boundary) are largely differentiated by differences in the various economic activities practiced in different areas. These regions include the Continental Core, the South, the Southwest, the West Coast, the Agricultural Heartland, French Canada, the New England/Maritime Provinces, and the Marginal Interior.

The general economic geography of Canada

As one of the world's wealthiest nations, Canada has a largely postindustrial economy, with employment concentrated in the service sector (particularly retail). However, unlike many developed countries, primary economic activities (specifically logging and oil production) are important aspects of the country's economy. Canada has a large and varied (though regionally variable) supply of natural resources, such as oil, nickel, and lead. Canadian agricultural products (especially wheat and grains) are exported in high levels to the United States, Europe, and East Asia. Another unusual aspect of Canada's economy (as compared to those of other highly-developed nations) is the historical secondary status of the manufacturing sector of industry. Though it is certainly not unimportant, manufacturing has never been as vital to the nation's economy as primary or tertiary activities. Many of Canada's industrial firms are branches of U.S. companies. Regional disparities in wealth and economy strength have increased regionalism throughout the region.

The general economic geography of the United States
As a current superpower, the United States has one of the most advanced economies in the world. Like Canada, the United States contains many deposits of natural resources. For instance, the North American realm has more coal reserves than any other. The spatial organization of regional agricultural production in the United States exists within the framework of a modified Von Thunen model, with the "megalopolis" of New England at its center, and belts of specialized activity extending westward. Though the manufacturing sector is less important in a postindustrial economy, this type of activity is still practiced in the United States, and tends to cluster around several urban-industrial nodes, especially within the Manufacturing Belt (located in the Northeast United States). Increased mechanization and advancements in technology have eliminated many "blue-collar" jobs in this region. Most laborers in the U.S. workforce are employed in quaternary economic activity. States offering noneconomic amenities (such as weather and proximity to urban centers and universities) have experienced higher levels of growth than other regions.

The geographic realm of Central America
The realm of Central America, which is sometimes referred to as Middle America, covers the territory between southern North America and the boundary between Panama and Colombia. The exact demarcations of the realm vary from source to source; however, the economic subregion recognized by the United Nations includes all mainland states of North America south of the U.S.-Mexico border in the realm. Basically, this definition counts Mexico and Belize as members of the Central America realm, while other definitions assign these countries to the North American realm. Due to the influence of Spanish and Portuguese colonialism in Central America, this realm and South America are often jointly referred to as Latin America. Central America is divided into four regions: Mexico, the seven states of Central America (Belize, Costa Rica, El Salvador, Guatemala, Honduras, Nicaragua, and Panama), the larger islands of the Caribbean (the Greater Antilles), and the smaller islands of the Caribbean (the Lesser Antilles).

The general economic geography of Central America
With the exception of Mexico, the territories of Central America are the least developed in the Americas. Under the Mainland-Rimland framework, Central America is divided into a Euro-Amerindian Mainland (made up of mainland Middle America from Mexico to Panama, excluding parts of the Caribbean coast) and a Euro-African rimland (consisting of the coastal zone and the Caribbean islands). Economic activity on the Mainland has historically been oriented around haciendas (privately-owned estates maintained more for prestige and self-sufficiency than maximum production), and is therefore less dependent on trade with other nations. Governmental and social pressures have led to the forced specialization of productive activity in or the parceling out of haciendas in this area.

The Rimland's economy has traditionally focused on plantation production, characterized by efficient production of one crop specifically for export and the importation of labor. The

Rimland's economy is thus more dependent on the fluctuating global market. Plantation systems, like hacienda systems, continue to metamorphose under internal and external pressures; still, their effects remain visible in the region.

The geographic realm of South America

South America and Central America are often collectively referred to as Latin America, due to the enduring cultural and social influences of former Spanish and Portuguese colonial presences in these realms. These influences are most visible in the languages, architecture, music, and visual arts of the peoples of South America. Roman Catholicism and traditional systems relating to land ownership, also transmitted from European countries, continue to be major factors in the evolution of South American societies. In addition, the cultural practices and beliefs of Native Americans have been and continue to be vital shaping forces in the realm. South America is made up of four regions: Brazil, the Northeastern countries, the West, and the Southern Cone.

The general economic geography of South America

The economic geography of South America is characterized by high levels of regional disparity. In many of the realm's countries (such as Brazil, Bolivia, and Venezuela), the richest 20% of the population may control over 60% of the nation's wealth, while the poorest 20% may own less than 5% of that wealth. Although several South American nations have become involved in the mining of oil, coal, and valuable minerals in high amounts, the realm's main economic focus is agriculture. The South American realm is unusual, because subsistence farming and commercial farming exist side by side; generally, a geographic realm is dominated by one or the other. Commercial farmers in this area tend to be involved in cattle ranching, wheat farming, grain farming (in a "Corn Belt" zone similar to that in the United States), or plantation-type agriculture. Commercial agricultural endeavors tend to be located near the coasts of the South American continent, with small pockets of activity in the interior. Subsistence level farming takes place on all other arable land.

The geographic realm of North Africa/Southwest Asia

The size and geographic diversity of the North Africa/Southwest Asia realm have spawned a number of different labels for the region, none of which are completely satisfactory. These labels include the Islamic realm, the Arab World, the dry world, and Afrasia. Though Islam and aridity do dominate the religious and climatic aspects of the realm, that domination is not complete, and the heterogeneity within these groups alone problematizes the notion of referring to the realm by a single characteristic. The use of relative location is seen as less divisive. The North Africa realm is composed of three regions (Egypt, the North Africa, and the Southwest), and Southwest Asia is composed of four (the Middle East [this label is also disputed, due to what some see as the pejorative connotations of the term], the Arabian Peninsula, the North, and the East).

Mesopotamia

Mesopotamia, a major historic culture hearth, is located in the Tigris-Euphrates lowland, from the northern edge of the Persian Gulf to present-day Turkey. Mesopotamia (literally the "land between the rivers") was an area of fertile alluvial soils and plentiful sunshine and water. This zone saw the development of advanced farming techniques, such as planned sowing and harvesting, irrigation, and the distribution of surplus crops for later consumption. Unfortunately for residents of the realm, much of the area's land is now desert; this climate change is thought to be related to glacial recession in the late

Pleistocene era. However, this realm is still home to the Nile and the fertile tell area (the northern coast of Morocco, Algeria, and Tunisia).

The general economic geography of North Africa/Southwest Asia

The majority of people in the realm of North Africa/Southwest Asia are involved in an agricultural economy. Through much of the fertile farmland associated with Mesopotamia and the Fertile Crescent (another ancient culture hearth characterized by its advanced agricultural activity) has dried up, many residents of this realm continue to produce resilient crops (particularly cereals), mostly at subsistence levels. Another important aspect of the economic geography of this realm is the vast oil reserves located on the southern Arabian Peninsula, in North Africa, and near the Caspian Sea. While oil is considered one of the most important natural resources on our planet, its presence in North Africa/Southwest Asia has improved the quality of life for only a small portion of the population. This realm exhibits a large gap between the rich and the poor.

The geographic realm of Sub-Saharan Africa

The geographic realm of Sub-Saharan Africa is composed of the territory between the southern border of the Sahara Desert and the southernmost coast of the country of South Africa. The boundary between the North Africa realm and the Sub-Saharan realm is a prime example of a transition zone; several states straddle this hypothetical divide. This area of the globe constitutes a fairly distinctive cultural realm, due to a fusion of traditional African beliefs and cultures with the influences of European colonialism. Many countries in this realm exhibit export-oriented transport systems and European concepts of political geography while retaining their traditional languages, religions, and social practices. The realm of Sub-Saharan Africa is the least developed realm in the world, and the majority of its residents engage in agricultural production. This realm is made up of four regions: West Africa, East Africa, Equatorial Africa, and Southern Africa.

The general economic geography of Sub-Saharan Africa

The majority of peoples living in the geographic realm of Sub-Saharan Africa rely on agriculture to meet their basic needs. Though many raw materials useful to industrialized countries (such as oil and diamonds) are located within this realm, most residents of Sub-Saharan Africa have little or no access to the technology needed to extract these resources, or to the world economy. Agriculturalists in this realm generally produce at the subsistence level (partially due to the harsh physical conditions—hot, dry weather—of the realm). Grain crops are produced more easily in drier areas, while root crops are grown in relatively wetter areas. Peoples in Sub-Saharan Africa also depend on pastoralism (especially the raising of goats, cattle, and chicken) and fishing for their livelihoods. Though this realm is the least developed in the world, farmers are attempting to better their situations by introducing cash crops to their land. Still, many in the area remain malnourished.

The geographic realm of South Asia

India is located at the center of the geographic realm of South Asia, which is one of the world's largest population agglomerations. This realm is delineated by natural boundaries: the Himalayan Mountains to the north and east, and the Arabian Sea and the Bay of Bengal to the south. India was once the cornerstone of civilization, and later a key part of the British colonial empire. Violent conflicts over the control of territory within South Asia have culminated in the creation of six states. This realm, with its many languages and variety of religious affiliations, contains deep cultural divisions. It contains five regions: the Ganges Plain, Pakistan, the mountainous North, Bangladesh, and the Dravidian South.

The general economic geography of South Asia

South Asia continues to experience the effects of former British colonialization. When they came to South Asia, European powers changed trade patterns in the realm; Europe replaced India as the provider of manufactured goods for the realm. This caused a decrease in South Asian industry. Colonialists also exploited raw materials in the realm. Today, each of the states in South Asia has a low-income economy, due largely to the fact that these economies tend to center on inefficient and relatively less productive agricultural methods. Most residents of this region live in villages and survive directly on their parcels of land (often measuring less than an acre). Low-technology production methods keep crop yields (both per acre and per worker) at the subsistence level. Also, local traditions of inheritance often subdivide already undersized plots, preventing the organization of progressive measures, such as cooperative farming and shared irrigation in many states. The lack of a strong official agricultural development policy at the state and federal levels also inhibits the maturation of agricultural production.

The geographic realm of East Asia

The geographic realm of East Asia has China at its center; this realm houses the largest concentration of human population in the world. Culturally, the 1.3 billion Chinese people dominate this realm, while the Japanese dominate economically. In fact, the economic activity and success of Japan have recently led to the tentative identification of the Pacific Rim region, a functional region with Japan as its anchor. The conceptualization of this region, as well as its practical development in the real world, continue to affect several realms and regions facing the Pacific Ocean. East Asia contains five regions: China Proper (eastern and northeastern China), which includes (somewhat precariously) North Korea, the mountains and plateaus of Xizang (the former Tibet), the deserts of Xinjiang, Mongolia, and the Pacific Rim (including Japan, Taiwan, South Korea, Thailand, and sometimes Malaysia), most of which was formerly referred to as the Jakota Triangle.

The general economic geography of East Asia

Economic conditions across the realm of East Asia are highly variable: Japan is one of the most developed countries on the globe, while Mongolia is one of the least developed. The wide inter- and intraregional variations in this realm's development level, therefore, demonstrate that it is inappropriate to label entire realms as "developed" or "underdeveloped." Agriculturalists in the realm tend to inhabit the fertile basins of the great rivers of the east, and produce grains such as wheat. East Asia is also home to large deposits of raw materials such as coal and natural gas. Economic development in the nations of the Jakota Triangle (Japan, South Korea, and Taiwan) is thought to presage the future growth and modernization of the other political entities in the region. Japan, in particular, has experienced rapid growth in all industrial sectors, and possesses long-established trading relationships with nations across the globe. China, the other giant of the realm, has developed a mixed-market economy which displays both capitalistic and communistic characteristics.

The geographic realm of Southeast Asia

The ethnic and linguistic groups which reside in the geographic realm of Southeast Asia are particularly diverse. The high occurrence of conflicts for territory and/or power in this realm throughout history has led some to refer to the realm as "the Eastern Europe of Asia." Some use the term Indochina synonymously with Southeast Asia; this is appropriate because it conveys the identities of the two major cultural contributors to the realm. The ethnic affinities of those in this realm tend to lie with China, while cultural influences (specifically religious) arrived in the region from India. The two major regions of Southeast Asia are differentiated by their spatial separation. Indochina is the eastern, mainland part of the region; the archipelagoes of the Philippines and Indonesia make up the other region.

The general economic geography of Southeast Asia

Like East Asia, the realm of Southeast Asia is a study in economic contrasts; like Eastern Europe, this realm is a shatter belt. Singapore, for example, has the second-busiest port in the world, and is a major banking and financial center. Indonesia, Thailand, and the Philippines have grown from foreign direct investments (a manner of transferring capital across political boundaries, in which the investor exercises control over the acquired asset) in local industries. Also, the islands of Southeast Asia contain large petroleum reserves. Countries such as Vietnam and Cambodia, on the other hand, are some of the least developed countries in the world. This is partially due to the effects of the transition from a planned economy to a market economy. Levels of unemployment tend to be high in both urban and rural areas, as masses of people leave their farmlands (typically rice and/or grains) for crowded cities with limited job opportunities. The lack of a cohesive infrastructure, coupled with political instability, continue to problematize economic growth in these countries.

The geographic realm of Australia

The geographic regions of Australia and New Zealand form the realm of Australia. This realm is distinguished from other areas of the world by its continental isolation and the strong influence of Western culture among its peoples, who are demographically unique. Today, the furthest northwestern points of Australia may be considered part of the Pacific Rim region of East Asia. Australia is anomalous alongside Southeast Asia and the regions of the Pacific, due to its relatively high level of economic development. Still, some of the peoples of New Zealand remain traditional societies. The realm of Australia is made up of four regions. Australia the state is divided into an urbanized core and an arid interior, and New Zealand is made up of two large islands which are physically and culturally distinct.

The general economic geography of Australia

The economies of both Australia and New Zealand rely principally on the exportation of livestock products; Australia is also participates in farming (especially wheat) and mining activities. Dependence on a constantly fluctuating world market places this realm's economy in a precarious position. Despite the plethora of advantages enjoyed by residents of the realm (plentiful farmlands, diverse mineral deposits, access to waterways, and underground water resources, as well as political stability), the Australian economy's growth has declined. Though it is considered one of the most developed realms in the world, Australia must now with the emerging Pacific Rim for trade opportunities. Australia has attempted to integrate itself into the Pacific Rim by exporting raw materials to countries in that region. Agriculturalists in this realm produce grains, rice, and certain fruits, while pastoralists produce wool and meat raising sheep. Manufacturing in Australia remains oriented to local domestic markets, partially due to the high costs of shipping and transportation to and from the relatively isolated realm.

The geographic realm of the Pacific

The Pacific Realm is made up of the thousands of islands (large and small) which are situated in the Pacific Ocean, between Asia and Australia to the west and the Americas to the east. This geographic realm is more fragmented than any other; it is also culturally heterogeneous. The Pacific Realm is traditionally subdivided into three regions: Melanesia (the most populous Pacific region), which is associated with New Guinea; Micronesia (so named for the small sizes of this region's constituent islands), which is located to the north; and Polynesia, which extends from the Hawaiian archipelago southward to Easter Island and southwestward to New Zealand. The regions of Melanesia and Polynesia meet in New Zealand (the residents of which are descended from Polynesian peoples) and Australia (whose indigenous population is Melanesian).

<u>The general economic geography of the Pacific Realm</u>
Tourism may be the single largest revenue earner for the economies of the countries which make up the Pacific Realm. Though this realm covers a larger total area than any other, it possesses the least land area. Coral atolls, ancient volcanoes, open sea, and tropical vegetation offer travelers one spectacular view after another. The region of Melanesia produces valuable export items such as palm oil, coffee, and cocoa, in addition to the subsistence-level production of root crops and bananas. Melanesia also houses large mineral deposits. Micronesia is also involved in agriculture; fertile soils in this region help to diversify crop production. Polynesia, the region which includes the Hawaiian Islands, has a highly developed tourism economy. Most states in the Pacific Realm have high or upper-middle income economies.

Regions of the United States

<u>Major land regions</u>
The United States can be divided into seven distinct major land regions: the Pacific Ranges and Lowlands; the Western Basins and Ranges; the Rocky Mountains; the Ozark-Ouachita Highlands; the Interior Plains; the Coastal Lowlands; and the Appalachian Highlands. Of course, this division does not include Alaska or Hawaii. Some geographers eliminate the Ozark-Ouachita Highlands from the total by classifying the Ozark Plateau as part of the Interior Plains and the Ouachita Mountains as part of the Appalachian Range. Similarly, some geographers combine the Rocky Mountains with the Pacific Ranges and Lowlands into the Pacific Cordillera. In any case, the United States has a total area of about 3,615,292 square miles, or about 9.5 million square kilometers.

<u>Outlying areas</u>
Two states, Hawaii and Alaska, are not part of the coterminous United States. Alaska is the largest state in the nation. It has proven to be an excellent source of natural resources, like gold and oil. Because of the frigid climate, though, it has a very small population. Hawaii is an archipelago, or collection of islands, in the Pacific Ocean. It is home to several important American military bases. The United States also has possession of several islands in the Pacific Ocean and Caribbean. Of these, Puerto Rico is the most closely aligned with the United States, though it is still largely autonomous. Puerto Rico is designated as a commonwealth. It sends a representative to Washington for committee votes, as do American Samoa, the Virgin Islands, and Guam.

<u>Pacific Ranges and Lowlands</u>
The Pacific Ranges and Lowlands region of the United States extends along the western border of the North American continent. On its eastern side, it is bordered by two mountain ranges, the Cascades and the Sierra Nevadas. The Cascade Range includes Lassen Peak (California) and Mount Saint Helens (Washington), both of which are active volcanoes. The Pacific Ranges and Lowlands region runs from northern Washington State to southern

California. To the west of the mountain ranges, there are expansive and fertile valleys. These include California's Central Valley, Oregon's Willamette Valley, and Washington's Puget Sound Lowland. To the west of the valleys, there are coastal ranges, some of which are quite dramatic and others of which are relatively low. The Pacific Coast features a number of large bays, including San Diego Bay, San Francisco Bay, Columbia River Bay, and the Puget Sound. In California, the San Andreas Fault extends along the length of the coastal ranges.

Western Basins and Ranges

The Western Basins and Ranges region of the United States is bordered on the west by the Cascades and Sierra Nevadas, and on the east by the Rockies. From north to south, it extends from central Washington to Mexico. This region is characterized by arid terrain, including several large deserts. Death Valley, in California, contains the lowest point in the United States, at a little less than 300 feet below sea level. To the north, the Great Basin is a large area with several salty and shallow lakes. The largest of these is the Great Salt Lake, which is adjoined by a desert composed in part of a salt bed. On the northern end of the Great Basin, the Columbia Plateau features exceptionally fertile soil, most of which derives from volcanic eruptions in the distant past. However, for the most part, the Western Basins and Ranges region is too dry for large-scale farming, though livestock may be sustained. In the southern part of the Great Basin lies the Colorado Plateau, which includes many deep river gorges, most notably the Grand Canyon.

Rocky Mountains

The Rocky Mountains region of the United States primarily consists of North America's largest mountain group. The Rocky Mountains run from northern New Mexico all the way to Alaska. Some of the peaks in the chain are higher than 14,000 feet. Along the lower slopes of the Rockies, there are deep forests, but above the timber line it is impossible for trees to grow. At the highest elevations, the only plant life that can be sustained is mosses, lichens, and grasses. These jagged mountain ranges include plentiful rivers and streams, and some of North America's most dramatic scenery. Geographers trace an imaginary line, known as the Continental Divide, along the range to separate those areas in which running water flows toward the Pacific Ocean and those in which it flows into the Gulf of Mexico, Atlantic Ocean, or Arctic Ocean. The Rocky Mountains region includes the headwaters of the Rio Grande, Colorado, Missouri, and Colorado Rivers. The first widely used pass through these mountains was at the Wyoming Basin.

Ozark-Ouachita Highlands

The Ozark-Ouachita Highlands region of the United States is not always considered an independent geographic region, though it is difficult to group it with any of the larger regions. The Ozark Plateau and Ouachita Mountains lie north of the Coastal Lowlands and south of the Interior Plains. They run through southern Missouri, eastern Oklahoma, and northwest Arkansas. The region is marked by rough, scrubby highlands interlaced with deep gorges. Perhaps the most noteworthy features of the region are the natural caves. There has also been a great deal of profitable mining in this region, primarily for coal and iron ore. Despite a network of springs, streams, and rivers, the land of the Ozark-Ouachita Highlands is not especially good for farming.

Interior Plains

The Interior Plains region of the United States is an enormous expanse of mostly flat land, extending from the Appalachians in the east to the Rockies in the west. This region was mainly formed by the slow passage of massive glaciers during the Ice Age. As these glaciers descended from the north, they removed topsoil in what are now Wisconsin, Minnesota, and Michigan. These glaciers were also responsible for carving out enormous depressions, among them the Great Lakes (Huron, Michigan, Erie, Superior, and Ontario), the largest system of freshwater lakes in the world. Farther south, the glaciers flattened the land and distributed the topsoil from the north, making the land in Indiana, Illinois, Iowa, and Ohio among the best in the world for farming. The region contains a network of rivers and streams, the greatest of which is the Mississippi River. The Mississippi begins in northern Minnesota and flows all the way to New Orleans. The western part of the Interior Plains region is known as the Great Plains; it is grassland used primarily for livestock grazing.

Coastal Lowlands
The Coastal Lowlands region of the United States runs in a strip along the Atlantic coast, expanding and heading west in the southeast until it terminates in eastern Texas. This region is typically divided into three subregions: the Gulf Coastal Plain, the Atlantic Coastal Plain, and the Piedmont. The Gulf Coastal Plain adjoins the Gulf of Mexico, and includes such major rivers as the Mississippi and Rio Grande. The land in this area is exceptionally fertile, and there are also rich deposits of petroleum. The Atlantic Coastal Plain runs from Maine to Florida, gradually widening as it heads south. This area is also fertile, and is primarily suited for cotton, peanuts, tobacco, and citrus fruits. The Atlantic Coastal Plain includes some large natural harbors, including those at Cape Cod, Boston, and the Chesapeake. The Piedmont lies just inland from the Atlantic Coastal Plain. It is characterized by gentle hills and rivers. Along the eastern border of the Piedmont is the Fall Line: rivers that run west across this line feature dramatic rapids and waterfalls, which makes shipping difficult.

Appalachian Highlands
The Appalachian Highlands region of the United States extends from northern Alabama all the way to northern Maine. It includes mountain ranges like the Blue Ridge, Smokies, Whites, Greens, and Adirondacks. The Blue Ridge Mountains are widely believed to be the oldest range in the world. They extend from northern Georgia to southern Pennsylvania. Several water gaps, or flat passages useful for transportation, are cut through the Blue Ridge by the Delaware, Potomac, and other rivers. To the west of the Blue Ridge, there is a series of high and lowlands known as the Ridge and Valley Region. It includes famous valleys like the Cumberland, Shenandoah, and Rome. The third major feature of this region is the Appalachian Plateau, which runs all the way from Alabama to New York. This area was formed by glaciers, and has been mined more extensively than any other area of the United States.

Grasslands and alpine tundra
The United States includes extensive grasslands, beginning in the Interior Plains region and stretching out into the basins and plateaus of the Rocky Mountains. These grasslands are covered with plants like side oat, buffalo grass, needle, wheat grass, and grama. There are also numerous wild herbs growing in these areas. Grasslands used to be grazed by huge populations of buffalo and cattle, but the buffalo were mostly hunted out of existence. The continental United States only has a few instances of alpine tundra, mostly in the Rocky Mountains above the tree line. In these regions, vegetation consists mostly of short grasses and flowers that bloom only for a brief period. Very few animals are hardy enough to live exclusively in the tundra.

Geomorphology

Geomorphology is a subdiscipline of physical geography. Geomorphologists study landforms, their origins, and their formative processes. Observation of weathering and erosion processes, the movement of tectonic plates, mass movements, and the effects of human activity on the environment all contribute to an understanding of the formation and evolution of landforms. Scholars of human geography are interested in the affects of the environment on human activity. Therefore, they often incorporate the findings of geomorphologists in their studies of places and their inhabitants. For example, the identification of the presence of natural waterways, such as rivers, in ancient societies provides clues about the organizations and economies of those societies.

Medical geography

Medical geography is the subfield of geography that studies the health of the global population in a spatial context. Most diseases which affect human beings originate in the natural environment. Certain environmental qualities facilitate the spread of disease. Tropical Africa, for instance, with its hot, humid climate, is the ideal habitat for carriers such as mosquitoes and flies. Cultural factors (such as personal hygiene, sexual behaviors, and food preparation techniques) can also contribute to disease diffusion. One virus which has its roots in the environment is the Ebola virus, which periodically breaks out randomly and violently in the region of Equatorial Africa. These viruses are born in source (core) areas and diffuse throughout surrounding population through hosts. Analysis of the spatial patterns of diseases and the geographic characteristics of the affected regions can provide vital information about the nature, prevention, and cure of diseases.

The Dust Bowl

The Dust Bowl (1930-1941) was a period of American history characterized by a high incidence of dust storms in the Oklahoma Panhandle region. The instability of the world agriculture market during World War I led to overproduction in the 1920's. Even lands previously considered unsuitable for agricultural use were leveled and developed. This excessive activity devastated the plains of the Oklahoma Panhandle, eliminating the natural vegetation which could have prevented the massive soil movement which occurred during the drought and strong winds of the 1930's. Thus, this ecological disaster occurred in large part due to the activities of humans in the region. In turn, the Dust Bowl led to a large intra-realm migration of humans in North America; hundreds of thousands of people migrated from Oklahoma to California. The events before, during, and after the Dust Bowl, as well as the environmental event itself, provide key examples of the complex processes of interaction between humans and their environments.

The environmental movement

The environmental movement is a global political association which advocates changes in human behavior and policy aimed at the protection, responsible management, and restoration of the natural environment. Members of this group feel that human activity is contributing to environmental degradation. The high consumption of increasingly scarce fossil fuels, deforestation, pollution (air, land, and water), and ozone deterioration are often-cited examples of the ill effects of human practices on the environment. The environmental movement espouses the belief that changes in harmful behaviors can assist in the restoration of environmental quality. Conservation, recycling, and the use of renewable fuel resources (such as hydroelectric power or wind) are touted as potential solutions to the environmental problem.

Practice Test

Practice Questions

1. Through which of the following does the prime meridian *not* pass?
   a. Equator
   b. Middle of the pacific ocean
   c. Greenwich, England
   d. Tropic of cancer

2. What is the name for a line that connects points with equal total rainfall?
   a. Isotherm
   b. Isoline
   c. Isobar
   d. Isohyet

3. The apparent distance between Greenland and Norway is greatest on a(n)
   a. Mercator Map.
   b. Conic Projection Map.
   c. Contour Map.
   d. Equal-Area Projection Map.

4. On a globe, the distance between Buenos Aires and Tokyo is 35 cm. If the globe has a scale of 1 cm for every 516 km, what is the real distance?
   a. 18,060 km
   b. 35 km
   c. 21,080 km
   d. 14,740 km

5. The shortest distance between New York and Paris goes
   a. over Florida and Spain.
   b. along the 42nd parallel.
   c. over Labrador and Greenland.
   d. over Philadelphia and London.

6. On which type of map are different countries represented in different colors, with no two adjacent countries sharing a color?
   a. Physical map
   b. Political map
   c. Climate map
   d. Contour map

7. Which of the following is a possible absolute location for New Orleans?
   a. 30° S, 90° E
   b. 30° N, 90° E
   c. 30° S, 90° W
   d. 30° N, 90° W

8. On a map of Africa, there is a small box around Nairobi. This city is depicted in greater detail in a box at the bottom of the map. What is the name for this box at the bottom of the map?
   a. Inset
   b. Legend
   c. Compass Rose
   d. Key

9. Which map describes the movement of people, trends, or materials across a physical area?
   a. Political Map
   b. Cartogram
   c. Qualitative Map
   d. Flow-line Map

10. How many intermediate directions are there?
   a. 2
   b. 4
   c. 8
   d. 16

11. Which of the following gives the clearest relative location of Milwaukee?
   a. in Wisconsin
   b. on Lake Michigan
   c. 44° N, 88° W
   d. 100 miles north of Chicago

12. Antarctica will appear the largest on a
   a. Mercator projection.
   b. Robinson projection.
   c. Homolosine projection.
   d. Azimuthal projection.

13. Which of the following is *not* a method of representing relief on a physical map?
   a. Symbols
   b. Color
   c. shading
   d. Contour Lines

14. Which of the following countries are separated by a geometric border?
   a. Turkish Cyprus and Greek Cyprus
   b. North Korea and South Korea
   c. France and Spain
   d. England and Ireland

15. On which type of map would Nigeria be bigger than Australia?
   a. Contour map of elevation
   b. Flow-line map of the spice trade
   c. Mercator projection
   d. Cartogram of population

16. On which of the following maps would the scale be largest?
    a. A map of Benelux nations
    b. A map of Senegal
    c. A map of Rio de Janeiro
    d. A map of Greenwich Village

17. Tracy needs to determine the shortest route between Lima and Lisbon. Which of the following maps should she use?
    a. Azimuthal projection with the North Pole at the center
    b. Azimuthal projection with Lisbon at the center
    c. Robinson projection of the Eastern Hemisphere
    d. Robinson projection of the Western Hemisphere

18. Which type of chart is best at representing the cycle of demographic transition?
    a. Pie chart
    b. Political map
    c. Line graph
    d. Flow-line map

19. What kind of chart would be best for representing the major events of World War I?
    a. Time line
    b. Bar graph
    c. Pie chart
    d. Political map

20. On a political map of India, the northernmost part of the border with Pakistan is represented as a dotted line. Why is this so?
    a. Pakistan does not have control of this border.
    b. This area has never been comprehensively mapped.
    c. Indian Sikhs are threatening to secede.
    d. The borders of the Kashmir region remain in dispute.

21. Which part of a hurricane features the strongest winds and greatest rainfall?
    a. Eye wall
    b. Front
    c. Eye
    d. Outward spiral

22. What is the most common type of volcano on earth?
    a. Lava dome
    b. Composite volcano
    c. Shield volcano
    d. Cinder cone

23. Which biome features scrubby plants and small evergreen trees and also has a hot, dry summer followed by a wetter winter?
    a. Taiga
    b. Coniferous forest
    c. Chaparral
    d. Savanna

24. Which type of rock is formed by extreme heat and pressure?
    a. Limestone
    b. Metamorphic
    c. Sedimentary
    d. Igneous

25. What is the name for a brief interval of coolness in between warm periods in the Pacific Ocean?
    a. La Niña
    b. Tropical gyre
    c. El Niño
    d. ENSO

26. The rocks and landmasses that make up the earth's surface are called the
    a. atmosphere.
    b. biosphere.
    c. hydrosphere.
    d. lithosphere.

27. Which of the following landmasses is *not* part of the Ring of Fire?
    a. Japan
    b. Cascade Mountains in Washington
    c. Andes Mountains in South America
    d. Mount Kilimanjaro

28. In the plate movement known as ____, an oceanic plate slides underneath a continental plate.
    a. faulting
    b. spreading
    c. subduction
    d. converging

29. Which of the following statements about loess is true?
    a. It is primarily carried by water.
    b. It has low mineral content.
    c. It is very dense.
    d. It has been essential to the success of farming in the American Midwest.

30. Which of the following currents is responsible for the climate of the British Isles?
    a. North Equatorial Current
    b. Canary Current
    c. Gulf Stream
    d. Labrador Current

31. What is the name for the pile of rocks and debris left behind by a glacier?
    a. Iceberg
    b. Col
    c. Fjord
    d. Moraine

32. According to Alfred Wegener, the earth originally had one continent called
    a. Pangaea.
    b. Eurasia.
    c. Transcontinentia.
    d. Africa.

33. Which of the following is an example of an isthmus?
    a. Central America
    b. the Aleutian Islands
    c. Northern Greenland
    d. Florida

34. Which of the following statements about the equator is true?
    a. It intersects four continents.
    b. It is to the north of both horse latitudes.
    c. It is located at 0° longitude.
    d. It is not very windy.

35. Which soil horizon consists of weathered rock?
    a. A horizon
    b. C horizon
    c. O horizon
    d. R horizon

36. What causes the motion of glaciers?
    a. Gravity
    b. Erosion
    c. Wind
    d. Temperature change

37. Which of the following is an example of chemical weathering?
    a. Frost wedging
    b. Heat expansion
    c. Acid rain
    d. Salt wedging

38. Which of the following statements about tropical rain forests is false?
    a. There are tropical rain forests on only two continents.
    b. The largest tropical rain forest is the Amazon River basin.
    c. Over half of the world's plant and animal species are found in the tropical rain forest.
    d. Tropical rain forests cover less than 10 percent of the earth's surface.

39. Which layer of the atmosphere is closest to the earth's surface?
    a. Thermosphere
    b. Troposphere
    c. Stratosphere
    d. Mesosphere

40. Which of the following soil types has the smallest grains?
    a. Sand
    b. Silt
    c. Clay
    d. Loam

41. Which type of precipitation results when warm, wet air is forced over mountains?
    a. Orographic precipitation
    b. Dorsal precipitation
    c. Convectional precipitation
    d. Frontal precipitation

42. During one year in Grassley County, there are 750 births, 350 deaths, 80 immigrations, and 50 emigrations. What is the natural increase rate for this year?
    a. 400
    b. 830
    c. 430
    d. More information is required.

43. Which of the following is *not* one of the world's four major population agglomerations?
    a. North Africa
    b. Eastern North America
    c. South Asia
    d. Europe

44. Thai food has become increasingly popular in the United States, though it is prepared in slightly different ways here. This is an example of
    a. Cultural Divergence.
    b. Assimilation.
    c. Cultural convergence.
    d. Acculturation.

45. Which government system vests almost all control in a central government?
    a. Federation
    b. Democracy
    c. Unitary system
    d. Confederation

46. To which language family does English belong?
    a. Romance
    b. Indo-European
    c. Amerindian
    d. Papuan

47. What is the name for the traditionally Arab district in a North African city?
    a. Souk
    b. Medina
    c. Wadi
    d. Bazaar

48. Which of the following languages is *not* alphabetic?
    a. Spanish
    b. Russian
    c. Chinese
    d. Arabic

49. Where is the greatest area of corn production?
    a. South Africa
    b. Kazakhstan
    c. United States
    d. Mexico

50. What has been one result of NAFTA?
    a. The border between the United States and Mexico has opened.
    b. There has been significant migration from Canada to Mexico.
    c. Trade barriers between the United States and Canada have increased.
    d. Mexico has sought to enter other trade agreements.

51. Last year, 4 residents of Henrytown died. The population of Henrytown is 500. What is the death rate of Henrytown (deaths per 1000)?
    a. 1
    b. 4
    c. 8
    d. 12

52. Which of the following locations would be considered a modern cultural hearth?
    a. New York City
    b. Baghdad
    c. Auckland
    d. Edmonton

53. According to Mark Jefferson, which of the following would be considered the primate city of England?
    a. London
    b. Manchester
    c. Brighton
    d. Salisbury

54. The popularity of hockey in Canada and the northern United States is an example of
    a. expansion diffusion.
    b. indirect diffusion.
    c. forced diffusion.
    d. direct diffusion.

55. Which of the following is *not* one of the criteria for nationhood?
   a. Defined territory
   b. Elections
   c. Government
   d. Sovereignty

56. Which form of religion includes the belief that the natural world is imbued with spirits?
   a. Monotheism
   b. Pantheism
   c. Animism
   d. Polytheism

57. When a foreign power has some political and economic control over a region in another country but does not directly govern, it is said to have a(n)
   a. Colony.
   b. Sphere Of Influence.
   c. Settlement.
   d. Enclave.

58. The town of Hamilton has 400 citizens living in 12 square miles. The town of Burrsville has 300 citizens living over 10 square miles. Which town has the greater population density?
   a. Hamilton
   b. Burrsville
   c. The towns have the same population density.
   d. The answer cannot be determined based on the information given.

59. When a person grows only enough food to feed himself and his family, he is engaged in
   a. nomadic herding.
   b. commercial farming.
   c. sharecropping.
   d. subsistence farming.

60. Which of the following exemplifies the multiplier effect of large cities?
   a. The presence of specialized equipment for an industry attracts even more business.
   b. The large population lowers the price of goods.
   c. Public transportation means more people can commute to work.
   d. A local newspaper can afford to give away the Sunday edition.

61. In which stage of demographic transition does fertility remain high while mortality declines?
   a. High stationary stage
   b. Early expanding stage
   c. Late expanding stage
   d. Low stationary stage

62. During which stage of spatial diffusion does the process slow to a stop?
    a. Primary
    b. Diffusion
    c. Condensing
    d. Saturation

63. In the United States, what is the correct term for a settlement with fewer than 100 inhabitants?
    a. Village
    b. Town
    c. Hamlet
    d. City

64. To communicate, traders from distant regions of the world settle on a(n)
    a. lingua franca.
    b. pidgin language.
    c. conurbation.
    d. activity space.

65. Juan has a mill, which he uses to grind wheat into flour. This is an example of
    a. primary economic activity.
    b. secondary economic activity.
    c. tertiary economic activity.
    d. quaternary economic activity.

66. Which of the following is *not* one of the necessary characteristics of a geographical region?
    a. Area
    b. Location
    c. Homogeneity
    d. Population

67. Stephen travels to the city every morning for work. Every evening, he returns to his home in the suburbs. What kind of movement is this?
    a. Cyclic movement
    b. Migratory movement
    c. Cross-boundary movement
    d. Periodic movement

68. Which of the following is *not* one of the demographic variables?
    a. Fertility
    b. Diversity
    c. Mortality
    d. Migration

69. Which of the following is an example of indirect diffusion?
    a. The Dutch and the Belgians both love soccer.
    b. Iran forbids its citizens from watching Western television programs.
    c. Japanese anime comics are popular in the United States.
    d. Many Native Americans have struggled with alcoholism.

70. Which of the following most closely resembles a communist society?
    a. Colony
    b. Ghetto
    c. Shtetl
    d. Kibbutz

71. The Russian city of St. Petersburg is crucial to the economy because of its
    a. timber reserves.
    b. access to the Baltic Sea.
    c. historic architecture.
    d. location on the Volga River.

72. Which of the following nations is *not* a member of OPEC?
    a. Saudi Arabia
    b. Venezuela
    c. Yemen
    d. Iraq

73. Which of the following was a consequence of the Mexican Revolution of 1910?
    a. Land redistribution
    b. National sovereignty
    c. Two-party rule
    d. The creation of railroads

74. For thousands of years, Africans have cultivated the grasslands south of the Sahara Desert, an area known as the
    a. Qattara Depression.
    b. Great Rift Valley.
    c. Congo Basin.
    d. Sahel.

75. What are the two regions of the Czech Republic?
    a. Chechnya and Slovakia
    b. Moravia and Slovakia
    c. Bohemia and Chechnya
    d. Bohemia and Moravia

76. Egypt is plagued by the sandstorms arising from a summer wind known as the
    a. khamsin.
    b. sirocco.
    c. zephyr.
    d. fellaheen.

77. What is the name of the highest habitable region in Middle and South America?
    a. *Tierra fria*
    b. *Puna*
    c. *Tierra helada*
    d. *Templada*

78. Identify one consequence of Zimbabwe's first free election in 1980.
   a. The government outlawed private property.
   b. The policy of apartheid was ended.
   c. The country ceased to be known as Rhodesia.
   d. The British government acknowledged the nation's sovereignty.

79. What do Marseilles and Genoa have in common?
   a. They are national capitals.
   b. They both border Germany.
   c. They are both in the south of France.
   d. They are both important ports on the Mediterranean.

80. Indian women often cover their faces in public, a tradition known as
   a. burqa.
   b. hijab.
   c. sari.
   d. purdah.

81. What is the most popular religion in Japan?
   a. Shinto
   b. Buddhism
   c. Confucianism
   d. A blend of these three religions

82. Why was Aksum able to become a powerful empire in Africa 2,000 years ago?
   a. It had access to major waterways.
   b. It was a Muslim nation.
   c. It had access to oil reserves.
   d. It was located in the center of the continent.

83. What is the name for the Muslims who live in northwestern China?
   a. Tibetans
   b. Mandarin
   c. Falun Gong
   d. Uighurs

84. Which religious group does *not* consider Jerusalem a holy city?
   a. Christians
   b. Buddhists
   c. Muslims
   d. Jews

85. Which of the following is *not* one of the Baltic states?
   a. Moldova
   b. Latvia
   c. Lithuania
   d. Estonia

86. Where do most Pakistanis live?
    a. Farming villages
    b. Karachi
    c. Baluchistan Plateau
    d. Khyber Pass

87. What is the best description of the Mongols?
    a. Grain farmers
    b. Nomadic herders
    c. Industrialists
    d. Tradesmen

88. Which state covers the most area?
    a. New York
    b. Texas
    c. California
    d. Alaska

89. Which of the following is a true statement about the Yucatan Peninsula?
    a. It is densely populated.
    b. It is more mountainous than the rest of Mexico.
    c. It was once inhabited by Aztecs.
    d. It has a number of large sinkholes.

90. Which two nations share the longest undefended border in the world?
    a. Chile and Argentina
    b. Canada and the United States
    c. Kazakhstan and Russia
    d. Egypt and Sudan

91. The reorganization of the USSR's economy under Gorbachev was known as
    a. glasnost.
    b. rubles.
    c. soviets.
    d. perestroika.

92. What is the best description of the pampas in Argentina and Uruguay?
    a. Migrant workers
    b. Jagged peaks
    c. Temperate grasslands
    d. Wild horses

93. Conflict between Sinhalese and Tamils has simmered for thousands of years in what is now
    a. Sri Lanka.
    b. Bhutan.
    c. Burma.
    d. Thailand.

94. Which of the following is *not* an official language of Switzerland?
    a. Italian
    b. Dutch
    c. French
    d. German

95. Which of the following statements about Kemal Ataturk is true?
    a. He increased the influence of Islam on the Turkish government.
    b. He outlawed English.
    c. He diminished the civil rights of women.
    d. He westernized Turkey in many ways.

96. What are the Atlantic provinces of Canada?
    a. Labrador, Prince Edward Island, New Brunswick, and Nova Scotia
    b. New Brunswick, Nunavut, Nova Scotia, and Labrador
    c. Prince Edward Island, Nova Scotia, Quebec, and Newfoundland
    d. Manitoba, Nunavut, Ontario, and Saskatchewan

97. Which country controlled Hong Kong before China?
    a. Japan
    b. United States
    c. Great Britain
    d. Korea

98. What is the name for a shantytown in Brazil?
    a. *Barrio*
    b. *Favela*
    c. *Maquiladora*
    d. *Ciudad*

99. In Holland, the lands reclaimed through a network of dikes and canals are known as
    a. polders.
    b. cantons.
    c. grabens.
    d. moors.

100. After the United States, which of the following nations imports the most oil?
    a. China
    b. Brazil
    c. Germany
    d. Japan

Answers and Explanations

1. C: The prime meridian does not pass through the middle of the Pacific Ocean. It is 0°, the line from which longitude is measured. There is no special reason why it passes through Greenwich, other than that the observatory there was one of the first to devise a system for measuring longitude and therefore put itself at the base of the system. The international date line is 180° longitude; it passes through the middle of the Pacific Ocean. Both the equator and the Tropic of Cancer are lines of latitude and therefore intersect the prime meridian. The equator circles the earth at its broadest circumference, equidistant from the North and South poles. The equator has a latitude of 0°. The Tropic of Cancer, 23°26′22″ North latitude, represents the northernmost point at which the sun is directly above the earth. In other words, at no point during the year will the sun be directly above any point north of the Tropic of Cancer. This line is mirrored in the Southern Hemisphere by the Tropic of Capricorn.

2. D: An isohyet is a line that connects points with equal total rainfall. On an isohyetal map then, a series of lines will indicate areas of greater or lesser rainfall. This is a form of contour map, the most common of which uses a series of lines to indicate changes in elevation. The other answer choices represent lines used in other forms of contour maps. An isotherm connects points with the same temperature. An isoline connects points with an equal value, as, for instance, on a contour map illustrating iron production. An isobar connects points with identical atmospheric pressure.

3. A: The apparent distance between Greenland and Norway will be greatest on a Mercator map. The Mercator map is a type of cylindrical projection map in which lines of latitude and longitude are transferred onto a cylindrical shape, which is then cut vertically and laid flat. For this reason, distances around the poles will appear increasingly great. The Mercator map is excellent for navigation because a straight line drawn on it represents a single compass reading. In a conic projection map, on the other hand, a hemisphere of the globe is transposed onto a cone, which is then cut vertically (that is, from rim to tip) and laid flat. The apparent distances on a conic projection will be smallest at the 45th parallel. A contour map uses lines to illustrate the features of a geographic area. For example, the lines on an elevation contour map connect areas that have the same altitude. An equal-area projection map represents landmasses in their actual sizes. To make this possible, the shapes of the landmasses are manipulated slightly, and the map is interrupted (divided into more than one part).

4. A: The distance between Buenos Aires and Tokyo is approximately 18,060 km. The process of converting a scaled distance to a real distance is fairly simple. In this case, multiply the number of centimeters by the number of kilometers represented by each of these centimeters. The calculation can be expressed as (35 cm) (516 km/1 cm). Because centimeters are in the numerator of the first term and the denominator of the second term, they cancel out, leaving kilometers as the unit.

5. C: The shortest distance between New York and Paris goes over Labrador and Greenland. This is not apparent on a projection map, in which a straight line drawn between the two cities would extend straight out across the Atlantic Ocean, roughly along the 42nd parallel. The illusion that this straight line is the shortest path is a result of the distortions inherent

in projection maps. On a globe, it would be easier to see that a plane flying from New York to Paris would cover the least ground by carving an arc, first up through eastern Canada and Greenland and then back down through the British Isles and northern France. This sort of path is known as a great circle route because it looks like an arc when it is drawn on a projection map.

6. B: On a political map, countries are represented in different colors, and countries that share a border are not given the same color. This is so that the borders between countries will be distinct. Political maps are used to illustrate those aspects of a country that have been determined by people: the capital, the provincial and national borders, and the large cities. Political maps sometimes include major physical features like rivers and mountains, but they are not intended to display all such information. On a physical, climate, or contour map, however, the borders between nations are more incidental. Colors are used on these maps to represent physical features, areas with similar climate, etc. It is possible that colors will overrun the borders and be shared by adjacent countries.

7. D: The only answer choice that represents a possible absolute location for New Orleans is 30° N, 90° W. When a location is described in terms of its placement on the global grid, it is customary to put the latitude before the longitude. New Orleans is north of the equator, so it has to be in the Northern Hemisphere. In addition, it is west of the prime meridian, which runs through Greenwich, England, among other places. So, New Orleans must be in the Western Hemisphere. It is possible, then, to deduce that 30° N, 90° W is the only possible absolute location for New Orleans.

8. A: A smaller box in which some part of the larger map is depicted in greater detail is known as an inset. Insets provide a closer look at parts of the map that the cartographer deems to be more important (for instance, cities, national parks, or historical sites). Often, traffic maps will include several insets depicting the roads in the most congested area of the city. Legends, also known as keys, are the boxes in which the symbols used in the map are explained. A legend, or key, might indicate how railroads and boundaries are depicted, for example. A compass rose indicates how the map is oriented along the north-south axis. It is common for cartographers to tilt a map for ease of display, such that up may not be due north.

9. D: A flow-line map describes the movement of people, trends, or materials across a physical area. The movements depicted on a flow-line map are typically represented by arrows. In more advanced flow-line maps, the width of the arrow corresponds to the quantity of the motion. Flow-line maps usually declare the span of time that is being represented. A political map depicts the man-made aspects of geography, such as borders and cities. A cartogram adjusts the size of the areas represented according to some variable. For instance, a cartogram of wheat production would depict Iowa as being much larger than Alaska. A qualitative map uses lines, dots, and other symbols to illustrate a particular point. For example, a qualitative map might be used to demonstrate the greatest expansion of the Persian Empire.

10. B: There are four intermediate directions. They are northwest, northeast, southwest, and southeast. The intermediate directions are midway between each set of adjacent cardinal directions. The cardinal directions are north, south, east, and west. On a compass rose, the cardinal directions are typically indicated by large points, while the intermediate directions are represented by smaller points.

11. D: A relative location for Milwaukee is 100 miles north of Chicago. Relative location is a description of placement in terms of some other location. The latitude and longitude of Milwaukee are its absolute location because they describe its placement relative to an arbitrary but inalterable system of positioning. To say that Milwaukee is in Wisconsin or on Lake Michigan does not provide as much detail as answer choice D because Wisconsin is a big state and because Lake Michigan is a large body of water.

12. A: Antarctica will appear the largest on a Mercator projection. This projection map converts the globe into a rectangle, such that lines of longitude and latitude are perpendicular to one another. This type of map depicts landforms near the equator at nearly their normal size but increasingly stretches out distances as it reaches the poles. A Robinson projection, on the other hand, rounds the edges of the Mercator projection, such that the polar regions are not so large. A homolosine projection renders the sizes and shapes of landmasses correctly, but it distorts the distances between them. An azimuthal projection represents one hemisphere as a circle, such that a straight line from the center to any point on the map would also be the shortest distance in the real world.

13. A: Symbols are not used to represent relief on a physical map. A physical map is dedicated to illustrating the landmasses and bodies of water in a specific region, so symbols do not provide enough detail. Color, shading, and contour lines, on the other hand, are able to create a much more complicated picture of changes in elevation, precipitation, etc. Changes in elevation are known in geography as relief.

14. B: North Korea and South Korea are separated by a geometric border, meaning that the boundary between the two nations is a straight line drawn on a map, without respect to landforms. Specifically, the boundary between the Koreas is the 38th parallel. Another example of a geometric border lies between the continental United States and Canada. The Turkish Cyprus–Greek Cyprus border is anthropogeographic, or drawn according to cultural reasons. The border between France and Spain is physiographic-political, a combination of the Pyrenees Mountains and European history. The Irish Sea separates England from Ireland.

15. D: On a cartogram of population, Nigeria would be bigger than Australia. Even though the area of Australia is several times greater than that of Nigeria, Nigeria has a much larger population. A cartogram is a map on which countries or regions are sized according to a certain variable. So, in a cartogram of population, the country with the most people will be the biggest. The countries would be depicted at their usual size in a contour map of elevation or in a flow-line map. On a Mercator projection, Nigeria would actually be smaller relative to Australia because it is closer to the equator.

16. D: The scale would be largest on a map of Greenwich Village. Scale is described as large when it is closer to life-sized; the smaller the region being depicted, the closer to actual size the map can be. Of the four answer choices, Greenwich Village, a neighborhood in Manhattan, is the smallest. Therefore, it must be depicted in the largest scale. Incidentally, Benelux is the name for the region of northern Europe that includes Belgium, the Netherlands, and Luxembourg.

17. B: To determine the shortest route between Lima and Lisbon, Tracy should use an azimuthal projection with Lisbon at the center. An azimuthal projection depicts one

hemisphere of the globe as a circle. A straight line drawn from the center of the map to any point represents the shortest possible distance between those two points. Tracy could obtain her objective, then, with an azimuthal projection in which either Lisbon or Lima were at the center. If the North Pole were at the center, the map would not include Lima because this city is in the Southern Hemisphere. A Robinson projection approximates the sizes and shapes of landmasses but does distort in some ways, particularly near the poles.

18. C: The cycle of demographic transition is best illustrated by a line graph. Demographic transition is a phenomenon in which a region's growth rate increases rapidly, peaks, and then decreases slowly over a long time. In the early phase of a region's development, both the birth and death rates are high, which can cause the population to fluctuate. As the people of the region become settled, the growth rate calms down, and the region enters a period of rapid increase. Political maps are better at depicting borders and the locations of cities, while pie charts are better at representing proportions. Flow-line maps are good for illustrating the movement of people, goods, or trends across a physical area.

19. A: A time line would be the best way to represent the major events of World War I. Time lines place events in chronological order, with the distance between the events correlated to their interval on the line. A time line can run in any direction. A thematic map or a flow-line map might also be good at representing this subject, but a political map is restricted to borders and cities; therefore, it would not be able to suggest the changes caused by the war. Bar graphs and pie charts are used to depict quantities and proportions rather than sequences of events.

20. D: The northernmost border between India and Pakistan is represented on political maps as a broken line because the borders of the Kashmir region remain in dispute. Both nations lay claim to this mountainous region, which has great water resources. This has been just one of the issues to complicate relations between these neighbors in South Asia. Although India controls most of Kashmir at present, the boundaries have not yet been fully resolved, and, on a political map, such undefined borders are usually represented with dotted lines.

21. A: The eye wall of a hurricane has the strongest winds and the greatest rainfall. The eye wall is the tower-like rim of the eye. It is from this wall that clouds extend out, which are seen from above as the classic outward spiral pattern. A hurricane front is the outermost edge of its influence; although there will be heavy winds and rain in this area, the intensity will be relatively small. The eye of a hurricane is actually a place of surprising peace. In this area, dry and cool air rushes down to the ground or sea. Once there, the air is caught up in the winds of the eye wall and is driven outward at a furious pace.

22. B: The composite volcano, sometimes called the stratovolcano, is the most common type of volcano on earth. A composite volcano has steep sides, so the explosions of ash, pumice, and silica are often accompanied by treacherous mudslides. Indeed, it is these mudslides that cause most of the damage associated with composite volcano eruptions. Krakatoa and Mount Saint Helens are examples of composite volcanoes. A lava dome is a round volcano that emits thick lava very slowly. A shield volcano, one example of which is Mt. Kilauea in Hawaii, emits a small amount of lava over an extended period of time. Shield volcanoes are not known for violent eruptions. A cinder cone has steep sides made of fallen cinders, which themselves are made of the lava that intermittently shoots into the air.

23. C: The chaparral biome features scrubby plants and small evergreen trees and also has a hot, dry summer followed by a wetter winter. This biome is mainly found around the Mediterranean Sea, though there are also chaparrals in Australia, South Africa, and the American Southwest. The taiga is a colder biome found primarily in northern Europe and Asia. The vegetation of the taiga is mainly scattered stands of coniferous trees. A coniferous forest, meanwhile, is a warmer forest composed of trees that have needles and cones rather than leaves. These trees are better suited for a cold climate than are deciduous trees. A savanna is a tropical grassland with only a few trees. Savannas are clustered around the equator.

24. B: Metamorphic rock is formed by extreme heat and pressure. This type of rock is created when other rocks are somehow buried within the earth, where they are subject to a dramatic rise in pressure and temperature. Slate and marble are both metamorphic rocks. Metamorphic rocks are created by the other two main types of rock: sedimentary and igneous. Sedimentary rock is formed when dirt and other sediment is washed into a bed, covered over by subsequent sediment, and compacted into rock. Depending on how they are formed, sedimentary rocks are classified as organic, clastic, or chemical. Igneous rocks are composed of cooled magma, the molten rock that emerges from volcanoes. Basalt and granite are two common varieties of igneous rock.

25. A: La Niña is a brief interval of coolness in between warm periods (El Niño) in the water of the Pacific Ocean. For a long time, La Niña was considered only in terms of its relation to El Niño. Increasingly, however, it is being studied as a climate event in its own right. A tropical gyre is a circle of winds made up of equatorial currents in one direction and countercurrents in the other direction. There are tropical gyres in both the Northern and Southern hemispheres. El Niño is an annual event, though some years it is considerably more pronounced. It is an increase in the temperature of coastal Pacific water, sometimes by as much as 2° Celsius. El Niño has a great impact on fishing and weather in the areas that border the Pacific Ocean. The El Niño–Southern Oscillation (ENSO) occurs during a particularly intense El Niño; the flow of equatorial wind and water during an ENSO actually reverses course.

26. D: The rocks and land formations that make up the earth's surface are collectively known as the lithosphere. The lithosphere does not include the core or mantle of the earth. The atmosphere is the air, water, and particles that are above the surface of the earth. The biosphere encompasses all the living things of the earth, such as animals, plants, fungi, and bacteria. The hydrosphere is all the water on and beneath the surface of the earth, including all the lakes, oceans, rivers, and creeks.

27. D: Mount Kilimanjaro is not part of the Ring of Fire, a circle of volcanoes that stretches around the Pacific Ocean. The Ring of Fire extends from islands east of Australia through Indonesia, Japan, the Aleutian Islands connecting Russia to Alaska, and down the western coast of the Americas. It includes such famous volcanoes as Mount Saint Helens and Krakatoa. Over 90 percent of earthquakes and over 80 percent of volcanic eruptions occur along the Ring of Fire.

28. C: In the plate movement known as subduction, an oceanic plate slides underneath a continental plate. Oceanic plates are denser, so they tend to go beneath when they are pressed against lighter continental plates. The edge of the oceanic plate will be melted by the earth's mantle and may reemerge as a volcano. The Cascade Range of the northwest

- 124 -

United States was formed by subduction. In faulting, the edges of two plates grind against each other laterally. The San Andreas Fault in California is perhaps the most famous example of this process. In spreading, plates pull apart from each other, typically creating a rift valley and the potential for earthquakes. In converging, two plates of similar density press against each other, creating mountain ranges where they meet.

29. D: Loess, a form of silt or dust, has been a major reason for the success of farming in the American Midwest. Loess is rich in minerals and is light enough to be moved by the wind. It has a very low density and is porous enough to retain a great deal of water. All of these attributes make it an ideal base for farm soil. There are also great deposits of loess in China, with similar benefits for agriculture.

30. C: The climate of the British Isles is mild for its latitude because of the Gulf Stream, an air current originating in the Gulf of Mexico. As this current of warm air makes its way northeast across the Atlantic, it divides, with the North Atlantic Current bringing moisture and mild temperatures to Ireland and the United Kingdom. Even though the latitude of the British Isles is roughly the same as that of Alaska, the land is arable, and the temperature remains warm for the most part. The North Equatorial Current, on the other hand, is a current of warm air that runs west just above the equator. The Canary Current brings cool air from western Europe down around the western tip of Africa, which includes the Canary Islands. The Labrador Current moves cool air from the water in between Canada and Greenland south to the northeastern United States.

31. D: A moraine is a pile of rocks and debris left behind by a glacier. As a glacier moves across the earth's surface, it churns up the ground beneath. The piles that remain after the glacier is gone become significant landmasses in their own right. For instance, Long Island off the coast of New York is the moraine of a long-ago glacier. An iceberg, meanwhile, is a mass of floating ice that has broken off of a glacier, typically near one of the poles. A col is a mountain pass, that is, the trough between two mountain peaks. A fjord is a narrow waterway cut out of the land by a glacier. A fjord typically has high walls on either side.

32. A: Alfred Wegener was a German scientist credited with developing the idea of Pangaea, the original supercontinent from which today's large landmasses were formed. Wegener created this name from the Greek words for *all* and *earth*. The continental drift theory asserts that Pangaea began to break up approximately 180 million years ago. Wegener was inspired in part by his observation that many of the continents seemed to fit together. He also discovered a number of prehistoric fossils that suggested similarities between animals and plants from different continents.

33. A: Central America is one example of an isthmus, a narrow strip of land connecting two larger landmasses. The strip of land should be bordered by water on either side. The nation of Panama is the most classic example of an isthmus in Central America because it is so narrow. This is why it was chosen as the site for a great canal connecting the Atlantic and Pacific Oceans. The Aleutian Islands are an example of an archipelago, or cluster of islands in an ocean. Northern Greenland is an example of a tundra, the coldest of the biomes. There are no trees in the tundra. Florida is an example of a peninsula, a strip of land extending out into a large body of water, in this case the Atlantic Ocean.

34. D: Around the world, the area around the equator is known for a relative lack of wind. Indeed, the equatorial belt is sometimes called the doldrums because the constant warm

water encourages the air to rise gently. To the north and south, however, there are trade winds that can become quite violent. The equator only intersects three continents: Asia, Africa, and South America. It is in between the north and south horse latitudes, which are belts known for calm winds. Finally, the equator is located at 0° latitude, not longitude, though the 0° line of longitude does intersect the equator.

35. B: The C horizon of soil consists of weathered rock. A soil that has been in the same place for a long time will begin to develop unique layers known as horizons. The bottom layer is called the R horizon; it consists of unweathered bedrock. Just above is the C horizon, which is composed of weathered rock fragments. Next up is the B horizon, made up of minerals and drier soil. Above that is the A horizon, or topsoil, which has a great deal of organic matter in it. The top layer is known as the O horizon. It is a thin layer of humus.

36. A: Glaciers move because they are incredibly heavy, and the force of gravity slowly pulls them lower. Erosion is a result rather than a cause of glacier movement. Although large glaciers may only move a few inches a year or may not move at all, some valley glaciers in Europe move as much as 600 feet annually. The result is a rounded valley and a trail of rock and soil debris known as a moraine. The Great Lakes in the United States were formed by the passage of glaciers long ago.

37. C: Acid rain is an example of chemical weathering. When acidic chemicals are evaporated and fall as rain, they can have devastating effects on plant and animal life. Although human activity is the primary cause of acid rain, weathering chemicals can also get into the atmosphere through oceanic bacteria and volcanoes. The other three answer choices are examples of mechanical weathering. Frost wedging occurs when water seeps into a narrow space within a rock formation and then freezes. Because water takes up more space as ice and frost than it does in its liquid state, this process can cause structural damage to the rock. Heat expansion occurs when rapid changes in temperature cause rocks to expand, leading to cracks and fissures. Salt wedging occurs when water flowing into a rock brings salt in with it. The water evaporates, but the salt is left behind, and over time the deposits of salt can create pressure within the rock.

38. A: There are tropical rain forests on all the continents except Europe and Antarctica. Indeed, the Congo River Basin in Africa is the site of the second-largest tropical rain forest. There are also tropical rain forests in Central America, northern Australia, and Southeast Asia. Of course, all these rain forests are close to the equator, where there is abundant heat and precipitation. All the other answer choices are true statements, though it could be said more specifically that tropical rain forests cover approximately 6 percent of the earth's surface.

39. B: The troposphere is the layer of the atmosphere closest to the earth's surface. It extends up from the ground about six miles, and it contains almost all clouds. Weather is a phenomenon of the troposphere. The thermosphere is the uppermost level of the atmosphere. There is very little air in the thermosphere. The stratosphere lies just above the troposphere and includes the ozone layer. The mesosphere is in between the stratosphere and the thermosphere, 30 to 50 miles above the surface of the earth.

40. C: Clay soil has the smallest grains. This is somewhat counterintuitive because clay tends to clump together when it is exposed to any moisture. However, the individual constituent parts of clay are finer than grains of sand. In fact, silty soils have smaller grains than sand as

well. Loam is a combination of sand, silt, and clay. In most cases, loam is the best soil for agriculture. Most soils are comprised of some mixture of sand, silt, and clay.

41. A: Orographic precipitation is caused by warm, wet air being forced upward so that it can pass over high landforms. The air cools rapidly as it gains elevation, and snow and cold rain begin to fall. This phenomenon occurs in the Andes Mountains, where warm air flowing over the Pacific Ocean is forced upward. The land on the other side of a range that receives orographic precipitation usually gets very little precipitation. There is no such thing as dorsal precipitation. Convectional precipitation results when warm air rises slowly and cools. As it cools, it expels some of its moisture. This kind of rainfall is common over tropical jungles. Frontal precipitation results when warm air encounters cooler air and is forced up.

42. D: More information is required to calculate the natural increase rate for Grassley County during this year. Natural increase rate is the growth in population measured as the surplus of live births over deaths for every thousand people. The calculation of natural increase rate does not take account of immigration or emigration. The natural increase rate for Grassley County cannot be calculated because the original population of the county is not given. As an example, if the beginning population of the county had been 10,000, the natural increase rate would be 40; 400 * 1,000/10,000 = 40.

43. A: North Africa is not one of the world's four major population agglomerations. These are eastern North America, South Asia, East Asia, and Europe. The largest of these is East Asia, which encompasses Korea, Japan, and the major cities of China. The second-largest population agglomeration is South Asia, which includes India and Pakistan. Most of the population in this area is near the coasts. The European agglomeration is spread across the largest piece of land, while the much smaller agglomeration in eastern North America is primarily focused on the string of cities from Boston to Washington, DC.

44. C: The increasing popularity of Thai food in the United States is an example of cultural convergence, or the intersection of traits or customs from two distinct cultures. Thailand's cuisine has been introduced to the United States, but it has undergone subtle changes as a result of the desires and practices of the American consumer. The phenomenon of cultural convergence is credited with much of the innovation in any society. Cultural divergence, on the other hand, is the practice of shielding one culture from the influence of another. France, for instance, seeks to limit the influence of American culture on its citizens. Assimilation is the process by which a minority group gradually adopts the culture of the majority group. For example, many Native Americans assimilated into the European-style culture of the early American settlers. Acculturation is the process of obtaining the practices and ideas of a culture. A child undergoes acculturation, wherein he or she learns to think and act appropriately for his or her setting.

45. C: In a unitary system of government, almost all control is held by the central government. The central government makes the laws, and the local governments are not allowed to overrule them. Although the unitary system is often associated with repressive regimes like that of North Korea, it also exists in countries like Japan and Great Britain. A unitary system tends to work better in countries with homogenous populations and relatively little cultural difference between regions. A federation, meanwhile, is a system in which the central government has some powers but grants others to local governments. The United States is a federation. A democracy is a system in which the people elect government officials. A democracy could be a unitary system, but it does not have to be. In a

confederation, the central government has much less power than the regional and local governments. In such a system, the central government is usually only responsible for defense and trade with other nations.

46. B: English is part of the Indo-European language family. This language family has its origins in the language spoken over 5,000 years ago by the inhabitants of what is now eastern Europe. Greek, Latin, and Sanskrit are all members of this language family. Romance languages are those derived from Latin. Spanish, French, and Italian are Romance languages. Latin is a member of the Indo-European language family, but it is not considered a direct antecedent of English. Amerindian languages are those of the indigenous peoples of the Americas. Navajo is one example of an Amerindian language. Finally, the Papuan language family includes all the dialects spoken by the inhabitants of Papua New Guinea and surrounding islands in the Pacific Ocean.

47. B: The Arab districts in North African cities are known as medinas. These are typically old neighborhoods surrounding a large mosque. Many Arabs who made their living in trade eventually settled in countries like Algeria, Tunisia, and Libya. There, they influenced culture by bringing Sunni Islam to the indigenous people. A souk, meanwhile, is a market area surrounding the mosque in the medina. A wadi is a dry North African creek bed, which becomes an essential source of water during the sporadic rains. The location of wadis has been a crucial factor in the political and economic history of North Africa. A bazaar, finally, is an open-air market in the Middle East.

48. C: Chinese is not an alphabetic language, which means that it is not written as a series of different sequences of letters. In English, for instance, all the words are made up of combinations of 26 letters. There are upper-case and lower-case forms of these letters, but these forms are constant. The same is true of all alphabetic languages, including Spanish, Russian, and Arabic. Chinese, on the other hand, is an orthographic language in which entire words are represented by pictures that are known as ideograms or characters. Learning to read an orthographic language requires the mastery of thousands of ideograms. In Chinese, a basic vocabulary includes 20,000 characters.

49. C: The greatest area of corn production is in the United States, specifically in the so-called Corn Belt that runs from northern Florida and eastern Texas all the way up to Iowa and Pennsylvania. Corn has traditionally been the specialty grain of the Americas, although it is now grown as a subsistence crop all over the world. Indeed, all the incorrect answer choices are areas that produce significant amounts of corn, though not as much as the Corn Belt. Corn is useful because it can grow in various climates and can be converted into a number of different products.

50. D: One result of NAFTA, the North American Free Trade Agreement, has been that Mexico has sought to enter into other trade agreements. This is because NAFTA has been a big success for Mexico. After the implementation of NAFTA in 1993, trade barriers among Canada, the United States, and Mexico were removed. The relative poverty of Mexico meant that it could create inexpensive centers of manufacturing, from which finished goods could be sent north. In fact, there are thousands of industrial centers along the northern border of Mexico. These factories are known as *maquiladoras*, and they make goods almost exclusively for sale in the United States and Canada. NAFTA has diminished unemployment and raised wages in Mexico over the last two decades.

51. C: The death rate of Henrytown is 8. Death rate is calculated as the number of deaths every year for every thousand people. Of course, the population of Henrytown is only 500, so it requires a quick calculation to obtain the death rate. This can be accomplished with the following equation: $4 / x = 500 / 1000$. This equation basically means "4 is to 500 as x is to 1000." The equation is solved by first cross multiplying, which yields $4,000 = 500x$. Then, both sides are divided by 500 to isolate the variable. This indicates that x is equal to 8.

52. A: Of the four answer choices, New York City is the most likely to be considered a modern cultural hearth. A cultural hearth is an area from which cultural trends emanate. Geographers suggest that there were seven original cultural hearths, including Mesoamerica and the Indus River Valley. The modes of living that originated in these areas emanated out into the rest of the world. These days, the cultural hearths tend to be the cities and countries with the most economic power. Of the four answer choices, New York City is clearly the wealthiest and the most influential. The styles and trends that originate in New York City find their way into communities all around the world.

53. A: According to Mark Jefferson, London would be considered the primate city of England. In 1939, Jefferson published an influential article, "The Law of the Primate City," in which he defined the primate city as that which most completely represents the culture of the nation it lies within. So, for instance, Paris would be the primate city of France, and Beijing would most likely be the primate city of China. In some cases, it can be difficult to name the primate city; for example, in the case of the United States, it might be hard to choose between Washington, DC and New York City. Many of the candidates for primate city status in Africa and South America are somewhat diminished by the heavy influence of foreign powers.

54. D: The popularity of hockey in Canada and the northern United States is an example of direct diffusion. Direct diffusion is the transfer of cultural practices and ideas between two groups living in close proximity to each other. Expansion diffusion, also known as forced diffusion, is the transfer of cultural practices from a subjugating culture to a subjugated culture. One example of expansion diffusion was the Western imposition of trading practices on China during the nineteenth and early twentieth centuries. Indirect diffusion is the spread of cultural traits over a long distance without there necessarily being any direct contact between the cultures. The popularity in the United States of henna tattoos, which originated in India, is an example of indirect diffusion.

55. B: Elections are not necessary to be recognized as a nation. Indeed, many nations are ruled by individuals or cabals who never allow elections to be held. Geographers assert that there are four criteria for nationhood: defined territory, government, sovereignty, and population. A nation must have land and other natural resources to exist. A nation also must have some form of government, whether it be tyrannical or democratic. Some level of central administration indicates the unity of the nation. A nation must have sovereignty; that is, it must not be directly controlled by some other country. Finally, and perhaps most obviously, a nation must have a population.

56. C: Animistic religions include the belief that the natural world is imbued with spirits. Animists believe, for example, that trees, rocks, and animals are divine in some way. This sort of belief system is typical of Native Americans and the indigenous peoples of West Africa (for instance, the Asante). Many sociologists have noted that animist cultures often demonstrate greater reverence for the natural world. Monotheism is a belief that there is

only one God. Christianity, Judaism, and Islam are all monotheistic religions. Pantheism is the belief that everything is a manifestation of the Divine Spirit. Polytheism is a belief in multiple gods. Hinduism is the most popular polytheistic religion.

57. B: A sphere of influence is a region in which a foreign power has some political and economic control but does not directly govern. One classic example is the sphere of influence held by European nations in China in the nineteenth and early twentieth centuries. These regions were ostensibly still part of China but had their politics and trade manipulated by the governments of foreign nations. Spheres of influence are less formal than colonies or settlements, which are directly under the control of the foreign government. An enclave, meanwhile, is a country that is entirely surrounded by some other country.

58. A: Hamilton has the greater population density. Population density is a measure of the number of people living in a particular area. It is usually calculated in units of citizens per square mile or square kilometer. The respective population densities of these two towns, then, can be calculated by dividing the number of citizens by the number of area units. So, the population density of Hamilton is 400 / 12 = 33 citizens per square mile, and the population of Burrsville is 300 / 10 = 30 citizens per square mile.

59. D: When a person grows only enough food to feed himself and his family, he is engaged in subsistence farming. The peasants of undeveloped countries are often forced to rely on subsistence farming because they lack the equipment and water resources to expand their crop. Of course, subsistence farming is not an ideal arrangement because a drought or monsoon can wipe out an entire crop and endanger the lives of the farmers. Nomadic herding is constant migration accompanied by livestock, particularly cows or sheep. Commercial farming is large scale enough to allow some or all the crops to be sold in a market. Sharecropping is a system wherein a landowner allows tenant farmers to use his or her land in exchange for a portion of the harvest.

60. A: One example of the multiplier effect of large cities would be if the presence of specialized equipment for an industry attracted even more business. Large cities tend to grow even larger for a number of reasons: they have more skilled workers, they have greater concentrations of specialized equipment, and they have already-functioning markets. These factors all make it easier for a business to begin operations in a large city than elsewhere. Thus, the populations and economic productivity of large cities tend to grow quickly. Some governments have sought to mitigate this trend by clustering groups of similar industries in smaller cities.

61. B: In the early expanding stage of demographic transition, the fertility rate remains high, while the mortality rate declines sharply. Demographic transition is a model for how the population growth rate of a region changes over time. It consists of four stages. In the first, the high stationary stage, fertility and mortality rates are high, so the population rate varies, and there is little growth. In the second stage, some of the problems causing mortality have been solved, but fertility continues at the same rate. This means that the population begins to expand at a greater rate. In the third stage, the late expanding stage, the fertility rate begins to decline, but because the mortality rate remains low, there is continuing growth. In the low stationary stage, there are low rates of fertility and mortality, and consequently there is a low rate of growth.

62. D: In the saturation stage of spatial diffusion, the process slows down and eventually stops altogether. The Swedish geographer Torsten Hägerstrand outlined four stages in spatial diffusion, which is the spread of innovation throughout a geographical region. In the primary stage, the innovation first appears and is adopted in the immediate vicinity. In the diffusion stage, the innovation is used in increasingly far-flung areas. In the condensing stage, any areas that had not already received the innovation do so. In the saturation stage, the innovation is either replaced or abandoned because it is no longer believed to have utility.

63. C: In the United States, geographers typically define a hamlet as a settlement with fewer than 100 inhabitants. A hamlet may have a few businesses, but it is unlikely to have a post office or a government office. A village is slightly larger than a hamlet; it may contain about 500 to 1,000 people. A village is likely to have a grocery store. A town is larger than a village. It usually has about 2,500 inhabitants. A city is larger than a town.

64. A: Traders from distant regions of the world adopt a lingua franca, or a shared vocabulary of terms. The lingua franca used by ancient merchants often included words from many different languages. These days, English often serves as the lingua franca for global businessmen. There is no conscious organization of a lingua franca; it, like other languages, emerges in response to the communication needs of the people who use it. Pidgin languages are versions of English used by the natives in areas colonized by the British and the Americans. These languages typically have smaller vocabularies and less sophisticated grammar than standard English. A conurbation is a combination of two urban areas. Finally, in geography, an activity space is the physical place in which a person performs his or her daily tasks.

65. B: Grinding wheat into flour is an example of secondary economic activity. A secondary economic activity is one in which raw materials are converted into a more valuable product. Another secondary economic activity would be weaving cotton into yarn. A primary economic activity is a direct use of natural resources. Hunting is one example of a primary economic activity. Service jobs are considered to be tertiary economic activities. These jobs do not necessarily entail the acquisition and use of raw materials. Lawyers and bus drivers are just two examples of tertiary economic actors. Quaternary economic activities entail the acquisition, synthesis, and production of information. Teachers and writers are among those who make up the quaternary level of economic activity.

66. D: Population is not one of the necessary characteristics of a geographical region. A geographical region does not require people. Indeed, such regions as the Hindu Kush or Death Valley have few if any inhabitants. A region does need to have area and location, however. It must be capable of being mapped, and it must be able to be found by travelers. A region also needs homogeneity, which means that it needs some sort of consistent features. It makes sense for a region to include a group of nearby mountains, but it does not make sense for it to include a mountain and an island hundreds of miles away. In human geography, it is necessary for the inhabitants of a region to share some cultural characteristics, such as religion or language.

67. A: Stephen's routine is considered by geographers to be cyclic movement. This type of movement happens regularly, does not involve traveling over a great distance, and does not require a change of residence. Because Stephen returns home every evening, he cannot be said to be changing residence. A migratory movement is a permanent change of residence,

especially from one country or region to another. A cross-boundary movement is any change in location that involves crossing a national border. A periodic movement is similar to a cyclic movement, except it takes place over a longer time. Going to college for a semester is an example of periodic movement.

68. B: Diversity is not one of the demographic variables. Demographers, or those who study population, rely on fertility, mortality, and migration to determine the number of people in a region. The general equation is *Total Population = Original Population + Births – Deaths + Immigration – Emigration*. The natural increase, on the other hand, is calculated only with the number of births and deaths. The diversity of a population may be relevant to subsequent research performed by the demographer, but it is not considered one of the essential three demographic variables.

69. C: The popularity of Japanese anime comics in the United States is an example of indirect diffusion. Indirect cultural diffusion is the spread of ideas or practices from one culture to a distant culture. Indeed, the primary difference between direct and indirect diffusion is distance, or adjacency. Because the United States and Japan are not close to each other, trends that begin in Japan and take root in the United States are examples of indirect diffusion. The Internet has made indirect diffusion a much more common phenomenon.

70. D: A kibbutz is a collective farm in Israel in which the economy closely resembles that of a communist society. Those who live on a kibbutz do not own private property; rather, they share living space with one another. Children are raised by the entire community. Although the kibbutz has become slightly less popular in recent years, there are still many of these arrangements in Israel. A colony is any settlement controlled by the government in another country. A colony could be administered like a communist society, but it need not be so. A ghetto is an impoverished urban district primarily populated by people of a certain race, religion, or ethnicity. A shtetl is a Jewish community, especially one in eastern Europe, that existed over the past few centuries.

71. B: St. Petersburg is crucial to the Russian economy because of its location along the Baltic Sea. Access to the Baltic has been a driving force throughout Russian history. Peter the Great finally conquered lands adjacent to the Baltic in the early eighteenth century, and he built there the magnificent city that bears his name. After the Russian Revolution and the creation of the USSR, St. Petersburg became known as Leningrad. The name reverted to St. Petersburg after the fall of the Soviet Union. The city remains an essential outlet to the rest of the world.

72. C: Yemen is not a member of OPEC, the Organization of Petroleum Exporting Countries. Yemen has some deposits of oil, but the nation has only recently begun developing them. This, along with a desperate water shortage, accounts for Yemen's position as the poorest nation in the Middle East. OPEC was established in 1960 to set oil prices and production. Until the formation of OPEC, many oil-producing nations felt they were being exploited by Western oil companies. This organization has obtained a great deal of power and is held responsible for the gas shortages that wracked the United States during the late 1970s.

73. A: Land redistribution was one consequence of the Mexican Revolution of 1910. Up to that point, all the arable land in the country was controlled by a select group of aristocrats. There were approximately 8,000 haciendas, which could only be farmed by certain people. After the Mexican Revolution ended in 1920, the newly formed government moved to

purchase these haciendas and provide access to peasant farmers. Much of this land is distributed in what are called *ejidos*, or collective farms owned and operated by several people. Nevertheless, to date, the Mexican government has only succeeded in redistributing about half of the original haciendas. As for the other answer choices, Mexico had already become a sovereign nation in 1821 after a long struggle with Spain. The Mexican Revolution did not usher in a period of multi-party rule; in fact, it was not until the election of Vicente Fox in 2000 that the country had a president who was not a member of the Institutional Revolutionary Party. Finally, the massive construction of railroads in Mexico had already taken place during the late nineteenth century, mainly to provide foreign economic interests with access to Mexico's natural resources.

74. D: The Sahel, a belt of grasslands just south of the Sahara Desert, has long been a focus of agricultural efforts in Africa. This semiarid region has provided sustenance to people and animals for thousands of years. In the last thousand years, stores of salt and gold were found there, giving rise to empires in Ghana and Mali. Changes in climate have expanded the Sahara, however, and pushed the Sahel farther south. The Qattara Depression is a low-lying desert in Egypt. The Great Rift Valley is a region of faults and rocky hills that extends along the southeastern coast of Africa. The Congo Basin is a repository of sediment from the Ubangi and Congo rivers. It is in the northern half of what is now called the Democratic Republic of the Congo.

75. D: The two regions of the Czech Republic are Bohemia and Moravia. Bohemia is the western half of the country, including Prague. There are excellent mineral resources in this area of the country. The Czech economy is in large part supported by the export of coal, copper, lead, and iron ore. Moravia is the eastern half of the Czech Republic. It is less advanced than Bohemia and is currently struggling to bring its industrial infrastructure up to date. Czechoslovakia became two separate nations, the Czech Republic and Slovakia, in 1993. This separation was spurred by Slovak resentment of the domination of the government by the Czech majority.

76. A: In the early summer, a desert wind known as the khamsin stirs up sandstorms throughout Egypt. These storms can be so strong that they effectively blot out the sky. The possibility of these storms makes it extremely difficult for any serious agriculture or animal husbandry to be performed. They are another reason why 99 percent of the Egyptian population lives in the Nile Valley. A sirocco is any hot and dry wind originating in North Africa but felt in the southern Mediterranean nations of Europe. A zephyr is a gentle western wind. The fellaheen are the peasant farmers of Egypt.

77. B: The highest habitable region in Middle and South America is known as the *puna*, or *páramos*. This region ranges in altitude between 12,000 and 15,000 feet and lies primarily in the Andes Mountains. Only sheep and other rugged livestock can be herded at this height, so there is very little economic activity. *Tierra fria* lies just below the *puna*, between 6,000 and 12,000 feet in elevation. It is possible to cultivate wheat at this height. The *tierra helada* is an uninhabitable region over 15,000 feet high, just above the *puna*. This region is always covered in snow and ice. The *templada*, also known as the *tierra templada*, is a moderate region between 2,500 and 6,000 feet high. Coffee, corn, and tobacco can all be grown in this region.

78. C: Shortly after holding its first free election in 1980, the country formerly known as Rhodesia officially became Zimbabwe. Rhodesia was the name given to this land by the

British colonizers. Rhodesia had declared independence from Britain in 1965, but the country continued to be controlled by a white minority. After considerable pressure from the United States and Britain, Rhodesia finally democratized and elected a black president, Robert Mugabe. Unfortunately, under Mugabe, the country now known as Zimbabwe has slid into dictatorship and endured an almost total economic collapse.

79. D: Both Marseilles and Genoa are important ports on the Mediterranean. Marseilles is on the southern coast of France. It is known for its lively mix of French and North African cultures. Marseilles is the second busiest port in western Europe. Genoa, meanwhile, is a thriving port on the western coast of Italy. The shipping traffic in Genoa has increased in the past few decades, as the surrounding region, known as the Po Valley, has become a center of manufacturing.

80. D: In the Indian tradition known as purdah, women cover their faces in public. This veiling originally was limited to the Muslim community but subsequently spread to the Hindus as well. The other answer choices are terms related to this topic. A burqa is a whole-body covering worn by Muslim women. Only the eyes and hands are visible when a woman is wearing a burqa. A hijab is a head covering worn by Muslim women. There are many styles of hijab, though many are simple scarves. A sari is a traditional Indian garment composed of a long piece of cloth, which is wrapped around the body and draped over the shoulder.

81. D: The religious practice of most Japanese people incorporates elements of Shinto, Buddhism, and Confucianism. Shinto is the oldest religion in Japan; it focuses on the divinity of the natural world and the importance of honoring ancestors. Shinto has been influenced heavily by Buddhism and Confucianism, both of which were imported from China. The Zen school of Buddhism began in Japan. It emphasizes meditation and realization of life's impermanence. Japanese religion and culture are affected by Confucianism, which asserts the importance of hierarchical relationships between people and the natural world.

82. A: Aksum became an imperial power in Africa 2,000 years ago in large part because of its access to major waterways. Specifically, the lands held by Aksum, in what is now Ethiopia, bordered the Red Sea to the east and the Blue Nile to the west. This enabled Aksum to trade with Arabs, Persians, other Africans, and even Europeans. The growing economic power of Aksum was mirrored by military and political success. One major hindrance, however, was religion: Aksum became a Christian nation in the third century, and influential Arabs preferred to deal with fellow Muslims.

83. D: The Uighurs (pronounced WEE-gurs) are a minority group of Muslims in northwestern China. This group is discriminated against by the Chinese government; they are not allowed to practice their religion freely, and they are paid lower wages than the majority Han Chinese. Some Uighurs have declared a desire for independence, but this is unlikely to happen. Xinjiang Province, where most of the Uighurs live, is rich in natural resources, so the Chinese government will not let it go without a fight. The Tibetans are Buddhists from a region in what is now southwestern China. China's conquest of Tibet was frowned upon by most of the rest of the world. Mandarin is the official dialect of Chinese. It comes from the northern part of the country. The Falun Gong is a religion that combines Daoism, Buddhism, and other spiritual disciplines. It has been outlawed by the Chinese government.

84. B: Buddhists do not consider Jerusalem a holy city. Christians, Muslims, and Jews all do, though for different reasons. Christians honor Jerusalem as the city near which Jesus was crucified. For Muslims, it is the city from which Mohammed ascended into heaven. For Jews, Jerusalem is the former site of the Temple, which was originally built by King Solomon around 960 B.C. The struggle for control of Jerusalem has been going on for thousands of years. Currently, the city is divided between Israel and the Palestinian territory on the West Bank of the Jordan River.

85. A: Moldova is not one of the Baltic states. Latvia, Lithuania, and Estonia all border the Baltic Sea, which has enabled them to become major traders. Unfortunately, the smallness and advantageous locations of these nations has made them attractive to invaders. The Soviet Union took over these lands in 1939, and it was not until 1991 that they regained independence. All three of these nations are now struggling to establish themselves as viable economic actors.

86. A: Most Pakistanis live in farming villages. Indeed, the total population of the 68 largest cities in Pakistan is only about one quarter of the nation's citizenry. Karachi is the most populous city in Pakistan; it has approximately 12 million citizens. The Baluchistan Plateau encompasses most of southern Pakistan, but it is tough terrain and mainly unsuitable for farming. The Khyber Pass is one of the world's most famous mountain passes. It winds through the Hindu Kush mountains, connecting Peshawar in Pakistan with Kabul in Afghanistan. The winter climate of the Khyber Pass is much too forbidding to allow many permanent residents.

87. B: The Mongols are known as nomadic herders, meaning that they do not build permanent villages but move about the land with animals, usually sheep and goats. Mongolia is an enormous, dry country that is dominated by the Gobi Desert in the south and grasslands in the north. Mongols traditionally lived in portable tents, known as yurts. In recent decades, however, more Mongols have begun to migrate to the large cities of China and to the capital of Mongolia, Ulan Bator.

88. D: Alaska is the largest state in terms of area. It is about 660,000 square miles, while the second-largest state, Texas, is about 270,000 square miles. Despite its immensity, however, Alaska is sparsely populated, with fewer than 630,000 permanent residents. Much of the state is covered in ice year round, and there are several months during the winter in which the sun barely rises at all. Nevertheless, Alaska is an incredible source of natural resources for the continental United States. In particular, Alaska supplies large amounts of oil, timber, and fish to the rest of the nation. There is a continuous conflict between environmentalists and those who want to harvest the state's natural resources more aggressively.

89. D: One of the unique features of the Yucatan Peninsula in Mexico is its collection of sinkholes created by the collapse of limestone caverns beneath the surface. Unlike most of the rest of Mexico, which has firm bedrock, the Yucatan is supported by porous limestone. When this limestone becomes too weak, it creates deep sinkholes that can be used as wells. The other answer choices are all false statements about the Yucatan Peninsula. This region of Mexico is relatively unpopulated; the largest city, Merida, has only about 500,000 citizens. The Yucatan is much flatter than the rest of Mexico; indeed, it is this absence of prehistoric volcano sites that accounts for the difference in soil. Finally, the Yucatan was once inhabited by Mayans, not Aztecs. Some scholars believe that the modern name of the

- 135 -

peninsula is derived from the Mayan words for "I do not understand your words," which was merely the unrelated reply to questions from Spanish explorers.

90. B: The United States and Canada share the longest undefended border in the world. It is more than 5,000 miles long, stretching from the Atlantic to the Pacific. The fact that there is no fence or military guard on this border is evidence of the strong, friendly bond between these two nations. Indeed, Canada and the United States are also major trading partners. The United States buys about 85 percent of all Canadian exports, and Canada buys about a quarter of everything sold abroad by the United States. There has never been a significant problem with illegal migration between the United States and Canada, though there has been considerable smuggling.

91. D: Under Gorbachev, the Union of Soviet Socialist Republics (USSR) began a program of economic reorganization known as perestroika. This program included a shift in power from central bureaucrats to local governments. Glasnost was the general policy of openness and transparency adopted by the Soviet government under Gorbachev. Formerly, government actions had been shrouded in secrecy and were often marked by corruption. Rubles are the unit of currency in Russia, as they were in the USSR. Soviets were the legislative assemblies that represented communities, regions, and the nation during the existence of the USSR.

92. C: The pampas in Argentina and Uruguay are temperate grasslands. These enormous stretches of interior space feature rolling hills, mild temperatures, and fertile soil. For many years, cattle farming was the dominant economic focus on the pampas. The cowboys who worked this land were known as gauchos. In recent decades, however, the pampas have increasingly been used for the cultivation of wheat. Although the winters in this region can be cold, the pampas manage to supply more than 80 percent of the grain used in Argentina.

93. A: The South Asian nation of Sri Lanka, formerly known as Ceylon, has been the site of almost constant fighting between Sinhalese and Tamils. Sri Lanka is an island nation off the southeast coast of India. The Sinhalese arrived from northern India in about 500 BCE, and soon after, the Tamils arrived from southern India. Ever since, they have been in competition for control of the island. For the most part, the Sinhalese have remained in control of the government. However, the Tamils maintained a guerilla campaign against the government for decades. In late 2009, the Sri Lankan military finally succeeded in quashing this insurgency.

94. B: Dutch is not one of the three official languages in Switzerland, a nation unique in Europe for having several distinct cultures within its borders. The official name of the country is the Swiss Federation. The majority of Swiss speak German, and cities like Zurich and Bern are predominately German in architecture and culture. Geneva, on the other hand, is a largely French-speaking city. There is a local Swiss dialect, known as Romansch, which is spoken by many people despite not being one of the official languages.

95. D: Kemal Ataturk was responsible for the rapid westernization of Turkey in the early twentieth century. He had spent considerable time in western Europe, and in 1923, soon after becoming president, he threw out the Islamic government structures and declared Turkey a republic. He went on to replace the Arabic alphabet and calendar with the Western versions. He also added to the rights of women, giving them the power to divorce their

husbands, vote, and seek office. Even today, Turkey remains the Muslim nation with the closest similarities to the nations of western Europe.

96. A: The Atlantic provinces of Canada are Labrador, Prince Edward Island, New Brunswick, and Nova Scotia. All of these provinces have a coastline on the Atlantic Ocean. Although these four provinces represent only about 5 percent of Canada's total landmass, they have played a major role in the development of the nation. In particular, the fishing industry off the coasts of Nova Scotia and Newfoundland has long been a solid component of the Canadian economy. There is also a great deal of agriculture in Nova Scotia and Prince Edward Island.

97. C: Before China took control of Hong Kong in 1997, the island was administrated by Great Britain. This transfer of power had been planned for a long time. One of the conditions for the transfer was that Hong Kong will retain political and economic independence from China. Hong Kong is referred to as a Special Administrative Region of China, and its citizens are given much more leeway than other Chinese citizens. To date, China has been successful in harnessing the economic power of Hong Kong and allowing two systems of governance to coexist within one nation.

98. B: A *favela* is a shantytown in Brazil. These communities begin when a parcel of vacant or abandoned land is taken over by squatters. Over time, small villages crop up, featuring rudimentary architecture and local government. In many cases, *favelas* are outside of the control of the Brazilian government and are instead managed by criminal syndicates and gangs. The problem of the *favela* is one of the greatest facing modern Brazil as it attempts to join the top tier of nations. A *barrio* may be just a neighborhood, but it typically refers to a low-income district in Central or South America. A *maquiladora* is an industrial district in northern Mexico. These areas manufacture goods for sale mostly in the United States. Finally, *ciudad* is the Spanish word for *city*.

99. A: The Dutch lands reclaimed through a network of dikes and canals are known as polders. This process has been ongoing since the 1200s when the Dutch first began using windmills to dry the land. About a third of Holland is below sea level, so it has taken a great deal of engineering ingenuity to keep the land inhabitable. The entire country is dotted with dikes, or thick earthen embankments that keep back the encroaching waters. Cantons are the states in Switzerland and Austria. Grabens are the narrow, sunken strips of land that lie between faults. There are a number of grabens in Greece. Moors are treeless, boggy patches of land.

100. D: Japan imports the second-highest amount of oil after the United States. Following World War II, Japan rapidly became one of the foremost industrial powers. Despite thriving economically, however, Japan is not especially rich in natural resources. Only slightly more than 10 percent of the nation's land can be farmed, and there are no significant oil deposits. For this reason, Japan must import most of the raw materials it needs for its manufacturing base.

Secret Key #1 - Time is Your Greatest Enemy

Pace Yourself

Wear a watch. At the beginning of the test, check the time (or start a chronometer on your watch to count the minutes), and check the time after every few questions to make sure you are "on schedule."

If you are forced to speed up, do it efficiently. Usually one or more answer choices can be eliminated without too much difficulty. Above all, don't panic. Don't speed up and just begin guessing at random choices. By pacing yourself, and continually monitoring your progress against your watch, you will always know exactly how far ahead or behind you are with your available time. If you find that you are one minute behind on the test, don't skip one question without spending any time on it, just to catch back up. Take 15 fewer seconds on the next four questions, and after four questions you'll have caught back up. Once you catch back up, you can continue working each problem at your normal pace.

Furthermore, don't dwell on the problems that you were rushed on. If a problem was taking up too much time and you made a hurried guess, it must be difficult. The difficult questions are the ones you are most likely to miss anyway, so it isn't a big loss. It is better to end with more time than you need than to run out of time.

Lastly, sometimes it is beneficial to slow down if you are constantly getting ahead of time. You are always more likely to catch a careless mistake by working more slowly than quickly, and among very high-scoring test takers (those who are likely to have lots of time left over), careless errors affect the score more than mastery of material.

Secret Key #2 - Guessing is not Guesswork

You probably know that guessing is a good idea. Unlike other standardized tests, there is no penalty for getting a wrong answer. Even if you have no idea about a question, you still have a 20-25% chance of getting it right.

Most test takers do not understand the impact that proper guessing can have on their score. Unless you score extremely high, guessing will significantly contribute to your final score.

Monkeys Take the Test

What most test takers don't realize is that to insure that 20-25% chance, you have to guess randomly. If you put 20 monkeys in a room to take this test, assuming they answered once per question and behaved themselves, on average they would get 20-25% of the questions correct.

Put 20 test takers in the room, and the average will be much lower among guessed questions. Why?

1. The test writers intentionally write deceptive answer choices that "look" right. A test taker has no idea about a question, so he picks the "best looking" answer, which is often wrong. The monkey has no idea what looks good and what doesn't, so it will consistently be right about 20-25% of the time.
2. Test takers will eliminate answer choices from the guessing pool based on a hunch or intuition. Simple but correct answers often get excluded, leaving a 0% chance of being correct. The monkey has no clue, and often gets lucky with the best choice.

This is why the process of elimination endorsed by most test courses is flawed and detrimental to your performance. Test takers don't guess; they make an ignorant stab in the dark that is usually worse than random.

$5 Challenge

Let me introduce one of the most valuable ideas of this course—the $5 challenge:

- *You only mark your "best guess" if you are willing to bet $5 on it.*
- *You only eliminate choices from guessing if you are willing to bet $5 on it.*

Why $5? Five dollars is an amount of money that is small yet not insignificant, and can really add up fast (20 questions could cost you $100). Likewise, each answer choice on one question of the test will have a small impact on your overall score, but it can really add up to a lot of points in the end.

The process of elimination IS valuable. The following shows your chance of guessing it right:

If you eliminate wrong answer choices until only this many remain:	Chance of getting it correct:
1	100%
2	50%
3	33%

However, if you accidentally eliminate the right answer or go on a hunch for an incorrect answer, your chances drop dramatically—to 0%. By guessing among all the answer choices, you are GUARANTEED to have a shot at the right answer.

That's why the $5 test is so valuable. If you give up the advantage and safety of a pure guess, it had better be worth the risk.

What we still haven't covered is how to be sure that whatever guess you make is truly random. Here's the easiest way:

- *Always pick the first answer choice among those remaining.*

Such a technique means that you have decided, **before you see a single test question**, exactly how you are going to guess, and since the order of choices tells you nothing about which one is correct, this guessing technique is perfectly random.

This section is not meant to scare you away from making educated guesses or eliminating choices; you just need to define when a choice is worth eliminating. The $5 test, along with a pre-defined random guessing strategy, is the best way to make sure you reap all of the benefits of guessing.

Secret Key #3 - Practice Smarter, Not Harder

Many test takers delay the test preparation process because they dread the awful amounts of practice time they think necessary to succeed on the test. We have refined an effective method that will take you only a fraction of the time.

There are a number of "obstacles" in the path to success. Among these are answering questions, finishing in time, and mastering test-taking strategies. All must be executed on the day of the test at peak performance, or your score will suffer. The test is a mental marathon that has a large impact on your future.

Just like a marathon runner, it is important to work your way up to the full challenge. So first you just worry about questions, and then time, and finally strategy:

Success Strategy

1. Find a good source for practice tests.
2. If you are willing to make a larger time investment, consider using more than one study guide. Often the different approaches of multiple authors will help you "get" difficult concepts.
3. Take a practice test with no time constraints, with all study helps, "open book." Take your time with questions and focus on applying strategies.
4. Take a practice test with time constraints, with all guides, "open book."
5. Take a final practice test without open material and with time limits.

If you have time to take more practice tests, just repeat step 5. By gradually exposing yourself to the full rigors of the test environment, you will condition your mind to the stress of test day and maximize your success.

Secret Key #4 - Prepare, Don't Procrastinate

Let me state an obvious fact: if you take the test three times, you will probably get three different scores. This is due to the way you feel on test day, the level of preparedness you have, and the version of the test you see. Despite the test writers' claims to the contrary, some versions of the test WILL be easier for you than others.

Since your future depends so much on your score, you should maximize your chances of success. In order to maximize the likelihood of success, you've got to prepare in advance. This means taking practice tests and spending time learning the information and test taking strategies you will need to succeed.

Never go take the actual test as a "practice" test, expecting that you can just take it again if you need to. Take all the practice tests you can on your own, but when you go to take the official test, be prepared, be focused, and do your best the first time!

Secret Key #5 - Test Yourself

Everyone knows that time is money. There is no need to spend too much of your time or too little of your time preparing for the test. You should only spend as much of your precious time preparing as is necessary for you to get the score you need.

Once you have taken a practice test under real conditions of time constraints, then you will know if you are ready for the test or not.

If you have scored extremely high the first time that you take the practice test, then there is not much point in spending countless hours studying. You are already there.

Benchmark your abilities by retaking practice tests and seeing how much you have improved. Once you consistently score high enough to guarantee success, then you are ready.

If you have scored well below where you need, then knuckle down and begin studying in earnest. Check your improvement regularly through the use of practice tests under real conditions. Above all, don't worry, panic, or give up. The key is perseverance!

Then, when you go to take the test, remain confident and remember how well you did on the practice tests. If you can score high enough on a practice test, then you can do the same on the real thing.

General Strategies

The most important thing you can do is to ignore your fears and jump into the test immediately. Do not be overwhelmed by any strange-sounding terms. You have to jump into the test like jumping into a pool—all at once is the easiest way.

Make Predictions

As you read and understand the question, try to guess what the answer will be. Remember that several of the answer choices are wrong, and once you begin reading them, your mind will immediately become cluttered with answer choices designed to throw you off. Your mind is typically the most focused immediately after you have read the question and digested its contents. If you can, try to predict what the correct answer will be. You may be surprised at what you can predict.

Quickly scan the choices and see if your prediction is in the listed answer choices. If it is, then you can be quite confident that you have the right answer. It still won't hurt to check the other answer choices, but most of the time, you've got it!

Answer the Question

It may seem obvious to only pick answer choices that answer the question, but the test writers can create some excellent answer choices that are wrong. Don't pick an answer just because it sounds right, or you believe it to be true. It MUST answer the question. Once you've made your selection, always go back and check it against the question and make sure that you didn't misread the question and that the answer choice does answer the question posed.

Benchmark

After you read the first answer choice, decide if you think it sounds correct or not. If it doesn't, move on to the next answer choice. If it does, mentally mark that answer choice. This doesn't mean that you've definitely selected it as your answer choice, it just means that it's the best you've seen thus far. Go ahead and read the next choice. If the next choice is worse than the one you've already selected, keep going to the next answer choice. If the next choice is better than the choice you've already selected, mentally mark the new answer choice as your best guess.

The first answer choice that you select becomes your standard. Every other answer choice must be benchmarked against that standard. That choice is correct until proven otherwise by another answer choice beating it out. Once you've decided that no other answer choice seems as good, do one final check to ensure that your answer choice answers the question posed.

Valid Information

Don't discount any of the information provided in the question. Every piece of information may be necessary to determine the correct answer. None of the information in the question is there to throw you off (while the answer choices will certainly have information to throw you off). If two seemingly unrelated topics are discussed, don't ignore either. You can be confident there is a relationship, or it wouldn't be included in the question, and you are probably going to have to determine what is that relationship to find the answer.

Avoid "Fact Traps"

Don't get distracted by a choice that is factually true. Your search is for the answer that answers the question. Stay focused and don't fall for an answer that is true but irrelevant. Always go back to the question and make sure you're choosing an answer that actually answers the question and is not just a true statement. An answer can be factually correct, but it MUST answer the question asked. Additionally, two answers can both be seemingly correct, so be sure to read all of the answer choices, and make sure that you get the one that BEST answers the question.

Milk the Question

Some of the questions may throw you completely off. They might deal with a subject you have not been exposed to, or one that you haven't reviewed in years. While your lack of knowledge about the subject will be a hindrance, the question itself can give you many clues that will help you find the correct answer. Read the question carefully and look for clues. Watch particularly for adjectives and nouns describing difficult terms or words that you don't recognize. Regardless of whether you completely understand a word or not, replacing it with a synonym, either provided or one you more familiar with, may help you to understand what the questions are asking. Rather than wracking your mind about specific detailed information concerning a difficult term or word, try to use mental substitutes that are easier to understand.

The Trap of Familiarity

Don't just choose a word because you recognize it. On difficult questions, you may not recognize a number of words in the answer choices. The test writers don't put "make-believe" words on the test, so don't think that just because you only recognize all the words in one answer choice that that answer choice must be correct. If you only recognize words in one answer choice, then focus on that one. Is it correct? Try your best to determine if it is correct. If it is, that's great. If not, eliminate it. Each word and answer choice you eliminate increases your chances of getting the question correct, even if you then have to guess among the unfamiliar choices.

Eliminate Answers

Eliminate choices as soon as you realize they are wrong. But be careful! Make sure you consider all of the possible answer choices. Just because one appears right, doesn't mean that the next one won't be even better! The test writers will usually put more than one good answer choice for every question, so read all of them. Don't worry if you are stuck between two that seem right. By getting down to just two remaining possible choices, your odds are now 50/50. Rather than wasting too much time, play the odds. You are guessing, but guessing wisely because you've been able to knock out some of the answer choices that you know are wrong. If you are eliminating choices and realize that the last answer choice you are left with is also obviously wrong, don't panic. Start over and consider each choice again. There may easily be something that you missed the first time and will realize on the second pass.

Tough Questions

If you are stumped on a problem or it appears too hard or too difficult, don't waste time. Move on! Remember though, if you can quickly check for obviously incorrect answer choices, your chances of guessing correctly are greatly improved. Before you completely give up, at least try to knock out a couple of possible answers. Eliminate what you can and then guess at the remaining answer choices before moving on.

Brainstorm

If you get stuck on a difficult question, spend a few seconds quickly brainstorming. Run through the complete list of possible answer choices. Look at each choice and ask yourself, "Could this answer the question satisfactorily?" Go through each answer choice and consider it independently of the others. By systematically going through all possibilities, you may find something that you would otherwise overlook. Remember though that when you get stuck, it's important to try to keep moving.

Read Carefully

Understand the problem. Read the question and answer choices carefully. Don't miss the question because you misread the terms. You have plenty of time to read each question thoroughly and make sure you understand what is being asked. Yet a happy medium must be attained, so don't waste too much time. You must read carefully, but efficiently.

Face Value

When in doubt, use common sense. Always accept the situation in the problem at face value. Don't read too much into it. These problems will not require you to make huge leaps of logic. The test writers aren't trying to throw you off with a cheap trick. If you have to go beyond creativity and make a leap of logic in order to have an answer choice answer the question, then you should look at the other answer choices. Don't overcomplicate the problem by creating theoretical relationships or explanations that will warp time or space. These are normal problems rooted in reality. It's just that the applicable relationship or explanation may not be readily apparent and you have to figure things out. Use your common sense to interpret anything that isn't clear.

Prefixes

If you're having trouble with a word in the question or answer choices, try dissecting it. Take advantage of every clue that the word might include. Prefixes and suffixes can be a huge help. Usually they allow you to determine a basic meaning. Pre- means before, post-means after, pro - is positive, de- is negative. From these prefixes and suffixes, you can get an idea of the general meaning of the word and try to put it into context. Beware though of any traps. Just because con- is the opposite of pro-, doesn't necessarily mean congress is the opposite of progress!

Hedge Phrases

Watch out for critical hedge phrases, led off with words such as "likely," "may," "can," "sometimes," "often," "almost," "mostly," "usually," "generally," "rarely," and "sometimes." Question writers insert these hedge phrases to cover every possibility. Often an answer choice will be wrong simply because it leaves no room for exception. Unless the situation calls for them, avoid answer choices that have definitive words like "exactly," and "always."

Switchback Words

Stay alert for "switchbacks." These are the words and phrases frequently used to alert you to shifts in thought. The most common switchback word is "but." Others include "although," "however," "nevertheless," "on the other hand," "even though," "while," "in spite of," "despite," and "regardless of."

New Information

Correct answer choices will rarely have completely new information included. Answer choices typically are straightforward reflections of the material asked about and will directly relate to the question. If a new piece of information is included in an answer choice that doesn't even seem to relate to the topic being asked about, then that answer choice is likely incorrect. All of the information needed to answer the question is usually provided for you in the question. You should not have to make guesses that are unsupported or choose answer choices that require unknown information that cannot be reasoned from what is given.

Time Management

On technical questions, don't get lost on the technical terms. Don't spend too much time on any one question. If you don't know what a term means, then odds are you aren't going to get much further since you don't have a dictionary. You should be able to immediately

- 144 -

recognize whether or not you know a term. If you don't, work with the other clues that you have—the other answer choices and terms provided—but don't waste too much time trying to figure out a difficult term that you don't know.

Contextual Clues

Look for contextual clues. An answer can be right but not the correct answer. The contextual clues will help you find the answer that is most right and is correct. Understand the context in which a phrase or statement is made. This will help you make important distinctions.

Don't Panic

Panicking will not answer any questions for you; therefore, it isn't helpful. When you first see the question, if your mind goes blank, take a deep breath. Force yourself to mechanically go through the steps of solving the problem using the strategies you've learned.

Pace Yourself

Don't get clock fever. It's easy to be overwhelmed when you're looking at a page full of questions, your mind is full of random thoughts and feeling confused, and the clock is ticking down faster than you would like. Calm down and maintain the pace that you have set for yourself. As long as you are on track by monitoring your pace, you are guaranteed to have enough time for yourself. When you get to the last few minutes of the test, it may seem like you won't have enough time left, but if you only have as many questions as you should have left at that point, then you're right on track!

Answer Selection

The best way to pick an answer choice is to eliminate all of those that are wrong, until only one is left and confirm that is the correct answer. Sometimes though, an answer choice may immediately look right. Be careful! Take a second to make sure that the other choices are not equally obvious. Don't make a hasty mistake. There are only two times that you should stop before checking other answers. First is when you are positive that the answer choice you have selected is correct. Second is when time is almost out and you have to make a quick guess!

Check Your Work

Since you will probably not know every term listed and the answer to every question, it is important that you get credit for the ones that you do know. Don't miss any questions through careless mistakes. If at all possible, try to take a second to look back over your answer selection and make sure you've selected the correct answer choice and haven't made a costly careless mistake (such as marking an answer choice that you didn't mean to mark). The time it takes for this quick double check should more than pay for itself in caught mistakes.

Beware of Directly Quoted Answers

Sometimes an answer choice will repeat word for word a portion of the question or reference section. However, beware of such exact duplication. It may be a trap! More than likely, the correct choice will paraphrase or summarize a point, rather than being exactly the same wording.

Slang

Scientific sounding answers are better than slang ones. An answer choice that begins "To compare the outcomes..." is much more likely to be correct than one that begins "Because some people insisted..."

Extreme Statements

Avoid wild answers that throw out highly controversial ideas that are proclaimed as established fact. An answer choice that states the "process should used in certain situations, if..." is much more likely to be correct than one that states the "process should be discontinued completely." The first is a calm rational statement and doesn't even make a definitive, uncompromising stance, using a hedge word "if" to provide wiggle room, whereas the second choice is a radical idea and far more extreme.

Answer Choice Families

When you have two or more answer choices that are direct opposites or parallels, one of them is usually the correct answer. For instance, if one answer choice states "x increases" and another answer choice states "x decreases" or "y increases," then those two or three answer choices are very similar in construction and fall into the same family of answer choices. A family of answer choices consists of two or three answer choices, very similar in construction, but often with directly opposite meanings. Usually the correct answer choice will be in that family of answer choices. The "odd man out" or answer choice that doesn't seem to fit the parallel construction of the other answer choices is more likely to be incorrect.

Special Report: How to Overcome Test Anxiety

The very nature of tests caters to some level of anxiety, nervousness, or tension, just as we feel for any important event that occurs in our lives. A little bit of anxiety or nervousness can be a good thing. It helps us with motivation, and makes achievement just that much sweeter. However, too much anxiety can be a problem, especially if it hinders our ability to function and perform.

"Test anxiety," is the term that refers to the emotional reactions that some test-takers experience when faced with a test or exam. Having a fear of testing and exams is based upon a rational fear, since the test-taker's performance can shape the course of an academic career. Nevertheless, experiencing excessive fear of examinations will only interfere with the test-taker's ability to perform and chance to be successful.

There are a large variety of causes that can contribute to the development and sensation of test anxiety. These include, but are not limited to, lack of preparation and worrying about issues surrounding the test.

Lack of Preparation

Lack of preparation can be identified by the following behaviors or situations:
- Not scheduling enough time to study, and therefore cramming the night before the test or exam
- Managing time poorly, to create the sensation that there is not enough time to do everything
- Failing to organize the text information in advance, so that the study material consists of the entire text and not simply the pertinent information
- Poor overall studying habits

Worrying, on the other hand, can be related to both the test taker, or many other factors around him/her that will be affected by the results of the test. These include worrying about:
- Previous performances on similar exams, or exams in general
- How friends and other students are achieving
- The negative consequences that will result from a poor grade or failure

There are three primary elements to test anxiety. Physical components, which involve the same typical bodily reactions as those to acute anxiety (to be discussed below). Emotional factors have to do with fear or panic. Mental or cognitive issues concerning attention spans and memory abilities.

Physical Signals

There are many different symptoms of test anxiety, and these are not limited to mental and emotional strain. Frequently there are a range of physical signals that will let a test taker know that he/she is suffering from test anxiety. These bodily changes can include the following:

- Perspiring
- Sweaty palms
- Wet, trembling hands
- Nausea
- Dry mouth
- A knot in the stomach
- Headache
- Faintness
- Muscle tension
- Aching shoulders, back and neck
- Rapid heart beat
- Feeling too hot/cold

To recognize the sensation of test anxiety, a test-taker should monitor him/herself for the following sensation

- The physical distress symptoms as listed above
- Emotional sensitivity, expressing emotional feelings such as the need to cry or laugh too much, or a sensation of anger or helplessness
- A decreased ability to think, causing the test-taker to blank out or have racing thoughts that are hard to organize or control.

Though most students will feel some level of anxiety when faced with a test or exam, the majority can cope with that anxiety and maintain it at a manageable level. However, those who cannot are faced with a very real and very serious condition, which can and should be controlled for the immeasurable benefit of this sufferer.

Naturally, these sensations lead to negative results for the testing experience. The most common effects of test anxiety have to do with nervousness and mental blocking.

Nervousness

Nervousness can appear in several different levels:

- The test-taker's difficulty, or even inability to read and understand the questions on the test
- The difficulty or inability to organize thoughts to a coherent form
- The difficulty or inability to recall key words and concepts relating to the testing questions (especially essays)
- The receipt of poor grades on a test, though the test material was well known by the test taker

Conversely, a person may also experience mental blocking, which involves:
- Blanking out on test questions
- Only remembering the correct answers to the questions when the test has already finished.

Fortunately for test anxiety sufferers, beating these feelings, to a large degree, has to do with proper preparation. When a test taker has a feeling of preparedness, then anxiety will be dramatically lessened.

The first step to resolving anxiety issues is to distinguish which of the two types of anxiety are being suffered. If the anxiety is a direct result of a lack of preparation, this should be considered a normal reaction, and the anxiety level (as opposed to the test results) shouldn't be anything to worry about. However, if, when adequately prepared, the test-taker still panics, blanks out, or seems to overreact, this is not a fully rational reaction. While this can be considered normal too, there are many ways to combat and overcome these effects.

Remember that anxiety cannot be entirely eliminated, however, there are ways to minimize it, to make the anxiety easier to manage. Preparation is one of the best ways to minimize test anxiety. Therefore the following techniques are wise in order to best fight off any anxiety that may want to build.

To begin with, try to avoid cramming before a test, whenever it is possible. By trying to memorize an entire term's worth of information in one day, you'll be shocking your system, and not giving yourself a very good chance to absorb the information. This is an easy path to anxiety, so for those who suffer from test anxiety, cramming should not even be considered an option.

Instead of cramming, work throughout the semester to combine all of the material which is presented throughout the semester, and work on it gradually as the course goes by, making sure to master the main concepts first, leaving minor details for a week or so before the test.

To study for the upcoming exam, be sure to pose questions that may be on the examination, to gauge the ability to answer them by integrating the ideas from your texts, notes and lectures, as well as any supplementary readings.

If it is truly impossible to cover all of the information that was covered in that particular term, concentrate on the most important portions, that can be covered very well. Learn these concepts as best as possible, so that when the test comes, a goal can be made to use these concepts as presentations of your knowledge.

In addition to study habits, changes in attitude are critical to beating a struggle with test anxiety. In fact, an improvement of the perspective over the entire test-taking experience can actually help a test taker to enjoy studying and therefore improve the overall experience. Be certain not to overemphasize the significance of the grade - know that the result of the test is neither a reflection of self worth, nor is it a measure of intelligence; one grade will not predict a person's future success.

To improve an overall testing outlook, the following steps should be tried:
- Keeping in mind that the most reasonable expectation for taking a test is to expect to try to demonstrate as much of what you know as you possibly can.
- Reminding ourselves that a test is only one test; this is not the only one, and there will be others.
- The thought of thinking of oneself in an irrational, all-or-nothing term should be avoided at all costs.
- A reward should be designated for after the test, so there's something to look forward to. Whether it be going to a movie, going out to eat, or simply visiting friends, schedule it in advance, and do it no matter what result is expected on the exam.

Test-takers should also keep in mind that the basics are some of the most important things, even beyond anti-anxiety techniques and studying. Never neglect the basic social, emotional and biological needs, in order to try to absorb information. In order to best achieve, these three factors must be held as just as important as the studying itself.

Study Steps

Remember the following important steps for studying:
- Maintain healthy nutrition and exercise habits. Continue both your recreational activities and social pass times. These both contribute to your physical and emotional well being.
- Be certain to get a good amount of sleep, especially the night before the test, because when you're overtired you are not able to perform to the best of your best ability.
- Keep the studying pace to a moderate level by taking breaks when they are needed, and varying the work whenever possible, to keep the mind fresh instead of getting bored.
- When enough studying has been done that all the material that can be learned has been learned, and the test taker is prepared for the test, stop studying and do something relaxing such as listening to music, watching a movie, or taking a warm bubble bath.

There are also many other techniques to minimize the uneasiness or apprehension that is experienced along with test anxiety before, during, or even after the examination. In fact, there are a great deal of things that can be done to stop anxiety from interfering with lifestyle and performance. Again, remember that anxiety will not be eliminated entirely, and it shouldn't be. Otherwise that "up" feeling for exams would not exist, and most of us depend on that sensation to perform better than usual. However, this anxiety has to be at a level that is manageable.

Of course, as we have just discussed, being prepared for the exam is half the battle right away. Attending all classes, finding out what knowledge will be expected on the exam, and knowing the exam schedules are easy steps to lowering anxiety. Keeping up with work will remove the need to cram, and efficient study habits will eliminate wasted time. Studying should be done in an ideal location for concentration, so that it is simple to become interested in the material and give it complete attention. A method such as

SQ3R (Survey, Question, Read, Recite, Review) is a wonderful key to follow to make sure that the study habits are as effective as possible, especially in the case of learning from a textbook. Flashcards are great techniques for memorization. Learning to take good notes will mean that notes will be full of useful information, so that less sifting will need to be done to seek out what is pertinent for studying. Reviewing notes after class and then again on occasion will keep the information fresh in the mind. From notes that have been taken summary sheets and outlines can be made for simpler reviewing.

A study group can also be a very motivational and helpful place to study, as there will be a sharing of ideas, all of the minds can work together, to make sure that everyone understands, and the studying will be made more interesting because it will be a social occasion.

Basically, though, as long as the test-taker remains organized and self confident, with efficient study habits, less time will need to be spent studying, and higher grades will be achieved.

To become self confident, there are many useful steps. The first of these is "self talk." It has been shown through extensive research, that self-talk for students who suffer from test anxiety, should be well monitored, in order to make sure that it contributes to self confidence as opposed to sinking the student. Frequently the self talk of test-anxious students is negative or self-defeating, thinking that everyone else is smarter and faster, that they always mess up, and that if they don't do well, they'll fail the entire course. It is important to decreasing anxiety that awareness is made of self talk. Try writing any negative self thoughts and then disputing them with a positive statement instead. Begin self-encouragement as though it was a friend speaking. Repeat positive statements to help reprogram the mind to believing in successes instead of failures.

Helpful Techniques

Other extremely helpful techniques include:
- Self-visualization of doing well and reaching goals
- While aiming for an "A" level of understanding, don't try to "overprotect" by setting your expectations lower. This will only convince the mind to stop studying in order to meet the lower expectations.
- Don't make comparisons with the results or habits of other students. These are individual factors, and different things work for different people, causing different results.
- Strive to become an expert in learning what works well, and what can be done in order to improve. Consider collecting this data in a journal.
- Create rewards for after studying instead of doing things before studying that will only turn into avoidance behaviors.
- Make a practice of relaxing - by using methods such as progressive relaxation, self-hypnosis, guided imagery, etc - in order to make relaxation an automatic sensation.
- Work on creating a state of relaxed concentration so that concentrating will take on the focus of the mind, so that none will be wasted on worrying.
- Take good care of the physical self by eating well and getting enough sleep.

- Plan in time for exercise and stick to this plan.

Beyond these techniques, there are other methods to be used before, during and after the test that will help the test-taker perform well in addition to overcoming anxiety.

Before the exam comes the academic preparation. This involves establishing a study schedule and beginning at least one week before the actual date of the test. By doing this, the anxiety of not having enough time to study for the test will be automatically eliminated. Moreover, this will make the studying a much more effective experience, ensuring that the learning will be an easier process. This relieves much undue pressure on the test-taker.

Summary sheets, note cards, and flash cards with the main concepts and examples of these main concepts should be prepared in advance of the actual studying time. A topic should never be eliminated from this process. By omitting a topic because it isn't expected to be on the test is only setting up the test-taker for anxiety should it actually appear on the exam. Utilize the course syllabus for laying out the topics that should be studied. Carefully go over the notes that were made in class, paying special attention to any of the issues that the professor took special care to emphasize while lecturing in class. In the textbooks, use the chapter review, or if possible, the chapter tests, to begin your review.

It may even be possible to ask the instructor what information will be covered on the exam, or what the format of the exam will be (for example, multiple choice, essay, free form, true-false). Additionally, see if it is possible to find out how many questions will be on the test. If a review sheet or sample test has been offered by the professor, make good use of it, above anything else, for the preparation for the test. Another great resource for getting to know the examination is reviewing tests from previous semesters. Use these tests to review, and aim to achieve a 100% score on each of the possible topics. With a few exceptions, the goal that you set for yourself is the highest one that you will reach.

Take all of the questions that were assigned as homework, and rework them to any other possible course material. The more problems reworked, the more skill and confidence will form as a result. When forming the solution to a problem, write out each of the steps. Don't simply do head work. By doing as many steps on paper as possible, much clarification and therefore confidence will be formed. Do this with as many homework problems as possible, before checking the answers. By checking the answer after each problem, a reinforcement will exist, that will not be on the exam. Study situations should be as exam-like as possible, to prime the test-taker's system for the experience. By waiting to check the answers at the end, a psychological advantage will be formed, to decrease the stress factor.

Another fantastic reason for not cramming is the avoidance of confusion in concepts, especially when it comes to mathematics. 8-10 hours of study will become one hundred percent more effective if it is spread out over a week or at least several days, instead of doing it all in one sitting. Recognize that the human brain requires time in order to assimilate new material, so frequent breaks and a span of study time over several days will be much more beneficial.

Additionally, don't study right up until the point of the exam. Studying should stop a minimum of one hour before the exam begins. This allows the brain to rest and put things in their proper order. This will also provide the time to become as relaxed as possible when going into the examination room. The test-taker will also have time to eat well and eat sensibly. Know that the brain needs food as much as the rest of the body. With enough food and enough sleep, as well as a relaxed attitude, the body and the mind are primed for success.

Avoid any anxious classmates who are talking about the exam. These students only spread anxiety, and are not worth sharing the anxious sentimentalities.

Before the test also involves creating a positive attitude, so mental preparation should also be a point of concentration. There are many keys to creating a positive attitude. Should fears become rushing in, make a visualization of taking the exam, doing well, and seeing an A written on the paper. Write out a list of affirmations that will bring a feeling of confidence, such as "I am doing well in my English class," "I studied well and know my material," "I enjoy this class." Even if the affirmations aren't believed at first, it sends a positive message to the subconscious which will result in an alteration of the overall belief system, which is the system that creates reality.

If a sensation of panic begins, work with the fear and imagine the very worst! Work through the entire scenario of not passing the test, failing the entire course, and dropping out of school, followed by not getting a job, and pushing a shopping cart through the dark alley where you'll live. This will place things into perspective! Then, practice deep breathing and create a visualization of the opposite situation - achieving an "A" on the exam, passing the entire course, receiving the degree at a graduation ceremony.

On the day of the test, there are many things to be done to ensure the best results, as well as the most calm outlook. The following stages are suggested in order to maximize test-taking potential:
- Begin the examination day with a moderate breakfast, and avoid any coffee or beverages with caffeine if the test taker is prone to jitters. Even people who are used to managing caffeine can feel jittery or light-headed when it is taken on a test day.
- Attempt to do something that is relaxing before the examination begins. As last minute cramming clouds the mastering of overall concepts, it is better to use this time to create a calming outlook.
- Be certain to arrive at the test location well in advance, in order to provide time to select a location that is away from doors, windows and other distractions, as well as giving enough time to relax before the test begins.
- Keep away from anxiety generating classmates who will upset the sensation of stability and relaxation that is being attempted before the exam.
- Should the waiting period before the exam begins cause anxiety, create a self-distraction by reading a light magazine or something else that is relaxing and simple.

During the exam itself, read the entire exam from beginning to end, and find out how much time should be allotted to each individual problem. Once writing the exam, should more time be taken for a problem, it should be abandoned, in order to begin another problem. If there is time at the end, the unfinished problem can always be returned to and completed.

Read the instructions very carefully - twice - so that unpleasant surprises won't follow during or after the exam has ended.

When writing the exam, pretend that the situation is actually simply the completion of homework within a library, or at home. This will assist in forming a relaxed atmosphere, and will allow the brain extra focus for the complex thinking function.

Begin the exam with all of the questions with which the most confidence is felt. This will build the confidence level regarding the entire exam and will begin a quality momentum. This will also create encouragement for trying the problems where uncertainty resides.

Going with the "gut instinct" is always the way to go when solving a problem. Second guessing should be avoided at all costs. Have confidence in the ability to do well.

For essay questions, create an outline in advance that will keep the mind organized and make certain that all of the points are remembered. For multiple choice, read every answer, even if the correct one has been spotted - a better one may exist.

Continue at a pace that is reasonable and not rushed, in order to be able to work carefully. Provide enough time to go over the answers at the end, to check for small errors that can be corrected.

Should a feeling of panic begin, breathe deeply, and think of the feeling of the body releasing sand through its pores. Visualize a calm, peaceful place, and include all of the sights, sounds and sensations of this image. Continue the deep breathing, and take a few minutes to continue this with closed eyes. When all is well again, return to the test.

If a "blanking" occurs for a certain question, skip it and move on to the next question. There will be time to return to the other question later. Get everything done that can be done, first, to guarantee all the grades that can be compiled, and to build all of the confidence possible. Then return to the weaker questions to build the marks from there.

Remember, one's own reality can be created, so as long as the belief is there, success will follow. And remember: anxiety can happen later, right now, there's an exam to be written!

After the examination is complete, whether there is a feeling for a good grade or a bad grade, don't dwell on the exam, and be certain to follow through on the reward that was promised...and enjoy it! Don't dwell on any mistakes that have been made, as there is nothing that can be done at this point anyway.

Additionally, don't begin to study for the next test right away. Do something relaxing for a while, and let the mind relax and prepare itself to begin absorbing information again.

From the results of the exam - both the grade and the entire experience, be certain to learn from what has gone on. Perfect studying habits and work some more on confidence in order to make the next examination experience even better than the last one.

Learn to avoid places where openings occurred for laziness, procrastination and day dreaming.

Use the time between this exam and the next one to better learn to relax, even learning to relax on cue, so that any anxiety can be controlled during the next exam. Learn how to relax the body. Slouch in your chair if that helps. Tighten and then relax all of the different muscle groups, one group at a time, beginning with the feet and then working all the way up to the neck and face. This will ultimately relax the muscles more than they were to begin with. Learn how to breathe deeply and comfortably, and focus on this breathing going in and out as a relaxing thought. With every exhale, repeat the word "relax."

As common as test anxiety is, it is very possible to overcome it. Make yourself one of the test-takers who overcome this frustrating hindrance.

Additional Bonus Material

Due to our efforts to try to keep this book to a manageable length, we've created a link that will give you access to all of your additional bonus material.

Please visit http://www.mometrix.com/bonus948/priigeo to access the information.